THE
MADE THING

THE

MADE THING

AN ANTHOLOGY OF
CONTEMPORARY SOUTHERN POETRY

Edited by Leon Stokesbury

THE UNIVERSITY OF ARKANSAS PRESS

FAYETTEVILLE   1987

DESIGNER: Chiquita Babb
TYPEFACE: Linotron 202 Palatino
TYPESETTER: G & S Typesetters, Inc.
PRINTER: Thomson-Shore, Inc.
BINDER: John H. Dekker & Sons, Inc.

The paper used in this publication meets the minimum requirements of the American
National Standard for Permanence of Paper for Printed Library Materials Z39.48-1984.∞™

LIBRARY OF CONGRESS CATALOGING-IN-PUBLICATION DATA

The Made thing.

   Includes index.
   1. American poetry—Southern States.   2. American poetry—20th cen-
tury.   3. Southern States—Poetry.
I. Stokesbury, Leon, 1945–
PS551.M29   1987   811'.54'080975   86–19220
ISBN 0-938626-77-9
ISBN 0-938626-78-7 (pbk.)

——— ACKNOWLEDGMENTS ———

RALPH ADAMO: "My Answer" and "The Great Escape" from *Sadness at the Private University* copyright © by Ralph Adamo, published by Lost Roads Publishing Company.

BETTY ADCOCK: "Roller Rink," "Walking Out," "Twentieth Anniversary," and "Southbound" reprinted by permission of Louisiana State University Press.

JAMES APPLEWHITE: "My Grandfather's Funeral" reprinted by permission of the University of Georgia Press. "White Lake," "Marriage Portrait," and "Barbecue Service" reprinted by permission of Louisiana State University Press.

ALVIN AUBERT: "Economics," "How It's Done," and "Silence" reprinted by permission of The Lunchroom Press.

GERALD BARRAX: " 'I had a terror—since September' " and "Gift" reprinted by permission of the University of Georgia Press. "Two Figures on Canvas" reprinted by permission of the author.

JOHN BENSKO: "Watching TV, the Elk Bones Up on Metaphysics," "The Wild Horses of Assateague Island," "The Elk Uncovers the Heavens," and "The Elk on Mutability" reprinted by permission of the author. "The Wild Horses of Assateague Island" first appeared in *Poetry*.

DC BERRY: "To the Woodville Depot" and "Road" reprinted by permission of the author.

WENDELL BERRY: "The Peace of Wild Things," "To Know the Dark," "The Grandmother," and "Grief" excerpted from : *The Collected Poems of Wendell Berry 1957–1982* copyright © 1984 by Wendell Berry. Published by North Point Press and reprinted by permission. All rights reserved.

DAVID BOTTOMS: "Sign for My Father, Who Stressed the Bunt," "The Boy Shepherds' Simile," "Under the Boathouse," "The Drowned," and "In a U-Haul North of Damascus" from *In a U-Haul North of Damascus* by David Bottoms copyright © 1981, 1982, 1983 by David Bottoms, by permission of William Morrow & Company. "The Desk" and "Under the Vulture-Tree" reprinted by permission of the author. "The Desk" first appeared in *Poetry*. "Under the Vulture-Tree" first appeared in *The Atlantic Monthly*. "Under the Boathouse" first appeared in *The New Yorker*.

EDGAR BOWERS: "The Stoic: For Laura von Courten," "An Afternoon at the Beach," "Autumn Shade, Part 1," and "An Elegy: December, 1970," from *Living Together* by Edgar Bowers copyright © 1973 by the author. Reprinted by permission of David R. Godine, Publisher, Boston.

VAN K. BROCK: "Novas," "Departure," "Lying on a Bridge," and "The Man in the Rain" reprinted by permission of the author. "Novas" first appeared in *The Southern Review*.

JACK BUTLER: "Preserves," "No News at All," "Subplot," "Afterglow," and "One Reason for Stars" from *The Kid Who Wanted to Be a Spaceman*, reprinted by permission of August House. "No News at All," "Subplot," and "Afterglow" copyright © 1974, 1972, and 1979, respectively, *The New Yorker*. "One Reason for Stars" first appeared in *Poetry*.

TURNER CASSITY: "U-24 Anchors off New Orleans (1938)" and "Flying Friendly Skies" from *The Hurricane Lamp* by Turner Cassity. Reprinted by permission of the University of Chicago Press. "Professionals" from *Steeplejacks in Babel* by Turner Cassity copyright © 1974 by the author. Reprinted by permission of David R. Godine, Publisher, Boston.

FRED CHAPPELL: "My Grandmother Washes Her Feet," "Cleaning the Well," "My Grandmother Washes Her Vessels," "Second Wind," "My Mother Shoots the

Breeze," "My Father Washes His Hands," and "Narcissus and Echo" reprinted by permission of Louisiana State University Press.

JOHN WILLIAM CORRINGTON: "For a Woodscolt Miscarried" and "On the Flesh of Christ" reprinted by permission of the author.

JAMES DICKEY: "The Heaven of Animals," "In the Mountain Tent," "Cherrylog Road," "The Hospital Window," "The Shark's Parlor," "The Sheep Child," "Adultery," and "Falling" copyright © 1961, 1962, 1963, 1965, 1967 by James Dickey. Reprinted from *Poems: 1957–1967* by permission of Wesleyan University Press. "False Youth: Autumn: Clothes of the Age" copyright © 1983 by James Dickey. Reprinted from *The Central Motion* by permission of Wesleyan University Press. "The Heaven of Animals," "In the Mountain Tent," "Cherrylog Road," "The Shark's Parlor," and "Falling" appeared originally in *The New Yorker.*

R.H.W. DILLARD: "The Mullins Farm" and "Meditation for a Pickle Suite" reprinted by permission of the University of Utah Press.

GEORGE GARRETT: "The Magi," "Revival," "Bubbles," "Luck's Shining Child," "York Harbor Morning," and "Buzzard" reprinted by permission of The University of Arkansas Press.

MARGARET GIBSON: "The Onion," "Invisible Work," and "Country Woman Elegy" are reprinted by permission of Louisiana State University Press.

R. S. GWYNN: "1916" by R. S. Gwynn was first published in the *Sewanee Review* 94 (Spring 1986). Copyright © 1986 by R. S. Gwynn. Reprinted by permission of the editor. "Among Philistines" was first published in *Poetry.* Reprinted by permission of the author.

JIM HALL: "Maybe Dats Your Pwoblem Too," "White Trash," and "Preposterous" are reprinted by permission of the Carnegie-Mellon University Press.

ANDREW HUDGINS: "Around the Campfire" and "Burial Detail" first appeared in *The Southern Review.* Reprinted by permission of the author.

T. R. HUMMER: "What Shines in Winter Burns" and "Where You Go When She Sleeps" are reprinted by permission of Louisiana State University Press. "Sorrow" and "The Beating" are reprinted by permission of the University of Illinois Press. "Inner Ear" is reprinted by permission of the author.

RANDALL JARRELL: "When I Was Home Last Christmas . . . ," "90 North," "The Death of the Ball Turret Gunner," and "The Player Piano" from *The Complete Poems* by Randall Jarrell copyright © 1941, 1945, 1948. Renewed copyright © 1967, 1968, 1972, 1975 by Mrs. Randall Jarrell. Reprinted by permission of Farrar, Straus, and Giroux, Inc. In England, reprinted by permission of Faber and Faber Publishers.

RODNEY JONES: "Sweep," "The Mosquito," and "The First Birth" reprinted by permission of The Atlantic Monthly Press. From *The Unborn,* copyright © 1985, by Rodney Jones.

DONALD JUSTICE: "The Poet at Seven" and "In Bertram's Garden" copyright © 1954, 1959 by Donald Justice. Reprinted from *The Summer Anniversaries* by permission of Wesleyan University Press. "Heart" and "Men at Forty" copyright © 1966, 1967 by Donald Justice. Reprinted from *Night Light* by permission of Wesleyan University Press. "First Death," "Tremayne" and "Thinking about the Past" from *Selected Poems* copyright © 1979 by Donald Justice. Reprinted by permission of Atheneum Publishers, Inc. "Variations on Southern Themes" (part 1) first appeared in *The Atlantic Monthly.* "Epilogue: Henry James at the Pacific" first appeared in *The Atlantic Monthly.* "Variations on Southern Themes" (part 2) and "American Scenes (1904)" reprinted by permission of the author. "Tremayne," "The Insomnia of Tremayne," "Tremayne Autumnal," and "Variations on Southern Themes" (part 3) appeared originally in *The New Yorker.*

ETHERIDGE KNIGHT: "He Sees Through Stone," "The Warden Said to Me the Other Day," and "As You Leave Me" reprinted by permission of the author.

YUSEF KOMUNYAKAA: "We Never Know," "Ia Drang Valley," "Saigon Bar Girls, 1975," and "Facing It" reprinted by permission of the author.

SUSAN LUDVIGSON: "Some Notes on Courage," "The Widow," "Man Arrested in Hacking Death Tells Police He Mistook Mother-in-Law for Raccoon," "The Punishment," and "Jeanne d'Arc" reprinted by permission of Louisiana State University Press.

EVERETTE MADDOX: "The Great Man's Death: An Anecdote," "Breakfast," and "1941" reprinted by permission of The New Orleans Poetry Journal Press.

CLEOPATRA MATHIS: "Elegy for the Other" reprinted by permission of the Sheep Meadow Press.

WALTER MCDONALD: "Never in My Life" reprinted by permission of Texas Tech University Press. "Hauling over Wolf Creek Pass in Winter" and "Starting a Pasture" reprinted by permission of the author. "Hauling over Wolf Creek Pass in Winter" first appeared in *Tri Quarterly*, a publication of Northwestern University.

HEATHER ROSS MILLER: "Minor Things" and "Girl, Prince, Lizard" reprinted by permission of the author.

JIM WAYNE MILLER: "Closing the House," "Hanging Burley," "Squirrel Stand," and "The Hungry Dead" reprinted by permission of Green River Press.

VASSAR MILLER: "Adam's Footprint," "Reciprocity," "Beside a Deathbed," and "Bout with Burning" copyright © 1960 by Vassar Miller. Reprinted from *Wage War on Silence* by permission of Wesleyan University Press. "Lord, hush this ego as one stops a bell" and "Of praying may (in mercy become prayer)" reprinted by permission of The New Orleans Poetry Journal Press.

WILLIAM MILLS: "Pity," "Motel," "Rituals Along the Arkansas," and "The Necessity of Falling" reprinted by permission of Louisiana State University Press.

ROBERT MORGAN: "The Hollow," "Mountain Bride," "Death Crown," and "Walnutry" from *Groundwork*. Reprinted by permission of Gnomon Press. "Passenger Pigeons" and "The Gift of Tongues" reprinted by permission of the author.

NAOMI SHIHAB NYE: "New Year," "Sure," "The Traveling Onion," "Hello," and "Going for Peaches, Fredericksburg, Texas" reprinted by permission of the author. "New Year" first appeared in *The Georgia Review*. "Hello" first appeared in *The Pacific Review*.

BRENDA MARIE OSBEY: "The Wastrel-Woman Poem," "'In These Houses of Swift Easy Women,'" and "Portrait" reprinted by permission of the author. "The Wastrel-Woman Poem" and "In These Houses of Swift Easy Women" first appeared in *The Southern Review*. "Portrait" first appeared in *Tendril*.

THOMAS RABBITT: from *The Booth Interstate* copyright © 1981 by the author. "Gargoyle," "The Old Sipsey Valley Road," and "Coon Hunt" reprinted by permission of Alfred A. Knopf, Inc.

BIN RAMKE: "Nostalgia," "Victory Drive, Near Fort Benning, Georgia," and "Georgia" reprinted by permission of the University of Georgia Press.

PAULA RANKIN: "Hot Bath in an Old Hotel" and "Middle Age" reprinted by permission of the Carnegie-Mellon University Press.

PATTIANN ROGERS: from *Expectations of Light* copyright © 1981 by Princeton University Press. "Concepts and Their Bodies (The Boy in the Field Alone)," previously published in *Poetry*; "Suppose Your Father Was a Redbird," previously published in *Poetry Northwest*; "Achieving Perspective," previously published in *The Southern Review*; "A Giant Has Swallowed the Earth," previously published in *The Southern Review*, reprinted with permission of Princeton University Press. "The Possible Salvation of Continuous Motion," "Discovering Your Subject," and "Finding the Tattooed Lady in the Garden" copyright © 1986 by Pattiann Rogers. Reprinted from *The Tattooed Lady in the Garden* by permission of Wesleyan University Press.

GIBBONS RUARK: "The Visitor," "The Muse's Answer," "Sleeping Out with My Father," and "Postscript to an Elegy" reprinted by permission of the author. "Lament" reprinted by permission of Texas Tech University Press. "Lost Letter to James Wright, With Thanks for a Map of Fano," "For a Suicide, a Little Early Morning Music," and "Basil" reprinted by permission of Johns Hopkins University Press. "Postscript to an Elegy" first appeared in *Poetry*.

LARRY RUBIN: "The Manual," "The Brother-in-Law," and "Dinner at the Mongoloid's" from *All My Mirrors Lie* by Larry Rubin copyright © 1975 by the author. Reprinted by permission of David R. Godine, Publisher, Boston.

JAMES SEAY: "It All Comes Together Outside the Restroom in Hogansville" copyright © 1974 by James Seay. Reprinted from *Water Tables* by permission of Wesleyan University Press. "When Our Voices Broke Off" and "Clouds over Islands" reprinted by permission of Deerfield Press.

DAVE SMITH: "Mending Crab Pots" reprinted by permission of the author. "Sailing the Back River" from *Cumberland Station* (University of Illinois Press) © 1975 by Dave Smith; "Rain Forest" and "The Roundhouse Voices" from *Goshawk, Antelope* (University of Illinois Press) © 1978 and 1979, respectively, by Dave Smith; "An Antipastoral Memory of One Summer," from *The Roundhouse Voices: Selected and New Poems* by Dave Smith copyright © 1984 by the author, reprinted by permission of Harper & Row, Publishers, Inc.; originally appeared in *The New Yorker*.

FRANK STANFORD: "The Intruder" and "Allegory of Death and Night" reprinted by permission of Lost Roads Publishers. "Inventory," "Place on a Grave," "Between Love and Death," and "Island Funeral" reprinted by permission of Ginny Crouch Stanford.

JAMES STILL: "Spring," "On Double Creek," "Ballad," and "Wolfpen Creek" reprinted from *The Wolfpen Poems* copyright © 1986 by James Still. Reprinted by permission of Berea College Press.

LEON STOKESBURY: "The Luncheon of the Boating Party," "Day Begins at Governor's Square Mall," "Adventures in Bronze," and "To Laura Phelan: 1880–1906" reprinted by permission of The University of Arkansas Press.

JOHN STONE: "The Girl in the Hall," "Death," "After Love," and "Early Sunday Morning" reprinted by permission of Louisiana State University Press.

DABNEY STUART: "The Ballad of the Frozen Field" and "Mining in Killdeer Alley" reprinted by permission of Louisiana State University Press. "The Soup Jar" from *The Diving Bell*, Alfred A. Knopf, Inc. 1966, copyright © Dabney Stuart, 1966. Reprinted by permission of the author.

HENRY TAYLOR: "Taking to the Woods," "The Way It Sometimes Is," "Artichoke," "As on a Darkling Plain," and "At the Swings" reprinted by permission of Louisiana State University Press.

RICHARD TILLINGHAST: "The Knife" and "Summer Rain" copyright © 1980 by Richard Tillinghast. Reprinted from *The Knife* by permission of Wesleyan University Press. "Envoi" copyright © 1984 by Richard Tillinghast. Reprinted from *Our Flag Was Still There* by permission of Wesleyan University Press.

ELLEN BRYANT VOIGT: "Farm Wife" copyright © 1972 by Ellen Bryant Voigt. Reprinted from *Claiming Kin* by permission of Wesleyan University Press. "Jug Brook," "Daughter," and "Sweet Everlasting" are reprinted from *The Forces of Plenty*, by Ellen Bryant Voigt, by permission of the author, and the publisher, W.W. Norton & Company, Inc. Copyright © 1983 by Ellen Bryant Voigt. "Landscape, Dense with Trees," "The Lotus Flowers," "The Farmer," and "The Last Class" are reprinted by permission of the author. "Landscape, Dense with Trees" and "The Lotus Flowers" originally appeared in *The New Yorker*. Copyright © 1984 and 1983 by Ellen Bryant Voigt.

ALICE WALKER: "My Husband Says," "Your Soul Shines," "Even as I Hold You" from *Goodnight Willie Lee, I'll See You in the Morning* copyright © 1977, 1979 by Alice Walker. Reprinted by permission of Doubleday & Company, Inc.

ROBERT PENN WARREN: "The Spider" from *Tale of Time: Poems 1960–1966*, by Robert Penn Warren. Copyright © 1966 by Robert Penn Warren. Reprinted from *Selected Poems 1923–1975*, by Robert Penn Warren, by permission of Random House, Inc. "Tell Me a Story" from *Audubon: A Vision* by Robert Penn Warren, copyright © 1969 by the author. Reprinted by permission of Random House, Inc. "Evening Hour," "Sister Water," "Last Laugh," "Heat Lightning," "Heart of Autumn," and "Heart of the Backlog" from *Now and Then: Poems 1976–1978* by Robert Penn Warren, copyright © 1978 by the author. Reprinted by permission of Random House, Inc. "What Voice at Moth-Hour" from *Rumor Verified: Poems 1979–1980*, by Robert Penn Warren, copyright © 1981 by the author. Reprinted by permission of Random House, Inc. "The Spider," "Heart of the Backlog," "Last Laugh," and "What Voice at Moth-Hour" appeared originally in *The New Yorker.* "Tell Me a Story" and "The Spider" from *Selected Poems 1923–1975* by Robert Penn Warren. Reprinted by permission of Martin Secker & Warburg, Limited, London.

JAMES WHITEHEAD: "A Local Man Goes to the Killing Ground," "A Local Man Remembers Betty Fuller," "A Local Contractor Flees His Winter Trouble and Saves Some Lives in a Knoxville Motel Room," "About a Year After He Got Married He Would Sit Alone in an Abandoned Shack in a Cotton Field Enjoying Himself," "He Remembers How He Didn't Understand What Lieutenant Dawson Meant," "Long Tour: The Country Music Star Explains Why He Put off the Bus and Fired a Good Lead Guitar in West Texas," "Good Linemen Live in a Closed World," and "A Natural Theology" reprinted by permission of the author.

MILLER WILLIAMS: "The Caterpillar," "Why God Permits Evil: For Answers to This Question of Interest to Many Write Bible Answers Dept. E–7," "Love and How It Becomes Important in Our Day to Day Lives," and "The Firebreathers at the Café Deux Magots" reprinted by permission of Louisiana State University Press. "Ruby Tells All," "On a Photograph of My Mother at Seventeen," "A Poem for Emily," "The Aging Actress Sees Herself a Starlet on the Late Show," and "After the Revolution for Jesus a Secular Man Prepares His Final Remarks" reprinted by permission of the author. "A Poem for Emily" first appeared in *Poetry.* "Ruby Tells All" first appeared in *The Georgia Review.*

C. D. WRIGHT: "Birth of the Cool" reprinted by permission of Lost Roads Publishers. "Tours," "Obedience of the Corpse," and "The Beautiful Urinals of Paris" reprinted from *Translations of the Gospel Back Into Tongues* by C. D. Wright, by permission of the State University of New York Press copyright © 1982 by the author. "Slag" reprinted by permission of the author.

CHARLES WRIGHT: "April," "Clear Night," "Cloud River," copyright © 1982 by Charles Wright. Reprinted from *Country Music* by permission of Wesleyan University Press. "October" reprinted from *Southern Cross.* Copyright © 1979 by Charles Wright, reprinted by permission of Random House, Inc. "Arkansas Traveller" and "The Other Side of the River" reprinted from *The Other Side of the River.* Copyright © 1984 by Charles Wright, reprinted by permission of Random House, Inc. "Arkansas Traveller," "Clear Night," and "October" appeared originally in *The New Yorker.*

CONTENTS

PREFACE

I should say a word about the selection of poets for *The Made Thing*. As a minimum standard, I have included only poets who have published at least one full-length book. In addition, to keep the collection contemporary, I limited the selections to poets who published their major works in the past thirty years. Although a few poems in the book were published earlier, their authors went on to write substantial volumes within this period. I restricted myself to poets who were either born and raised in the South or who have lived in the South at least since they began publishing their mature work.

My intent in compiling *The Made Thing* was not to verify any restrictive definition of Southern poetry. Still, as I read the hundreds of books by the more than one hundred poets I considered for inclusion I recognized tendencies of theme and form that give a distinctive flavor to the poems. The most distinctive theme, perhaps, is a preoccupation with the past as history. I was also struck by how much of the poetry is centered around a profound relationship to the natural world. Add to this that Southern poets in general are somewhat conservative in their approach to form. But finally, what this anthology says about contemporary Southern poets and their work is to be found in the poetry. It speaks convincingly for itself.

So my reason for compiling the poems was simply to bring to as many people as possible the best poetry by what I believe to be the largest and most talented group of poets this region of the United States has known, and to share the enjoyment I have found in them. In less than a generation there will be need for another collection with many new poets and poems. I look forward to that.

I want to thank Susan Thurman, my wife, for her assistance and support during the last two years. And for her patience. When I began this, neither of us realized how much time and how many obstacles would be involved before the book could be finished. Her help was essential to the making of *The Made Thing*.

—Leon Stokesbury
1987

THE
MADE THING

Ralph Adamo lives in New Orleans, where he was born in 1948. He holds an M.F.A. from the University of Arkansas, and has made his living as a journalist, screenwriter, music critic, and teacher. His recent books include *Sadness at the Private University* and *The End of the World*, both from Lost Roads Publishers.

Photo Credit: David Richmond

My Answer

The big impression left on me
By the story of Cain and Abel
Was that meat is better than vegetables.
This is a point raised time
And time again in the Old Testament.

I know how it was.
There was Cain, older, part of the number three,
An important number, and yet forced
To ponder the number four
Most of his life. This drove him crazy.
But not just this. There he was,
Close enough to the well that he could hear
Adam and Eve puttering and rocking in the house.
He turned the field with a scythe
Strapped to his back. He moved his feet
Along slowly while the ground
Opened up behind him. Did he look back ever

To see the worms like so many exposed nerves
Undulating in their chunks of sod? Nah.
But once in a while, oh yes, he did look up
To gaze at the unterraced hills and ponder
The needles and blades of green, but all at one time.
You can bet Adam and Eve leaned on that boy,
Not that they were harsh about it.
Adam was a kind old gentleman
With a well-meaning wife.
So what if she'd gotten them into this.
It wasn't the end of the world.
Things needed doing and the field was close to the house.
But Abel, that Abel—sometimes
He wouldn't come back for three days and three nights.
Not that he didn't wish to help out.
You try keeping a bunch of lambs
From getting lost looking for that sweeter taste
Without a dog to help you. Can't be done.
You can't walk away from the other lambs either.
You've got to lead them back and forth
Across the hills while you keep an eye
Peeled for the last one that just got lost.
You develop a sixth sense about which one's missing.
You brood about it. Who's missing?
Then you go off in one direction or another
Trying not to lose the next one.
But it's still a fair time out there.
The hills are full of surprises, not one thing
Quite looks like it did before. Plus,
There are other animals, most of them friendly,
A sackful of corn and onions and potatoes,
And berries to be found among the scrub and heather.
Plus not to have to talk all the time.
Especially when your mother feels guilty about something,
And your father acts obscurely embarrassed,
And your brother seems a little bit frenzied.
It's nice to lay way outside at night,
With the animals snoring very quietly, and watch
Light pour through the pinholes in the fabric.
Plus, the slaughter won't have to be done for weeks.
So you can relax, even though you can't go to sleep.

The Great Escape

for John Stoss

Everything's still on down the rows of cells of beds with men
    asleep
Who dream dreams in prison about prison life

But one man is awake and digs at the floor of his cell
With a spoon: one spoonful by the week

Everyone knows what he is doing and no one cares:
The rock floor is built on rocks, everyone knows

He has a special relationship with the moon
Which one guard exploits who sells the spoons

He has imagined the deaths of enemies,
Bicycles used to fall apart under him

He gets packages in which are steaming pots of the foods of
    his native region,
Then all the hungry and all the greedy are fed

Everyone is grateful for his witlessness, but especially
For the dreamless music of his spoon against the stones

BETTY
ADCOCK

Born in rural east Texas in 1938, Betty Adcock has lived in North Carolina for most of her life. Her first collection, *Walking Out,* won the Great Lakes Colleges Associations' New Writing Award. *Nettles,* her second, won North Carolina's Roanoke-Chowan Award. She is Kenan Writer-in-Residence at Meredith College in Raleigh.

Roller Rink

That summer it just appeared,
like a huge canvas butterfly
pinned to McNaughton's field.
All of us half-grown came every day
to watch and try, in love
with unlikely motion, with ourselves
and the obscure brother
who was older and came from a nameless far end
of the country. He knew, from somewhere,
how to do it, the dance of it turning
faster than music, could bend
and glide smooth as a fish where we fell,
could leap, land and roll on
squatting, backward, one-footed.
We loved him for looking blade-boned and frail,
for being always alone with nothing to tell.

In August the old man who'd taken our change
hefted sections of floor and his tent
and his music into a truckbed and left.
The autumn that came after
rose for us with so perfectly clear
a cry of wild geese and amber light
on its early winds, with so many stars
let loose, and leaves in the rain—
even our shambling, hopeless town
seemed good, just in that turn
before the wheel of the year came down.

Of course it never came again.
But there was the round brown place
where grass wouldn't grow in that field,
but would grow next year with great ghost wheels
of queen anne's lace.
That summer was a line we'd stumbled over,
and so we were free to fall and gather
the dear, unskillful, amazing losses
departure needs. We took them all,
our bodies shooting crazily
into and through each other. And finally past
to army, city, anyplace far.
We took any road out we could take;
but none of us with the sweet-lifting grace
and ease of the promise that farm boy made
who went and stayed.

Walking Out

Fishing alone in a frail boat
he leaned too far, lost hold,
was turned out of the caulked world.
Seventy years he had lived without learning
how surfaces keep the swimmer up.

In that green fall, the churn of fear
slowing to pavane,
one breath held precious and broken,
he counted oar-strokes backward:

shore was not far.
This coin he took from the pocket of terror.

Starting over, over his head,
he reached for the earth.
As creatures of water once called on the future
locked in their bodies, he called on his past.
He walked. Walked. And there was enough
time, just enough, and luck.
Touching greenfingered sand, rising and touching,
body bursting with useless knowledge,
he came at the world from its other direction
and came to his place in air.

Back in his life now, he measures
distances one breath long,
talks less, flexes
the oars of his legs.

Things shimmer where he is,
his house, his earthcolored wife and sons.
Every place raises walls around him
the color of old glass.
Heaven is a high clear skin.

Beneath the drift of flesh his bones remember
trying for bottom.

Twentieth Anniversary

This is the silence known, a place
like the kitchen of an old, high-ceilinged house
where summer's heat has a layering
coolness as if there were woods
or a river close enough by.
When the woman who uses such a place has gone
out of the body of bread dough into her own,
when the man has walked his way to a porch,
and the child has opened the last door,
there is this.

Crumbs swept from the table
glow in a wedge of sun. As in heaven
or the time before birth,
here there is neither eating nor drinking.
The faucet holds one drop imperceptibly
growing, holds precisely the one note
it will let fall.

And whatever singing, forgetting or nightmare
howled in the house between man and woman,
the child laughing or stifling
in a clenched sleep, here
it is summer and cool, the shelves
green with okra, beans, pears in clear jars.

So clear to each other we see clean through,
we've put away whole pieces of the world
that grew in us. We are this late
quiet light that holds all afternoon,
color of those sharp yellow weedflowers
we look for when the trees begin to bare
the rest of things. Even winter
can wear such still shining,
this pair of rings.

Southbound

You can go back in a clap of blue metal
tracked by stewardesses with drinks and virginal masks.
These will work whether you breathe or not. And this
is the first part. The way is farther
into thin roads that sway with the country.
Through the shine of a rented car the red towns rise
and crumble, leaving faces stuck to you like dust.
Following the farms, houses the color of old women,
you gather a cargo from yards full of lapsed
appliances, tin cans, crockery, snapped wheels,
weedy, bottomless chairs. These float through the air
to rest on the sleek hood, the clean seats.
Things broken out of their forms
move to you, their owner, their own.

You slow under weight. The windshield blurs
with the wingbeat of chickens. The hound's
voice takes over your horn.
A green glass vase from a grave in a field
comes flowerless to your hand, holds a smell
of struck matches, of summer on rust, of running
water, of rabbits, of home.

Then the one place flung up like a barrier,
the place where you stop, the last
courthouse and gathering of garrulous stores.
You have brought the town.
It walks in your skin like a visitor.
Here, under the wooden tongue of the church,
by the paths with their toothed gates,
in the light of the drunk as he burns
past hunkered children reaching
for the eyes of their fathers, these fading
and coming like seasons,
you are the tall rooms of your dead.

Merchants still ring small furious bells
and the window of the moviehouse opens,
and the girls who will, open.
Men still stand jack-knifed to trace
deer trails in the dirt.
And blacks scythe the lawns, not singing,
keeping their flag hidden.

You may house again these weathers worn thin
as coins that won't spend, worn smooth
as the years between two who are old
and not fooled any longer. You may stand
beneath the cafe's blue sign where it steps
on the face like a fly. You may bend
to finger the cracked sidewalk,
the shape of stilled lightning, every fork
the same as it was when you thought that map
led to the rim of the world.

You may listen for thunder.

JAMES
APPLEWHITE

James Applewhite was born in 1935 in Stantonsburg, North Carolina, and received his Ph.D. from Duke University. He has published four books of poetry, most recently *Ode to the Chinaberry Tree and Other Poems*. *Following Gravity* was the winner of the 1979 Associated Writing Programs Award.

Photo Credit: Harold Moore
Copyright © 1985 Durham Herald Co., Inc.

My Grandfather's Funeral

I knew the dignity of the words:
"As for man, his days are as grass,
As a flower of the field so he flourisheth:
For the wind passeth, and he is gone"—
But I was not prepared for the beauty
Of the old people coming from the church,
Nor for the suddenness with which our slow
Procession came again in sight of the awakening
Land, as passing white houses, Negroes
In clothes the color of the earth they plowed,
We turned, to see bushes and rusting roofs
Flicker past one way, the stretch of fields
Plowed gray or green with rye flow constant
On the other, away to unchanging pines
Hovering over parallel boles like
Dreams of clouds.

At the cemetery the people
Surprised me again, walking across
The wave of winter-bleached grass and stones
Toward his grave; grotesques, yet perfect
In their pattern: Wainwright's round head,
His bad shoulder hunched and turning
That hand inward, Luby Paschal's scrubbed
Square face, lips ready to whistle to
A puppy, his wife's delicate ankles
Angling a foot out, Norwood Whitley
Unconsciously rubbing his blue jaw,
Locking his knees as if wearing boots;
The women's dark blue and brocaded black,
Brown stockings on decent legs supporting
Their infirm frames carefully over
The wintry grass that called them down,
Nell Overman moving against the horizon
With round hat and drawn-back shoulders—
Daring to come and show themselves
Above the land, to face the dying
Of William Henry Applewhite,
Whose name was on the central store
He owned no more, who was venerated,
Generous, a tyrant to his family
With his ally, the God of Moses and lightning
(With threat of thunder clouds rising in summer
White and ominous over level fields);
Who kept bright jars of mineral water
On his screened, appled backporch, who prayed
With white hair wispy in the moving air,
Who kept the old way in changing times,
Who killed himself plowing in his garden.
I seemed to see him there, above
The bleached grass in the new spring light,
Bowed to his handplow, bent-kneed, impassive,
Toiling in the sacrament of seasons.

White Lake

Rimmed in by cypresses, tin water flashed
Like the top of a can, in fields still buzzing
With cicadas: electrical August short-circuiting.
The surface slicked over us like oil, shone
Silver with clouds. We walked, holding hands,
Toward the rides. Roller Coaster. Dive Bomber.
We sat in the Ferris Wheel, throbbing
With its engine, as it hurried us backward,
To show a black polish, the lake like marble
Under the stars, bulbs on its opposite shore
Rolling across reflection in miniature pearls.

With a wince of thrill in the quick of our spines,
We offered up ourselves to a turning as enormous
As the seasons or desire, whirled down to search
Shadows, where water lapped subtly at roots,
For a place we could lie down together, wandered
Through glare from the lighted piers.
In the rides park afterward, there were dolls
To be won by rings or thrown balls. Pandas,
Like drunken guests at a wedding, faced
A tree-tall whirling as if spun by a giant.

Marriage Portrait

Nowhere else does screened porch wire
Gray the light so steadily, do moths
Circle bulbs at noon, pecan leaves wave
As in a paperweight's fluid. Here is
Childhood's landscape, glassed in a frame.

Caught in this jewel focus, the one
Bright place squeezes water from our eyes.
I pose as the little master, apple
Of an eye, who reads, spins tales for brother.
You are the lovely outsiders' daughter,

Blond and patronized. You mouth "yes m'am."
We skip down streets holding hands
In the yellow pinafore, knee britches—
Buildings, porches, enormous with shadow.
This says spicery from houses with pickles.

This is the world of mysterious feelings
Whose echo comes through the bedroom door:
The keys, the shortbread, small hands held,
An outgrown glove that seems a doll's.
A Europe of grown-ups far as the sky.

We look back now from that other country
Of secrets, overcoats, canes, prophylactics—
At a home town preserved in preciousness
Like peaches sealed in a Mason jar.
The rooms of that house which was houses

And rooms held in a different knowledge:
Dreams of flying, books that enclosed us
Whole days pavemented by sun.
The large space of staircases during a rain.
Innocence of violets. The cat's ruff, silver.

Trees of ordinary height made those
Summers mountainous. One cavernous hall
Kept the Roles in a trunk of treasures:
Paper silk hat, champagne slippers.
The two still try on costumes—high heels

Sharpening her steps beside his clumsy sword.
We see it a playhouse but cannot part.
As twilight mixes with perennial sun,
We recede from our vision. Like dolls gone gray.

Barbecue Service

I have sought the elusive aroma
Around outlying cornfields, turned corners
Near the site of a Civil War surrender.
The transformation may take place
At a pit no wider than a grave,
Behind a single family's barn.
These weathered ministers
Preside with the simplest of elements:
Vinegar and pepper, split pig and fire.
Underneath a glistening mountain in air,
Something is converted to a savor: the pig
Flesh purified by far atmosphere.
Like the slick-sided sensation from last summer,
A fish pulled quick from a creek
By a boy. Like breasts in a motel
With whiskey and twilight
Now a blue smoke in memory.
This smolder draws the soul of our longing.

I want to see all the old home folks,
Ones who may not last another year.
We will rock on porches like chapels
And not say anything, their faces
Impenetrable as different barks of trees.
After the brother who drank has been buried,
The graveplot stunned by sun
In the woods,
We men still living pass the bottle.
We barbecue pigs.
The tin-roofed sheds with embers
Are smoking their blue sacrifice
Across Carolina.

ALVIN AUBERT

Alvin Aubert was born in 1930 in Lutcher, Louisiana. He has taught at Southern University in Baton Rouge and now teaches at Wayne State University in Detroit. His *South Louisiana: New and Selected Poems* was published in 1985. He is the founding editor of the journal *Obsidian*.

Economics

I remember the boy, pink hand
Clutching the pull of a red wagon
Filled with gutted coons
And possoms kept from flies
And delicate eyes
By old newspapers,
        minus coats
His paw's gray skinning hand
Tagged for another end—
        the boy,
Crossing the line
To our side of town where each
Fat-streaked corpse brought
Twenty-five to a half
Money down on a new red bike.

How It's Done

palm the head just so. then
quick, before it comes to its senses
and plant a set of prying claws
in your wrist, a rapid twirl, a deft
snap and the headless weight shoots up
and out in a flurry. the lifeless head
left warm in your hand, eyes fixed
in a cold surprise. and when the frantic
flap flopping about is through
and you go forth with a dishpan
to retrieve the prize, ignore the mysterious
dark leavings, the damp hieroglyphics
in the back yard dust.

Silence

every one of us saw it
but none of us ever spoke of it
not even the widow Commere:

the fly
trapped beneath the closing lid
of the young soldier's coffin.

GERALD
BARRAX

Gerald Barrax was born in Attalla, Ala-
bama in 1933. He now teaches at North
Carolina State University in Raleigh,
where he is the editor of *Obsidian II:
Black Literature in Review*. His three vol-
umes of poetry are *Another Kind of Rain*,
An Audience of One, and *The Deaths of
Animals and Lesser Gods*.

Gift

What does it mean
that there is a snake lying among the wild strawberries;
   Spring has laid smooth stones
     at the edge of the pool;
   there are birds who see farther at night
     than the warm things under cover of purple leaves?
Some god has bitten this mottled apple.
We swim in these summer days, its juices.
What does it matter where the snake hides:
     I was out of place until a blue jay
     in return for my seed
     left that black banded feather from his wing
     in my back yard.

"I had a terror—since September"

First a terror of choice, but that was done
By September—Renunciation my chosen word.
I hope she knows the troubles, what pools I wade,
What an old romantic ass I've become—
To remember each stage of that delirium
I bought the albums and use the music we heard
To keep us in time together out of handmade
Memories of loving and scrooving in double-tongue.
Double-stopped now, it's all I can do to hum
The tunes and hang on to what I can, less
Each September, channeling raw music into the wound—
Afraid when she appears in the room
As out of time as music from all this sound
I might say yes this time goddamn I'd say yes.

Two Figures on Canvas

Here in this foreground of sunny Italian fields
She accepts exile as obligation to art.
This one, as all the others,
Has brought her here for his own need
From her harsher land beyond those background towers
Where even a stable and clean straw served
The kind of need they all understand.
He smiles in appreciation at his image of her.
And she, in spirit, must smile because she is aware
Of her renascence among women,
And is woman enough to smile.

She takes and comforts the child.
She assumes her pose from habit, endurance.
She accepts the gambit of heavy satin gown
In fashion with a wistful fancy
For the extravagant cascade of solemn Latin and feudal music:
But she laughs at his need for those moons,
For those pancake haloes.

JOHN BENSKO

John Bensko, born in Birmingham, Alabama in 1949, has degrees from the University of Alabama (B.A. 1973, M.F.A. 1979), and Florida State University (Ph.D., 1985). His first book, *Green Soldiers* (Yale University Press), won the Yale Series of Younger Poets Prize. He currently teaches at Rhodes College in Memphis.

Photo Credit: Rosemary Bensko

The Wild Horses of Assateague Island

Although the sign says
Do not feed the horses,

my husband cannot help but admire
their docile looks, the delicate size

of their bodies, and the ease
with which they nibble

the crackers from his hands.
He says: *Why waste stale crackers*

when the least we can do
is make friends?

They lean across the picnic table
and stretch their lips.

Losing its fear, a small herd
drifts across the road toward us.

From behind the dunes
a string of ten or twelve

breaks into a run.
The car, he says, *run for it!*

The home movie later shows
tongues licking the windows,

lips and teeth caressing
the hood. My husband's mouth opens.

He is saying: *Sign? What sign?*
Under the perspective

of wild brown eyes peering in.

Watching TV, the Elk Bones Up on Metaphysics

He loves it when the lawyer shouts:
Irrelevant and immaterial!
and slaps his palms on the courtroom table.
Hushed, the jurors shift in their chairs.
Their faces strain with confusion.

The question is: How can the defendant
be two places at once? Both guilty
and innocent? Mowing the lawn
to the satisfaction of his wife
while he also slips into the living room
and plunges in the knife? Perhaps

the answer lies in the shapely legs
of the secretary. She smiles
and denies everything. Or in the sly
looks of the detective. He claims
he watched the house for hours,
and while the crime came and went,
he saw nothing.

The Elk knows this is the point
to turn off the set, before the crafty
lawyer saves his client. Now
the mystery is complete: he has done in
his wife, but she still lives, seen
by shoppers, loading groceries
into the trunk of her car.

It is only a matter of time
until she comes up the driveway, looks
at the half-mowed lawn, and sees him there,
smiling, pushing the mower,
the perfect husband, struggling as always,
sweating out the wretched truth
of his innocence.

The Elk on Mutability

Time was he went for weeks without
changing his shirt. His wife naturally bitched;
his dog was, undeniably, a bit
too friendly; but the shirt never itched;

never came back from the cleaner's too stiff,
suggesting to his wife
that they go out for dinner.
Such friendships, he felt, should not alter.

The fair shapes of his arms embraced him. At night
guarding him on the chair, the gentle, hunched curve
was the air of his shoulders made light,
his second body. The doctor said: *Drive*

him home, and gave his wife the pills to cure
his doldrums. The shirt came clean. His heart went bare.

The Elk Uncovers the Heavens

He lifts the heavy tube
of the telescope to the roof of his house
and climbs above the trees, above his wife
sitting in the dark living room
with her TV game show.
He can forget she calls him
a child. As if her string
of situation comedies were more

important. The moon: to her
it's just another place
the boys have put their feet on.
Saturn is a child's spun top.
Undiscovered planets, he told her.
Explosions out of time. She laughed
and imitated the TV preacher: *It's Satan.*
Science makes men mad.

He listens to the tree frogs
with their song like an answer:
Don't think . . . don't pray . . . don't care . . .
hum along. Should he believe
like the Indians that the frogs
with their rising and falling song
will turn a man's spirit into evening?
The ancients searched the stars

for the will of God.
What will I inherit? he wonders . . .
just a cloud. But the white smear
focuses to a bright point:
The Elk's Comet, his name in the stars.

DC
BERRY

DC Berry was born in Vicksburg, Mississippi in 1942, and grew up in Woodville and Greenville. He teaches at the University of Southern Mississippi and is the author of *Saigon Cemetery*.

To the Woodville Depot

1. The Death Hog

Before I drove Davy to nursery school,
he left his daffodil on garbage can #8.
He sometimes used the lid as a shield.
It was the only one left in the morning shade.

When we returned in the afternoon,
the death hog had the daffodil,
now dead and shriveled, a scar
on our faces mirrored in the lid.

> The schoolhouse emptied each fall
> when Grandpa Hays and the dogs
> drove 500 slaughter hogs fifteen miles
> from Hays Hollow to the Woodville Depot.

Davy pouted, his lips making two small tusks.
We're all on the way to the Woodville Depot.

2. The Gut Bucket

So, let that siren sing, driver, let her whine,
that bloody light on top sling a bucket of blood
for every bottle of wine Old Man Hays sucked
until his teeth cracked the head of the copperhead
crawling up the dream that held his legs in the weeds,

whine for Davy fighting for his life,
clubbing #8 with the daffodil
as if he could beat the death hog to death
there mirrored in the garbage lid,

Davy marble-eyed at himself,
at the sight of so much dancing
in the dust of The Woodville Depot,
where even in the gut bucket the heart,
stomping and sidestepping the death hog,
keeps on stumbling the old two-step.

Road

Between Vicksburg and Rolling Fork,
the sun purpled
like the plum of shock
around embedded bird shot.

> A smoky sleeve
> reached from a chimney.

Now, at the Bon Ton in Yazoo City,
I can't remember what it was
when I thought of you,
Walter Whitman,

when the wind wrinkled
the edge of a cottonfield
as though to blow it off a lap,
and a hand quickly snatched it back.

WENDELL

BERRY

Wendell Berry was born in Kentucky in 1934 and received a B.A. and an M.A. from the University of Kentucky. Mr. Berry has published ten books of poetry, most recently *Collected Poems* (North Point Press, 1985). Although he taught in universities for many years, since 1977 he has made his living as a writer and farmer in Port Royal, Kentucky.

Photo Credit: Tanya Berry

The Peace of Wild Things

When despair for the world grows in me
and I wake in the night at the least sound
in fear of what my life and my children's lives may be,
I go and lie down where the wood drake
rests in his beauty on the water, and the great heron feeds.
I come into the peace of wild things
who do not tax their lives with forethought
of grief. I come into the presence of still water.
And I feel above me the day-blind stars
waiting with their light. For a time
I rest in the grace of the world, and am free.

To Know the Dark

To go in the dark with a light is to know the light.
To know the dark, go dark. Go without sight,
and find that the dark, too, blooms and sings,
and is traveled by dark feet and dark wings.

The Grandmother

Better born than married, misled,
in the heavy summers of the river bottom
and the long winters cut off by snow
she would crave gentle dainty things,
"a pretty little cookie or a cup of tea,"
but spent her days over a wood stove
cooking cornbread, kettles of jowl and beans
for the heavy, hungry, hard-handed
men she had married and mothered, bent
past unbending by her days of labor
that love had led her to. They had to break her
before she would lie down in her coffin.

Grief

The morning comes. The old woman, a spot
of soot where she has touched her cheek, tears
on her face, builds a fire, sets water to boil,
puts the skillet on. The man in his middle years,
bent by the work he has done toward the work
he will do, weeps as he eats, bread in his mouth,
tears on his face. They shape the day for its passing
as if absent from it—for what needs care, caring,
feeding what must be fed. To keep them, there are only
the household's remembered ways, etched thin
and brittle by their tears. It is a sharp light
that lights the day now. It seems to shine,
beyond eyesight, also in another day
where the dead have risen and are walking
away, their backs forever turned. What
look is in their eyes? What do they say
as they walk into the fall and flow of light?
It seems that they must know where they are going.
And the living must go with them, not knowing,
a little way. And the dead go on, not turning,
knowing, but not saying. And the living
turn back to their day, their grieving and staying.

DAVID ——

BOTTOMS

David Bottoms was born in Canton, Georgia in 1949. His first book, *Shooting Rats at the Bibb County Dump*, was chosen by Robert Penn Warren as winner of the 1979 Walt Whitman Award of the Academy of American Poets. *In a U-Haul North of Damascus*, his second collection, was named Book of the Year by the Dixie Council of Authors and Journalists. He teaches at Georgia State University.

Photo Credit: Michael Pugh

In a U-Haul North of Damascus

1

Lord, what are the sins
I have tried to leave behind me? The bad checks,
the workless days, the scotch bottles thrown across the fence
and into the woods, the cruelty of silence,
the cruelty of lies, the jealousy,
the indifference?

What are these on the scale of sin
or failure
that they should follow me through the streets of Columbus,
the moon-streaked fields between Benevolence
and Cuthbert where dwarfed cotton sparkles like pearls
on the shoulders of the road. What are these
that they should find me half-lost,
sick and sleepless
behind the wheel of this U-Haul truck parked in a field
   on Georgia 45

a few miles north of Damascus,
some makeshift rest stop for eighteen wheelers
where the long white arms of oaks slap across trailers
and headlights glare all night through a wall of pines?

2

What was I thinking, Lord?
That for once I'd be in the driver's seat, a firm grip
on direction?

So the jon boat muscled up the ramp,
the Johnson outboard, the bent frame of the wrecked Harley
chained for so long to the back fence,
the scarred desk, the bookcases and books,
the mattress and box springs,
a broken turntable, a Pioneer amp, a pair
of three-way speakers, everything mine
I intended to keep. Everything else abandon.

But on the road from one state
to another, what is left behind nags back through the distance,
a last word rising to a scream, a salad bowl
shattering against a kitchen cabinet, china barbs
spiking my heel, blood trailed across the cream linoleum
like the bedsheet that morning long ago
just before I watched the future miscarried.

Jesus, could the irony be
that suffering forms a stronger bond than love.

3

Now the sun
streaks the windshield with yellow and orange, heavy beads
of light drawing highways in the dew-cover.
I roll down the window and breathe the pine-air,
the after-scent of rain, and the far-off smell
of asphalt and diesel fumes.

But mostly pine and rain
as though the world really could be clean again.

Somewhere behind me,
miles behind me on a two-lane that streaks across
west Georgia, light is falling
through the windows of my half-empty house.
Lord, why am I thinking about this? And why should I care
so long after everything has fallen
to pain that the woman sleeping there should be sleeping alone?
Could I be just another sinner who needs to be blinded
before he can see? Lord, is it possible to fall
toward grace? Could I be moved
to believe in new beginnings? Could I be moved?

The Boy Shepherds' Simile

Wind rose cold under our robes, and straw blew loose
from the stable roof.
We loved the cow tied to the oak, her breath rising
in the black air, and the two goats trucked
from the Snelling farm, the gray dog shaking with age
and weather.
                    Over our scene a great star hung
its light, and we could see in the bleached night
a crowd of overcoats peopling the chairs.
A coat of black ice glazed the street.

This was not a child or a king,
but Mary Sosebees's Christmas doll of a year ago.
We knelt in that knowledge on the wide front lawn
of the First Baptist Church
while flashbulbs went off all around us
and a choir of angels caroled from their risers.
This was not a child wrapped in the straw
and the ragged sheet, but since believing was an easy thing
we believed it was like a child,
a king who lived in the stories we were told.
For this we shivered in adoration. We bore the cold.

Sign for My Father, Who Stressed the Bunt

On the rough diamond,
the hand-cut field below the dog lot and barn,
we rehearsed the strict technique
of bunting. I watched from the infield,
the mound, the backstop
as your left hand climbed the bat, your legs
and shoulders squared toward the pitcher.
You could drop it like a seed
down either base line. I admired your style,
but not enough to take my eyes off the bank
that served as our center-field fence.

Years passed, three leagues of organized ball,
no few lives. I could homer
into the left-field lot of Carmichael Motors,
and still you stressed the same technique,
the crouch and spring, the lead arm absorbing
just enough impact. That whole tiresome pitch
about basics never changing,
and I never learned what you were laying down.

Like a hand brushed across the bill of a cap,
let this be the sign
I'm getting a grip on the sacrifice.

Under the Boathouse

Out of my clothes, I ran past the boathouse
to the edge of the dock
and stood before the naked silence of the lake,
on the drive behind me, my wife
rattling keys, calling for help with the grill,
the groceries wedged into the trunk.
Near the tail end of her voice, I sprang
from the homemade board, bent body
like a hinge, and speared the surface,
cut through water I would not open my eyes in,

to hear the junked depth pop in my ears
as my right hand dug into silt and mud,
my left clawed around a pain.
In a fog of rust I opened my eyes to see
what had me, and couldn't but knew
the fire in my hand and the weight of the thing
holding me under, knew the shock of all
things caught by the unknown
as I kicked off the bottom like a frog,
my limbs doing fearfully strange strokes,
lungs collapsed in a confusion of bubbles,
all air rising back to its element.
I flailed after it, rose toward the bubbles
breaking on light, then felt down my arm
a tug running from a taut line.
Halfway between the bottom of the lake
and the bottom of the sky, I hung like a buoy
on a short rope, an effigy
flown in an underwater parade,
and imagined myself hanging there forever,
a curiosity among fishes, a bait hanging up
instead of down. In the lung-ache,
in the loud pulsing of temples, what gave first
was something in my head, a burst
of colors like the blind see, and I saw
against the surface a shadow like an angel
quivering in a dead-man's float,
then a shower of plastic knives and forks
spilling past me in the lightened water, a can
of barbecued beans, a bottle of A.1., napkins
drifting down like white leaves,
heavenly litter from the world I struggled toward.
What gave then was something on the other end,
and my hand rose on its own and touched my face.
Into the splintered light under the boathouse,
the loved, suffocating air hovering over the lake,
the cry of my wife leaning dangerously
over the dock, empty grocery bags at her feet,
I bobbed with a hook through the palm of my hand.

The Drowned

Arms finned-out across the water,
he floated face down in the crotch of a fallen oak.
I cut the outboard
and rode the current, paddle-steered
toward the water stilled in the limbs of the tree.

In the bend where the river pooled and deepened,
my stomach jumped like something caught
and I pulled up short,
waited for breath, let my eyes follow water downstream
where the string of plastic milk jugs
floating my trotline
bobbed like heads on the surface of the river.

Then I drew the boat closer,
watched the slack of his blue jeans roll in my wake,
his head nod gently against the thick oak branch,
long hair tangled in the branch-twigs.
I eased the paddle out and touched his heel.
He didn't turn or move, only gazed straight down
into the deepest part of the Etowah
as though fascinated by something I couldn't see.

Under the Vulture-Tree

for Mary Oliver

We have all seen them circling pastures,
have looked up from the mouth of a barn, a pine clearing,
the fences of our own backyards, and have stood
amazed by the one slow wing beat, the endless dihedral drift.
But I had never seen so many so close, hundreds,
every limb of the dead oak feathered black,

and I cut the engine, let the river grab the jon boat
and pull it toward the tree.
The black leaves shined, the pink fruit blossomed

red, ugly as a human heart.
Then, as I passed under their dream, I saw for the first time
its soft countenance, the raw fleshy jowls
wrinkled and generous, like the faces
of the very old who have grown to empathize with everything.

And I drifted away from them, slow, on the pull of the river,
reluctant, looking back at their roost,
calling them what I'd never called them, what they are,
those dwarfed transfiguring angels,
who flock to the side of the poisoned fox, the mud turtle
crushed on the shoulder of the road,
who pray over the leaf-graves of the anonymous lost,
with mercy enough to consume us all and give us wings.

The Desk

Under the fire escape, crouched, one knee in cinders,
I pulled the ball peen hammer from my belt,
cracked a square of window pane,
the gummed latch, and swung the window,
crawled through that stone hole into the boiler room
of Canton Elementary School, once Canton High,
where my father served three extra years
as star halfback and sprinter.
                              Behind a flashlight's
cane of light, I climbed a staircase almost a ladder
and found a door. On the second nudge of my shoulder,
it broke into a hallway dark as history,
at whose end lay the classroom I had studied
over and over in the deep obsession of memory.

I swept that room with my light—an empty blackboard,
a metal table, a half-globe lying on the floor
like a punctured basketball—then followed
that beam across the rows of desks,
the various catalogs of lovers, the lists
of all those who would and would not do what,
until it stopped on the corner desk of the back row,
and I saw again, after many years, the name
of my father, my name, carved deep into the oak top.

To gauge the depth I ran my finger across that scar,
and wondered at the dreams he must have lived
as his eyes ran back and forth
from the cinder yard below the window
to the empty practice field
to the blade of his pocket knife etching carefully
the long, angular lines of his name,
the dreams he must have laid out one behind another
like yard lines, in the dull, pre-practice afternoons
of geography and civics, before he ever dreamed
of Savo Sound or Guadalcanal.
                                        In honor of dreams
I sank to my knees on the smooth, oiled floor,
and stood my flashlight on its end.
Half the yellow circle lit the underedge of the desk,
the other threw a half-moon on the ceiling,
and in that split light I tapped the hammer
easy up the overhang of the desk top. Nothing gave
but the wall's sharp echo, so I swung again,
and again harder, and harder still in half anger
rising to anger at the stubborn joint, losing all fear
of my first crime against the city, the county,
the state, whatever government claimed dominion,
until I had hammered up in the ringing dark
a salvo of crossfire, and on a frantic recoil glanced
the flashlight, the classroom spinning black
as a coma.
          I've often pictured the face of the teacher
whose student first pointed to that topless desk,
the shock of a slow hand rising from the back row,
their eyes meeting over the question of absence.
I've wondered, too, if some low authority of the system
discovered that shattered window,
and finding no typewriters, no business machines,
no audio-visual gear missing, failed to account for it,
so let it pass as minor vandalism.
                                        I've heard nothing.
And rarely do I fret when I see that oak scar leaning
against my basement wall, though I wonder what it means
to own my father's name.

EDGAR BOWERS

Born in Rome, Georgia in 1924, Edgar Bowers served in the U.S. Army from 1943 to 1946. He attended the University of North Carolina and received his Ph.D. from Stanford. He teaches in the English department at the University of California, Santa Barbara.

Photo Credit: Joshua Odell

The Stoic: For Laura von Courten

All winter long you listened for the boom
Of distant cannon wheeled into their place.
Sometimes outside beneath a bombers' moon
You stood alone to watch the searchlights trace

Their careful webs against the boding sky,
While miles away on Munich's vacant square
The bombs lunged down with an unruly cry
Whose blast you saw yet could but faintly hear.

And might have turned your eyes upon the gleam
Of a thousand years of snow, where near the clouds
The Alps ride massive to their full extreme,
And season after season glacier crowds

The dark, persistent smudge of conifers.
Or seen beyond the hedge and through the trees
The shadowy forms of cattle on the furze,
Their dim coats white with mist against the freeze.

Or thought instead of other times than these,
Of other countries and of other sights:
Eternal Venice sinking by degrees
Into the very water that she lights;

Reflected in canals, the lucid dome
Of Maria dell'Salute at your feet,
Her triple spires disfigured by the foam.
Remembered in Berlin the parks, the neat

Footpaths and lawns, the clean spring foliage,
Where just short weeks before, a bomb, unaimed,
Released a frightened lion from its cage,
Which in the mottled dark that trees enflamed,

Killed one who hurried homeward from the raid.
And by yourself there standing in the chill
You must, with so much known, have been afraid
And chosen such a mind of constant will,

Which, though all time corrode with constant hurt,
Remains, until it occupies no space,
That which it is; and passionless, inert,
Becomes at last no meaning and no place.

An Afternoon at the Beach

I'll go among the dead to see my friend.
The place I leave is beautiful: the sea
Repeats the winds' far swell in its long sound,
And, there beside it, houses solemnly
Shine with the modest courage of the land,
While swimmers try the verge of what they see.

I cannot go, although I should pretend
Some final self whose phantom eye could see
Him who because he is not cannot change.
And yet the thought of going makes the sea,
The land, the swimmers, and myself seem strange,
Almost as strange as they will someday be.

Autumn Shade, Part 1

The autumn shade is thin. Grey leaves lie faint
Where they will lie, and, where the thick green was,
Light stands up, like a presence, to the sky.
The trees seem merely shadows of its age.
From off the hill, I hear the logging crew,
The furious and indifferent saw, the slow
Response of heavy pine; and I recall
That goddesses have died when their trees died.
Often in summer, drinking from the spring,
I sensed in its cool breath and in its voice
A living form, darker than any shade
And without feature, passionate, yet chill
With lust to fix in ice the buoyant rim—
Ancient of days, the mother of us all.
Now, toward his destined passion there, the strong,
Vivid young man, reluctant, may return
From suffering in his own experience
To lie down in the darkness. In this time,
I stay indoors. I do my work. I sleep.
Each morning, when I wake, I assent to wake.
The shadow of my fist moves on this page,
Though, even now, in the wood, beneath a bank,
Coiled in the leaves and cooling rocks, the snake
Does as it must, and sinks into the cold.

An Elegy: December, 1970

Almost four years, and, though I merely guess
What happened, I can feel the minutes' rush
Settle like snow upon the breathless bed—
And we who loved you, elsewhere, ignorant.
From my deck, in the sun, I watch boys ride
Complexities of wind and wet and wave:
Pale shadows, poised a moment on the light's
Archaic and divine indifference.

VAN K.
BROCK

Van K. Brock was born in 1932 and raised near Moultrie, Georgia. He graduated from Emory University and the University of Iowa and co-directs the writing program at Florida State University. His collection, *The Hard Essential Landscape*, follows his complex South through World Wars and the social revolution he considers his home.

Novas

Who called flowers "mouths"?—these painted lips
of mimes frozen in imperceptible motion. Azaleas
hold the pose for days, weeks in temperate weather—
such reds, whites and purples, I lose my thread—
whispering essences, mouths that mock speech
with stillness, composing fuchsia symphonies
with fragrances so thin one is only an eighth note,
but here are the banks and reeds of Arcadia.

They surround me: I am theirs: wifewarp, childwoof,
birdflower, cloudtree. The porches of the poor
are propped up by azaleas. I am wrapped in woods.
The mouths say, *I am hungry.* They say, *Hum a thin song.*
In my yard, under a bush, the anthill streams red
stingers in and out. A city of law and industry.
All day and night their armies march to and from
their catacombs. I think they never sleep.

At night, when I fly into Los Angeles, spread
like a cancer of wisteria on the crumbling edge
of the continent, even its slums seem luminous.
Mouths! Mouths! What are they saying? The ripened
slums say, *Police are a state of mind, and we are
their colonies.* Just before dawn, after the rain
has washed the air, a pimp—raped, beaten, and OD'd—
comes to and sees his whore beside him, her throat cut,

the sky afloat with brilliant bones. Words of ash
and fire: star orchids and those black stellar flowers
forever collapsing inward and exploding outward in
rhythms that rock firmly in the center of yourself:
listen! They begin and end the long curve of eternity.
I am knocking on a wooden table in a dark seance.
Viewed from the moon, looking back, Earth's a blue
anthill throbbing like an orchid in a vast austerity

of fireants that have vaulted the woods of imagining:
here all worlds that ever existed still exist in an eye
for which time is merely the spatial lines of perspective,
and Plato, Dante, Einstein are silent red songs on a bush,
interlocking cones of perception, sequential, burning
together, telling what the stars say, what azaleas mime,
while I am trying to hear the song enabling the ant
with its load of contraband pollen to lift thrice its weight.

Departure

After I died I could not close my eyes,
And when everything appeared
In sweeping glares where people swayed
Like trees in dreaming blows,
I tried to say, "The horror is all yours."

A woman wailed when rocks fell on my house.
I never knew a gentler music.
I hear contrasting rhythms not of rain.
Quiet descends like lint;
The air is being absorbed.

I miss nothing yet unless it's God,
But I am breaking loose,
And as I wander through the stones
That churn like seas inside,
The terror is the getting lost in earth.

Lying on a Bridge

We saw anchored worlds in a shallow stream.
The current tugged at clouds, the sun, our faces.
And while we stared, as though into a dream,
The stream moved on; the anchors kept their places.
Even the white rose thorned into your hair
Stayed there, though its refracted, scattered aura
Circled your abstract face, like snow in air;
Then the rose fell onto that gentle water,
Shattering our faces with their mirror. But sun
And clouds, and all their height and depth of light,
Could not feel so involved, nor watch when one
Bloom touched that current and waltzed it out of sight.
Though rising, we saw how all things float in space:
The stars and clouds, ourselves, each other's face.

The Man in the Rain

"George," she said, "come out of the rain!"
All afternoon it had been raining,

The cat lying under the doorstep
And George in the lawn chair.
"George," she said, "come out of the rain!"

George, as if the sun were shining,
Face up, eyes closed, did not answer.
The cat, lying under the doorstep,

Opened his eyes on the second call,
But did not move except to stretch.
George, as if the sun were shining,

Lay there, face up, eyes closed, not answering.
All afternoon it had been raining.

JACK
BUTLER

Jack Butler is the author of two books of poetry, *West of Hollywood* and *The Kid Who Wanted to be a Spaceman*. He has degrees in English and mathematics and took an M.F.A. in creative writing at the University of Arkansas. Originally from Alligator, Mississippi, where he was born in 1944, Butler currently lives in Little Rock, where he makes his living as a statistical analyst.

Photo Credit: Bill Parsons

Preserves

Great love goes mad to be spoken: you went out
to the ranked tent-poles of the butterbean patch,
picked beans in the sun. You bent, and dug
the black ground for fat purple turnips.
You suffered the cornstalk's blades, to emerge
triumphant with grain. You spent all day in a coat
of dust, to pluck the difficult word
of a berry, plunk in a can. You brought home
voluminous tribute, cucumbers, peaches,
five-gallon buckets packed tightly with peas,
cords of sugar-cane, and were not content.

You had not yet done the pure, the completed,
the absolute deed. Out of that vegetable ore,
you wrought miracles: snap-beans broke
into speech, peas spilled from the long slit pod
like pearls, and the magical snap of your nail
filled bowls with the fat white coinage of beans.

Still, you were unfinished. Now fog swelled
in the kitchen, your hair wilted like vines.
These days drove you half-wild—you cried, sometimes,
for invisible reasons. In the yard, out of your way,
we played in the leaves and heard
the pressure-cooker blow out its musical shriek.

Then it was done: you had us stack up the jars
like ingots, or books. In the dark of the shelves,
quarts of squash gave off a glow like late sun.

That was the last we thought of your summer
till the day that even the johnson grass died.
Then, bent over sweet relish and black-eyed peas,
over huckleberry pie, seeing the dog outside
shiver with cold, we would shiver, and eat.

No News at All

The weather isn't news unless extreme,
though the news is a kind of grumbling weather—
fortunately far-off and dwindled, tinny
as voices remembered from a dream.
Men need freshness most: what can offer any?
Not memory and history together.

Only what's outside skin or brain
can make a difference to what's caught in it.
That difference might be nothing more than light,
the rusty odor of dust freckling with rain,
or the rain-drops, dust-floured, dusty white,
that roll about like mercury a minute.

Subplot

Accident or the gods,
processes busy about their own directions
touch you, transform you. I found myself
six feet tall,
dressed in coachman's piping, a whip coiled
in my right hand—and in my stomach,
the same half-digested cricket.
Oh, I remembered—the rat still crouched
in my brand-new brain, and I could almost
twitch my non-existent whiskers.
Far below, I saw the bricks of the floor
ripple for miles. Out the window
I saw, for the first time, hills,
truncated with evening light. Later,
when I drove up the road,
there would be brightnesses overhead
I thought of as stars.

It became dark. She bent over once
to put on her shoes, hand against the mantel,
each breast succulent, dependent
against her bodice, the fire
flickering on their curves. Her hair fell over
her shoulders like water.

Sitting in the coach outside the dance,
I had hours to settle it all.
Laughter rang from the lighted windows,
music drifted out. The horses
whuffled and shuddered. Water lapped
on the stones of the palace pool.
Leaves whispered. Mosquitoes whined and bit me.
I couldn't bring myself to kill them.
I had hours to settle it all.
If I had touched her or run away,
they would have changed me back.
I had hours, hours.

Then the doors burst open, flooding the yard
with light and clamor,
and she fled down the steps like a bird.
All the way back down that country road,
the silver, impassive moon

rode in the sky in front of me. I lashed blood
from those foaming backs,
I shouted scripture and algebra.
"I will turn blank eyes to the moon," I cried,
"the rest of my nights! I will be clubbed to death
gnawing on a dead child's foot!"

Afterglow

A light rustle of rain laid down now.
The saint augustine, the laurelcherry
out in the darkness drinking their lives,
roots dusty and cramped in new graves.

After transplanting, a little walk.
The darkness was swift as the shadow of a bird.
It came on us suddenly in the forest,
suddenly in the lemony air,
that diffuse glow near sunset
that comes of a cloudy day clearing
too late for sun, but not too late
for the amber, the umber, the orange and yellow
refracted off eastward cumulus.

It came on us suddenly in a green tunnel.
The day went grey, and then night.

I sit now in a manufactured storm of light,
the gutters talking quietly to puddles,
the nandena, the yaupon drinking,
a radiance decaying probably by halves
somewhere deep in my memory—

something of your face clean as an apple,
my hands that are now line drawings,
that were then rosy as angels—

something of green vivid as eyes after tears,
a floor of rusty pine-needles
like banked fires stirred with a poker.

One Reason for Stars

Stars and trouble, stars and trouble. Walk out
from the argument, and there, beyond the light
from the kitchen window, in the cool night roll the stars.

Spit at them for how they don't help and go back in
to the sort of thing that makes you hate yourself
even more than you hate who's crying behind the door she slammed.

And twenty weeks later, beside the rattling creek,
smoke-odor sharp in the frozen air and the dark
drawn down to a knot of coals, you'll gulp the last
scalding swallow of chocolate and sack in warmly,
to listen to pine sighing its friendly, night-long,
impersonal sigh, and stare up for an hour or two
thanking God they didn't, and couldn't, get involved.

TURNER
CASSITY

Turner Cassity was born in Jackson, Mississippi in 1929, and graduated from high school there. He has degrees from Millsaps College, Stanford University, and Columbia University. His latest book of poetry is *Hurricane Lamp* (University of Chicago Press). Since 1962 he has worked at Emory University Library.

U-24 Anchors off New Orleans (1938)

The only major city, one would hope,
Below the level of a periscope.
An air so wet, a sewer-damp so ill,
One had as well be under water still.

The muddy river cakes us, camouflages.
Maddened goats, my crew go off in barges.
At a distance—I do not refer
To feet and inches—I go too. To err

Defines the deckhands; not to is the Bridge.
Discretion is the sex of privilege.
The streetcars meet the levee four abreast;
I cleverly have picked the noisiest.

A mad mapmaker made this master plan,
To wring out, of his grid of streets, a fan.
One German restaurant, well meant but erring:
Ten kinds of shellfish; bouillabaisse; no herring.

Have my men fared better? Where they are
Becomes a high Weimar Republic bar.
There—lower Bourbonstrasse—lace and leather
Mingle in Louisiana weather.

Crack your whip, Old Harlot; pop your garter.
Who lives here is, by definition, martyr.
If I come back I'll think to pack libido.
For symbolism there will be torpedo.

Professionals

Itinerant astrologers of no great wealth,
We leave three gifts as winning teams might drink a health;
The whole point being, not the goal, however termed,
But how our distant calculation stands confirmed.

Our bright conjunction splits to its component stars;
We part. Dark Heaven, give again your text we parse,
That, by the well-loved exercise, the known arcane,
We keep our pride. If, through arcana now our own,

We still may end as fable, need true cameleers
Seem quack familiars? Substance of the gold, the years,
Become ourselves that which we are in other eyes:
Three kings of Orient, by reputation wise.

Flying Friendly Skies

Our left and right show red and green: mute phonics.
A two-light Christmas in a sky of onyx.
The 1011 is an hour from Phoenix.

The cabin lights are off, and at my side
A sleeping Pfc., his waking bride,
Have heads an airline pillow may divide,

But somewhat as a cut divides the cards—
In no essential. Having knitted yards,
My neighbor on the other side—her guard's

Up always—draws a game of solitaire.
"The point of Phoenix," says she, "is its *air*."
Sun City is for her the at, the where.

The two young people near the primal scene.
The solitary, tactful, has to screen
Her reading light. I? I fall in between.

Fred Chappell, winner of the Bollingen Prize in Poetry in 1985, was born in Canton, North Carolina in 1936, and received his B.A. and M.A. from Duke University. He teaches in the Writing Program at the University of North Carolina in Greensboro.

My Grandmother Washes Her Feet

I see her still, unsteadily riding the edge
Of the clawfoot tub, mumbling to her feet,
Musing bloodrust water about her ankles.
Cotton skirt pulled up, displaying bony
Bruised patchy calves that would make you weep.

Rinds of her soles had darkened, crust-colored—
Not yellow now—like the tough outer belly
Of an adder. In fourteen hours the most refreshment
She'd given herself was dabbling her feet in the water.

"You mightn't've liked John-Giles. Everybody knew
He was a mean one, galloping whiskey and bad women
All night. Tried to testify dead drunk
In church one time. That was a ruckus. Later
Came back a War Hero, and all the young men
Took to doing the things he did. And failed.
Finally one of his women's men shot him."

"What for?"

　　　"Stealing milk through fences. . . . That part
Of Family nobody wants to speak of.
They'd rather talk about fine men, brick houses,
Money. Maybe you ought to know, teach you
Something."

　　　　　"What *do* they talk about?"

　　　　　　　　　"Generals,
And the damn Civil War, and marriages.
Things you brag about in the front of Bibles.
You'd think there was arms and legs of Family
On every battlefield from Chickamauga
To Atlanta."

　　　　　"That's not the way it is?"

"Don't matter how it is. No proper way
To talk, is all. It was nothing they ever did.
And plenty they *won't* talk about . . . John-Giles!"

Her cracked toes thumped the tub wall, spreading
Shocklets. Amber toenails curled like shavings.
She twisted the worn knob to pour in coolness
I felt suffuse her body like a whiskey.

"Bubba Martin, he was another, and no
Kind of man. Jackleg preacher with the brains
Of a toad. Read the Bible upside down and crazy
Till it drove him crazy, making crazy marks
On doorsills, windows, sides of Luther's barn.
He killed hisself at last with a shotgun.
No gratitude for Luther putting him up
All those years. Shot so he'd fall down the well."

"I never heard."

　　　　　"They never mention him.
Nor Aunt Annie, that everybody called
Paregoric Annie, that roamed the highways
Thumbing cars and begging change to keep
Even with her craving. She claimed she was saving up
To buy a glass eye. It finally shamed them
Enough, they went together and got her one.

That didn't stop her. She lugged it around
In a velvet-lined case, asking strangers
Please to drop it in the socket for her.
They had her put away. And that was that.
There's places Family ties just won't stretch to."

Born then in my mind a race of beings
Unknown and monstrous. I named them Shadow-Cousins,
A linked long dark line of them,
Peering from mirrors and gleaming in closets, agog
To manifest themselves inside myself.
Like discovering a father's cancer.
I wanted to search my body for telltale streaks.

"Sounds like a bunch of cow thieves."

                              "Those too, I reckon,
But they're forgotten or covered over so well
Not even I can make them out. Gets foggy
When folks decide they're coming on respectable.
First thing you know, you'll have a Family Tree."

(I imagined a wind-stunted horse-apple.)

She raised her face. The moons of the naked bulb
Flared in her spectacles, painting out her eyes.
In dirty water light bobbed like round soap.
A countenance matter-of-fact, age engraved,
Mulling in peaceful wonder petty annals
Of embarrassment. Gray but edged with brown
Like an old photograph, her hair shone yellow.
A tiredness mantled her fine energy.
She shifted, sluicing water under instep.

"O what's the use," she said. "Water seeks
Its level. If your daddy thinks that teaching school
In a white shirt makes him a likelier man,
What's to blame? Leastways, he won't smother
Of mule-farts or have to starve for a pinch of rainfall.
Nothing new gets started without the old's
Plowed under, or halfway under. We sprouted from dirt,
Though, and it's with you, and dirt you'll never forget."

"No Mam."

"Don't you say me No Mam yet.
Wait till you get your chance to deny it."

Once she giggled, a sound like stroking muslin.

"You're bookish. I can see you easy a lawyer
Or a county clerk in a big white suit and tie,
Feeding the preacher and bribing the sheriff and the judge.
Second-generation-respectable
Don't come to any better destiny.
But it's dirt you rose from, dirt you'll bury in.
Just about the time you'll think your blood
Is clean, here will come dirt in a natural shape
you never dreamed. It'll rise up saying, Fred,
Where's that mule you're supposed to march behind?
Where's your overalls and roll-your-owns?
Where's your Blue Tick hounds and Domineckers?
Not all the money in this world can wash true-poor
True rich. Fatback just won't change to artichokes."

"What's artichokes?"

                    "Pray Jesus you'll never know.
For if you do it'll be a sign you've grown
Away from what you are, can fly to flinders
Like a touch-me-not . . . I may have errored
When I said *true-poor*. It ain't the same
As dirt-poor. When you got true dirt you got
Everything you need . . . And don't you say me
Yes Mam again. You just wait."

                    She leaned
And pulled the plug. The water circled gagging
To a bloody eye and poured in the hole like a rat.
I thought maybe their spirits had gathered there,
All my Shadow-Cousins clouding the water,
And now they ran to earth and would cloud the earth.
Effigies of soil, I could seek them out
By clasping soil, forcing warm rude fingers
Into ancestral jelly my father wouldn't plow.
I strained to follow them, and never did.
I never had the grit to stir those guts.
I never had the guts to stir that earth.

Cleaning the Well

Two worlds there are. One you think
You know; the Other is the Well.
In hard December down I went.
"Now clean it out good." Lord, I sank
Like an anchor. My grand-dad leant
Above. His face blazed bright as steel.

Two worlds, I tell you. Swallowed by stones
Adrip with sweat, I spun on the ache
Of the rope; the pulley shrieked like bones
Scraped merciless on violins.
Plunging an eye. Plunging a lake
Of corkscrew vertigo and silence.

I halfway knew the rope would break.

Two suns I entered. At exact noon
The white sun narrowly hung above;
Below, like an acid floating moon,
The sun of water shone.
And what beneath that? A monster trove

Of blinding treasure I imagined:
Rib cage of drowned warlock gleaming,
Rust-chewed chain mail, or a plangent
Sunken bell tolling to the heart
Of earth. (They'd surely chosen an art-
less child to sound this soundless dreaming

O.) Dropping like a meteor,
I cried aloud—"Whoo! It's *God
Damn* cold!"—dancing the skin of the star.
"You watch your mouth, young man," he said.
I jerked and cursed in a silver fire
Of cold. My left leg thrummed like a wire.

Then, numb. Well water rose to my waist
And I became a figure of glass,
A naked explorer of outer space.
Felt I'd fricasseed my ass.
Felt I could stalk through earth and stone,
Nerveless creature without a bone.

Water-sun shattered, jelly-
Bright wavelets lapped the walls.
Whatever was here to find, I stood
In the lonesome icy belly
Of the darkest vowel, lacking breath and balls,
Brain gummed mud.

"Say, Fred, how's it going down there?"
His words like gunshots roared; re-roared.
I answered, "Well—" (*Well well well* . . .)
And gave it up. It goes like Hell,
I thought. Precise accord
Of pain, disgust, and fear.

"Clean it out good." He drifted pan
And dipper down. I knelt and dredged
The well floor. Ice-razors edged
My eyes, the blackness flamed like fever,
Tin became nerve in my hand
Bodiless. *I shall arise never.*

What did I find under this black sun?
Twelve plastic pearls, monopoly
Money, a greenish rotten cat,
Rubber knife, toy gun,
Clock guts, wish book, door key,
An indescribable female hat.

Was it worth the trip, was it true Descent?
Plumbing my childhood, to fall
Through the hole in the world and become . . .
What? *He told me to go. I went.*
(Recalling something beyond recall.
Cold cock on the nether roof of Home.)

Slouch sun swayed like a drunk
As up he hauled me, up, up,
Most willing fish that was ever caught.
I quivered galvanic in the taut
Loop, wobbled on the solid lip
Of earth, scarcely believing my luck.

His ordinary world too rich
For me, too sudden. Frozen blue,
Dead to armpit, I could not keep

My feet. I shut my eyes to fetch
Back holy dark. Now I knew
All my life uneasy sleep.

Jonah, Joseph, Lazarus,
Were you delivered so? Ript untimely
From black wellspring of death, unseemly
Haste of flesh dragged forth?
Artemis of waters, succor us,
Oversurfeit with our earth.

My vision of light trembled like steam.
I could not think. My senses drowned
In Arctic Ocean, the Pleiades
Streaked in my head like silver fleas.
I could not say what I had found.
I cannot say my dream.

When life began re-tickling my skin
My bones shuddered me. Sun now stood
At one o'clock. Yellow. Thin.
I had not found death good.
"Down there I kept thinking I was dead."

"Aw, you're all right," he said.

My Grandmother Washes Her Vessels

In the white-washed medical-smelling milkhouse
She wrestled clanging steel; grumbled and trembled,
Hoisting the twenty-gallon cans to the ledge
Of the spring-run (six by three, a concrete grave
Of slow water). Before she toppled them in—
Dented armored soldiers booming in pain—
She stopped to rest, brushing a streak of damp
Hair back, white as underbark. She sighed.

"I ain't strong enough no more to heft these things.
I could now and then wish for a man
Or two . . . Or maybe not. More trouble, likely,
Than what their rations will get them to do."

The August six o'clock sunlight struck a wry
Oblong on the north wall. Yellow light entering
This bone-white milkhouse recharged itself white,
Seeped pristine into the dozen strainer cloths
Drying overhead.

        "Don't you like men?"

Her hand hid the corner of her childlike grin
Where she's dropped her upper plate and left a gap.
"Depends on the use you want them for," she said.
"Some things they're good at, some they oughtn't touch."

"Wasn't Grandaddy a good carpenter?"

She nodded absentminded. "He was fine.
Built churches, houses, barns in seven counties.
Built the old trout hatchery on Balsam . . .
Here. Give me a hand."

      We lifted down
Gently a can and held it till it drowned.
Gushed out of its headless neck a musky clabber
Whitening water like a bedsheet ghost.
I thought, Here spills the soldier's spirit out;
If I could drink a sip I'd know excitements
He has known; travails, battles, tourneys,
A short life fluttering with pennants.

           She grabbed
A frazzly long-handled brush and scrubbed his innards
Out. Dun flakes of dried milk floated up,
Streamed drainward. In his trachea water sucked
Obscenely, graying like a storm-sky.

"You never told me how you met."

          She straightened,
Rubbed the base of her spine with a dripping hand.
"Can't recollect. Some things, you know, just seem
To go clear from your mind. Probably
He spotted me at prayer meeting, or it could
Have been a barn-raising. That was the way
We did things then. Not like now, with the men
All hours cavorting up and down in cars."

[handwritten margin note: "disparity between past/present"]

Again she smiled. I might have sworn she winked.

"But what do you remember?"

                              "Oh, lots of things.
About all an old woman is good for
   Is remembering. . . . But getting married to Frank
Wasn't the beginning of my life.
I'd taught school up Greasy Branch since I
Was seventeen. And I took the first census
Ever in Madison County. You can't see
It now, but there was a flock of young men come
Knocking on my door. If I'd a mind
I could have danced six nights of the week."

We tugged the cleaned can out, upended it
To dry on the worn oak ledge, and pushed the other
Belching in. Slowly it filled and sank.

"Of course, it wasn't hard to pick Frank out,
The straightest-standing man I ever saw.
Had a waxed moustache and a chestnut mare.
Before I'd give my say I made him cut
That moustache off. I didn't relish kissing
A briar patch. He laughed when I said that,
Went home and shaved. . . . It wasn't the picking and saying
That caused me ponder, though. Getting married—
In church—in front of people—for good and all:
It makes you pause. Here I was twenty-eight,
Strong and healthy, not one day sick since I
Was born. What cause would I have to be waiting
On a man?"

       Suddenly she sat on the spring-run edge
And stared bewildered at empty air, murmuring.

"I never said this to a soul, I don't
Know why . . . I told my papa, 'Please hitch me
The buggy Sunday noon. I can drive
Myself to my own wedding.' That's what I did,
I drove myself. A clear June day as cool
As April, and I came to where we used to ford
Laurel River a little above Coleman's mill,
And I stopped the horse and I thought and thought.
If I cross this river I won't turn back. I'll join
To that blue-eyed man as long as I've got breath.

There won't be nothing I can feel alone
About again. My heart came to my throat.
I suppose I must have wept. And then I heard
A yellowhammer in a willow tree
Just singing out, ringing like a dance-fiddle
Over the gurgly river-sound, just singing
To make the whole world hush to listen to him.
And then my tears stopped dropping down, and I touched
Nellie with the whip, and we crossed over."

Second Wind

The day they laid your Grandfather away
Was as hot and still as any I recall.
Not the least little breath of air in hall
Or parlor. A glossy shimmering July day,
And I was tired, so tired I wanted to say,
"Move over, Frank-my-husband, don't hog all
The space there where you are that looks so cool";
But it's a sin to want yourself to die.

And anyhow there was plenty enough to do
To help me fend off thoughts I'd be ashamed
Of later. (Not that ever I'd be blamed.)
The house was full of people who all knew
Us from way back when. Lord knows how
They'd even heard he died. And so it seemed
I owed them to stand firm. I hadn't dreamed
There'd be so terrible many with me now.

I'd fancied, don't you see, we'd be alone.
A couple growing old, until at last
There's one of them who has to go on first,
And then the other's not entirely *one*.
Somehow I'd got it in my mind that none
Of the rest of the world would know. Whichever passed
Away would have the other to keep fast
By, and the final hours would be our own.

It wasn't like that. I suppose it never is.
Dying's just as public as signing a deed.
They've got to testify you're really dead
And haven't merely changed an old address;
And maybe someone marks it down: *One less.*
Because it doesn't matter what you did
Or didn't do, just so they put the lid
On top of someone they think they recognize.

All those people . . . So many faces strained
With the proper strain of trying to look sad.
What did they feel truly? I thought, what could
they feel, wearing their Sunday clothes and fresh-shined
Prayer-meeting shoes? . . . Completely drained,
For thoughts like that to come into my head,
And knowing I'd thought them made me feel twice bad . . .
Ninety degrees. And three weeks since it rained.

I went into the kitchen where your mother
And your aunts were frying chicken for the crowd.
I guess I had in mind to help them out,
But then I couldn't. The disheartening weather
Had got into my heart; and not another
Thing on earth seemed worth the doing. The cloud
Of greasy steam in there all sticky glued
My clothes flat to my skin. I feared I'd smother.

I wandered through the house to the bedroom
And sat down on the bed. And then lay back
And closed my eyes. And then sat up. A black
And burning thing shaped like a tomb
Rose up in my mind and spoke in flame
And told me I would never find the pluck
To go on with my life, would come down weak
And crazed and sickly, waiting for my time.

I couldn't bear that . . . Would I ever close
My eyes again? I heard the out-of-tune
Piano in the parlor and knew that soon
Aunt Tildy would crank up singing "Lo, How a Rose
E'er Blooming."—Now I'll admit Aunt Tildy tries,
But hadn't I been tried enough for one
Heartbreaking day? And then the Reverend Dunn
Would speak . . . *A Baptist preacher in my house!*

That was the final straw. I washed my face
And took off all my mourning clothes and dressed
Up in my everyday's, then tiptoed past
The parlor, sneaking like a scaredey mouse
From my own home that seemed no more a place
I'd ever feel at home in. I turned east
And walked out toward the barns. I put my trust
In common things to be more serious.

Barely got out in time. Aunt Tildy's voice
("Rough as a turkey's leg," Frank used to say)
Ran through the walls and through the oily day
Light and followed me. Lord, what a noise!
I walked a little faster toward where the rose
Vine climbed the cowlot fence and looked away
Toward Chambers Cove, out over the corn and hay,
All as still as in a picture pose.

What was I thinking? Nothing nothing nothing.
Nothing I could nicely put a name to.
There's a point in feeling bad that we come to
Where everything is hard as flint: breathing,
Walking, crying even. It's a heathen
Sorrow over us. Whatever we do,
It's nothing nothing nothing. We want to die,
And that's the bitter end of all our loving.

But then I thought I saw at the far end
Of the far cornfield a tiny stir of blade.
I held my breath; then, sure enough, a wade
Of breeze came row to row. One stalk would bend
A little, then another. It was the wind
Came tipping there, swaying the green sad
Leaves so fragile-easy it hardly made
A dimpling I could see in the bottom land.

I waited it seemed like hours. Already I
Felt better, just knowing the wind was free once more,
That something fresh rose out of those fields where
We'd worn off half our lives under the sky
That pressed us to the furrows day by day.
And I knew too the wind was headed here
Where I was standing, a cooling wind as clear
As anything that I might ever know.

It was the breath of life to me, it was
Renewal of spirit such as I could never
Deny and still name myself a believer.
The way a thing is is the way it is
Because it gets reborn; because, *because*
A breath gets in its veins strong as a river
And inches up toward light forever and ever.
As long as wind is, there's no such thing as *Was*.

The wind that turned the fields had reached the rose
Vine now and crossed the lot and brushed my face.
So fresh I couldn't hear Aunt Tildy's voice.
So strong it poured on me the weight of grace.

My Mother Shoots the Breeze

Hot horn hand in my face is all,
The old days. Not that I'm not glad you honor
Daddy and Mama by remembering.
But it wasn't eggs in clover by any means.
To belong like that to Old Times, you belong
To cruelty and misery . . . Oh,
I can't say just what I mean.

Whenever they talk to *you* they leave out hurting.
That's it, everybody hurt. The barns
Would hurt you, rocks in the field would bite like snakes.
And girls have skinny legs, eaten up
By rocks and briars. But I knew always a man
Was looking for me, there was a man would take me
Out of the bottom cornfield for my soul.
My Mama sent me to Carson-Newman College
And the University of Tennessee.
I came back home a schoolmarm, and could watch
Out my first grade windows women chopping
Tobacco, corn, and rocks in the first spring heat.
Two years before, and that was only me
There chopping, but now the pupils said me Yes Mam.
When I read Chaucer they learned to call me Mam.

I'd go back home and milk the cows and grade
A hundred papers. I'd have milked a thousand cows
And graded papers till my eyes went stone
To hear them call me Yes Mam before my Mama.
I taught how to read and write my first grade class
Of six-year-olds and big farm boys and grandmothers.
I'm not humble I was schoolbook proud.

First time I met your Pa he took my slip
Off. "Miss Davis, I want your pretty slip,
If you've got one loose about, for my Science class."
He was going to fly them Benjamin Franklin's kite.
I went to the women's room and squirmed it down
And sneaked it to him in a paper bag.
Under the table at lunch he grinned like a hound.
That afternoon he patched the kite together
And taught them about Electricity.
"Touch that, boys," he said, "if you want a shock.
We've got Miz Silverside's silk panties here."
(Jake Silverside was our Acting Principal.)

But I knew better what I couldn't say
And giggled like a chicken when that kite
Sailed up past my fifth period Spanish window.
I don't know what to tell you how I mean,
But I felt it was me, seeing my slip
Flying up there. It was a childish folly
But it made me warm. I know there's pictures now
Of people doing anything, whatever
Only a doctor could think of, but my slip,
Scented the way that I alone could know,
Flying past the windows made me warm.
J.T.'s the man I want, I thought, *because
He'd do anything* . . . And so he would.

But wouldn't stop . . . Everyday two weeks
In a row he ran that kite up past my window,
Long after he had worn Ben Franklin out.
It's time to show that man that I mean business,
I thought, it's time we both came down to earth.
The very next day I borrowed my daddy's 12 gauge
And smuggled it to school under a raincoat,
And when that kite came past me one more time
I propped and took my time and lagged and sighted
And blew the fool out of it, both barrels.

It floated up and down in a silky snow
Till there was nothing left. I can still remember
Your Pa's mouth open like the arch of a bridge.
"Quit troubling us maiden girls with your silly Science,"
I said, "while we're learning to talk to Mexico."

And one month later, after we were married,
He still called me Annie Mexico.

So. You're the offspring of a shotgun wedding,
But I don't blush about it much. Something
Your father taught me: *Never apologize,*
Never be ashamed, it's only life . . .
And then he was fired for creating life
From alfalfa in a jar on a window sill.

But look, I've told the story that was fun,
And I didn't mean that. What I meant to tell you:
It was hard, hard, hard, hard,
Hard.

My Father Washes His Hands

I pumped the iron handle and watched the water
Cough his knuckles clean. Still he kept rubbing,
Left hand in his right like hefting a baseball;
The freckles might have scaled off with the clay.
But didn't. They too were clay, he said, that mud
The best part maybe of apparent spirit.

"What spirit?" I asked.
                    He grinned and got the soap
Again and sloshed. A bubble moment I saw
Our two faces little in his palm.
"The Spirit of Farming," he said, "or the Soul of Damnfool."
Our faces went away and showed his lifeline.
"Damnfool why?"
                    "A man's a fool in this age
Of money to turn the soil. Never a dime
To call his own, and wearing himself away

Like a kid's pencil eraser on a math lesson.
I've got a mind to quit these fields and sell
Cheap furniture to poor folks. I've got a mind
Not to die in the traces like poor Honey."
(Our jenny mule had died two weeks before.)
"A man's not the same as a mule," I said.

He said, "You're right. A man doesn't have the heart . . .
We buried Honey, me and Uncle Joe,
While you were away at school. I didn't tell you.
Two feet down and we hit pipe clay as blue
And sticky as Buick paint. Octopus-rassling,
Uncle Joe called it. Spade would go down
Maybe two inches and with my whole weight behind
And come up empty. Blue glue with a spoon.
I soon decided to scale down the grave.
I told him straight, *I'm going to bust her legs*
And fold them under. His face flashed red at once.
My God, J.T., poor Honey that's worked these fields
For thirteen years, you'd bust her legs? I nodded.
She can't feel a thing, I said. He says,
By God I do. I told him to stand behind
The truck and stop his ears. I busted her legs.
I busted her legs with the mattock, her eyes all open
And watching me crack her bones and bulging out
Farther slightly with every blow. These fields
Were in her eyes, and a picture of me against
The sky blood-raw savage with my mattock.
I leaned and thumbed her eye shut and it was like
Closing a book on an unsatisfactory
Last chapter not pathetic and not tragic,
But angrifying mortifying sad.
The harder down I dug the bluer I got,
And empty as my shovel. It's not in me
To blubber, dont have Uncle Joe's boatload
Of whiskey in my blood yet. Heavy is how
I felt, empty-heavy and blue as poison.
So maybe it's time to quit. The green poison
Of money has leached into the ground,
And turned it blue . . . That grave is mighty shallow
That I dug, but I felt so out of heart I couldn't
Make myself go farther and farther down.
I stopped waist-high and we built up a mound
That will soak away by springtime and be level."

"Are you really going to quit the farm?" I asked.
"I wouldn't quit if I could get ahead,
But busting my behind to stay behind
Has got to be the foolishest treadmill a man
Could worsen on. The farm can wait; there's money
To be made these days, and why not me?
Better me than some cheap crooks I know of,
And that's a fact."
                                    "Whatever you say," I said,
"It's kind of sad, though . . . And now old Honey's gone."
"Gone? Six nights in a row I'd close my eyes
And see her pawing up on her broken legs
Out of that blue mud, her suffering hindquarters
Still swallowed in, and in her eyes the picture
Of me coming toward her with my mattock;
And talking in a woman's pitiful voice:
Don't do it, J.T., you're breaking promises. . . .
And wake up in a sweat. Honey's not gone,
She's in my head for good and all and ever."
"Even if you quit the farm?"
                                    "Even if."

I handed him the towel. He'd washed his hands
For maybe seven minutes by the clock,
But when he gave it back there was his handprint,
Earth-colored, indelible, on the linen.

Narcissus and Echo

Shall the water not remember   *Ember*
my hand's slow gesture, tracing above   *of*
its mirror my half-imaginary   *airy*
portrait? My only belonging   *longing;*
is my beauty, which I take   *ache*
away and then return, as love   *of*
teasing playfully the one being   *unbeing.*
whose gratitude I treasure   *Is your*
moves me. I live apart   *heart*
from myself, yet cannot   *not*
live apart. In the water's tone,   *stone?*
that brilliant silence, a flower   *Hour,*
whispers my name with such slight   *light:*
moment, it seems filament of air,   *fare*
the world become cloudswell.   *well.*

JOHN WILLIAM CORRINGTON

John William Corrington was born in Memphis in 1932, and raised in Shreveport, Louisiana. After study at Centenary College and Rice, he received a D.Phil. from the University of Sussex, and a J.D. from Tulane Law School. He is the author of several volumes of poetry, short stories and novels.

For a Woodscolt Miscarried

I know the barn where they got you
the night they tricked each other
and themselves.

In that season, the nights are
full of rain, the sky shakes
like a lost child and for an hour
it is cool enough to love.

Out of such cool love you came
to burgeon day by day,
carelessly made and moving darkly
like the land your most distant bending
fathers tilled, crying for Israel,
hoping for Jesus.

Your nearly mother felt trouble in her depths
where an ignorant angel stirred the waters
with his holy staff.
She sat big on a shack's long porch
watching cars dart South for Baton Rouge,
watching fingers of young pine fondle
tumid clouds above the field and shed
where you took place.

Cars throbbed toward the city. The shack
stayed where it was. And stayed
till her time came. And yours.

At the clinic they found something wrong;
her blood, his seed—your own blind weaving
of them both. They said that you were dead.
And it was so.

Some time in the sixth month you gave it up.
Maybe you heard some talk of what there was,
could feel the chill dissension in her gut:
her wanting and her fearing and her shame.
And gave it up. Collapsed, began to junk
limbs and fingers,
the tassel of your kind,
the piggish brooding something like a face.
Each cell dissolved, left off its yearning,
its moist prophecies.

In the Felicianas,
there are no coffins for what is not born
but loosed, a stewy discharge almost the same
as if the bowels went wrong.
Preachers, fine at birth, adroit at marriage,
inured to burial,
have no rite for those who almost were.
A near thing does not count.
A miss had just as well be fifty miles.

Just as well: no matter what they say
each coming and each leaving is a feast,
a celebration of the sun we squall to see
and weep to leave: a leaping forth,
a going down, each swings its own harsh joy
and the round of its perfection has no words.
But for you, what?

Who lay for a brief time within
the confines of her deep uneasy space,
your sun her heart thundering there above
red as the wounds of Jesus.
Who turned and turned amidst a tideless
inward sea as ghosts of her body
taught your spindrift hands to be
and made a tongue for speech and eyes to see.

For you, what?

Somewhere near in the fields your father
turns the land waiting for a first
bold thrust of green out of the earth's
confusion. Maybe relieved, as mute and
unaware as she, he will watch the stalks
and leaves spread out, will bless
the flower and the bole. Will shout and
carry the first opened fruit,
a pale victory, running down the rows
pulling its long staple through his fingers
like a sheaf of dollar bills.

And you who lost nothing that you had,
not trees or blooms or words
rising against Louisiana's sun, will stir,
if ever, in the evening breeze, a trouble missed,
a junction passed and never seen
like a field or shack at the edge of sight
down a highway to the Gulf.

On the Flesh of Christ

Flesh is the nag on which we make
the journey to Jerusalem.

—St. Augustine

He saw in every palm-leaf something new:
a burning in Toulouse, an ankle sprain
down south. He felt the sobbing women strew
a rhapsody of elemental pain
across millenia he'd never see.
Always like that: ahead of space and time,
His Father hence, the image of a tree
burning ahead, the print of Roman crime
stamped in his hands and feet, his ruptured side,
the dooms of Indians in Spanish cells,
a prioress raped to death, the awful ride
of children into bleak teutonic hells.

He closed his eyes and blessed them as he passed,
and bit his lip to make the magic last.

JAMES
DICKEY

James Dickey was born in Atlanta in 1923 and received degrees from Clemson and Vanderbilt. He was awarded the National Book Award for Poetry in 1966 and subsequently served two terms as Consultant in Poetry to the Library of Congress. He is the author of the novel *Deliverance* and collections of literary essays entitled *From Babel to Byzantium* and *Sorties*, as well as several volumes of poetry. Since 1969 he has been Poet in Residence and Carolina Professor at the University of South Carolina.

Photo Credit: William Mills

The Heaven of Animals

Here they are. The soft eyes open.
If they have lived in a wood
It is a wood.
If they have lived on plains
It is grass rolling
Under their feet forever.

Having no souls, they have come,
Anyway, beyond their knowing.
Their instincts wholly bloom
And they rise.
The soft eyes open.

To match them, the landscape flowers,
Outdoing, desperately
Outdoing what is required:
The richest wood,
The deepest field.

For some of these,
It could not be the place
It is, without blood.
These hunt, as they have done,
But with claws and teeth grown perfect,

More deadly than they can believe.
They stalk more silently,
And crouch on the limbs of trees,
And their descent
Upon the bright backs of their prey

May take years
In a sovereign floating of joy.
And those that are hunted
Know this as their life,
Their reward: to walk

Under such trees in full knowledge
Of what is in glory above them,
And to feel no fear,
But acceptance, compliance.
Fulfilling themselves without pain

At the cycle's center,
They tremble, they walk
Under the tree,
They fall, they are torn,
They rise, they walk again.

The Hospital Window

I have just come down from my father.
Higher and higher he lies
Above me in a blue light
Shed by a tinted window.
I drop through six white floors
And then step out onto pavement.

Still feeling my father ascend,
I start to cross the firm street,
My shoulder blades shining with all
The glass the huge building can raise.
Now I must turn round and face it,
And know his one pane from the others.

Each window possesses the sun
As though it burned there on a wick.
I wave, like a man catching fire.
All the deep-dyed windowpanes flash,
And, behind them, all the white rooms
They turn to the color of Heaven.

Ceremoniously, gravely, and weakly,
Dozens of pale hands are waving
Back, from inside their flames.
Yet one pure pane among these
Is the bright, erased blankness of nothing.
I know that my father is there,

In the shape of his death still living.
The traffic increases around me
Like a madness called down on my head.
The horns blast at me like shotguns,
And drivers lean out, driven crazy—
But now my propped-up father

Lifts his arm out of stillness at last.
The light from the window strikes me
And I turn as blue as a soul,
As the moment when I was born.
I am not afraid for my father—
Look! He is grinning; he is not

Afraid for my life, either,
As the wild engines stand at my knees
Shredding their gears and roaring,
And I hold each car in its place
For miles, inciting its horn
To blow down the walls of the world

That the dying may float without fear
In the bold blue gaze of my father.
Slowly I move to the sidewalk
With my pin-tingling hand half dead

At the end of my bloodless arm.
I carry it off in amazement,

High, still higher, still waving,
My recognized face fully mortal,
Yet not; not at all, in the pale,
Drained, otherworldly, stricken,
Created hue of stained glass.
I have just come down from my father.

In the Mountain Tent

I am hearing the shape of the rain
Take the shape of the tent and believe it,
Laying down all around where I lie
A profound, unspeakable law.
I obey, and am free-falling slowly

Through the thought-out leaves of the wood
Into the minds of animals.
I am there in the shining of water
Like dark, like light, out of Heaven.

I am there like the dead, or the beast
Itself, which thinks of a poem—
Green, plausible, living, and holy—
And cannot speak, but hears,
Called forth from the waiting of things.

A vast, proper, reinforced crying
With the sifted, harmonious pause,
The sustained intake of all breath
Before the first word of the Bible.

At midnight water dawns
Upon the held skulls of the foxes
And weasels and tousled hares
On the eastern side of the mountain.
Their light is the image I make

As I wait as if recently killed,
Receptive, fragile, half-smiling,
My brow watermarked with the mark
On the wing of a moth

And the tent taking shape on my body
Like ill-fitting, Heavenly clothes.
From holes in the ground comes my voice
In the God-silenced tongue of the beasts.
"I shall rise from the dead," I am saying.

Cherrylog Road

Off Highway 106
At Cherrylog Road I entered
The '34 Ford without wheels,
Smothered in kudzu,
With a seat pulled out to run
Corn whiskey down from the hills,

And then from the other side
Crept into an Essex
With a rumble seat of red leather
And then out again, aboard
A blue Chevrolet, releasing
The rust from its other color,

Reared up on three building blocks.
None had the same body heat;
I changed with them inward, toward
The weedy heart of the junkyard,
For I knew that Doris Holbrook
Would escape from her father at noon

And would come from the farm
To seek parts owned by the sun
Among the abandoned chassis,
Sitting in each in turn
As I did, leaning forward
As in a wild stock-car race

In the parking lot of the dead.
Time after time, I climbed in
And out the other side, like
An envoy or movie star
Met at the station by crickets.
A radiator cap raised its head,

Become a real toad or a kingsnake
As I neared the hub of the yard,
Passing through many states,
Many lives, to reach
Some grandmother's long Pierce-Arrow
Sending platters of blindness forth

From its nickel hubcaps
And spilling its tender upholstery
On sleepy roaches,
The glass panel in between
Lady and colored driver
Not all the way broken out,

The back-seat phone
Still on its hook.
I got in as though to exclaim,
"Let us go to the orphan asylum,
John; I have some old toys
For children who say their prayers."

I popped with sweat as I thought
I heard Doris Holbrook scrape
Like a mouse in the southern-state sun
That was eating the paint in blisters
From a hundred car tops and hoods.
She was tapping like code,

Loosening the screws,
Carrying off headlights,
Sparkplugs, bumpers,
Cracked mirrors and gear-knobs,
Getting ready, already,
To go back with something to show

Other than her lips' new trembling
I would hold to me soon, soon,
Where I sat in the ripped back seat

Talking over the interphone,
Praying for Doris Holbrook
To come from her father's farm

And to get back there
With no trace of me on her face
To be seen by her red-haired father
Who would change, in the squalling barn
Her back's pale skin with a strop,
Then lay for me

In a bootlegger's roasting car
With a string-triggered 12-gauge shotgun
To blast the breath from the air.
Not cut by the jagged windshields,
Through the acres of wrecks she came
With a wrench in her hand,

Through dust where the blacksnake dies
Of boredom, and the beetle knows
The compost has no more life.
Someone outside would have seen
The oldest car's door inexplicably
Close from within:

I held her and held her and held her,
Convoyed at terrific speed
By the stalled, dreaming traffic around us,
So the blacksnake, stiff
With inaction, curved back
Into life, and hunted the mouse

With deadly overexcitement,
The beetles reclaimed their field
As we clung, glued together,
With the hooks of the seat springs
Working through to catch us red-handed
Amidst the gray breathless batting

That burst from the seat at our backs.
We left by separate doors
Into the changed, other bodies
Of cars, she down Cherrylog Road
And I to my motorcycle
Parked like the soul of the junkyard

Restored, a bicycle fleshed
With power, and tore off
Up Highway 106, continually
Drunk on the wind in my mouth,
Wringing the handlebar for speed,
Wild to be wreckage forever.

The Shark's Parlor

Memory: I can take my head and strike it on a wall   on Cumberland
    Island
Where the night tide came crawling under the stairs   came up the first
Two or three steps   and the cottage stood on poles all night
With the sea sprawled under it   as we dreamed of the great fin circling
Under the bedroom floor. In daylight there was my first brassy taste of
    beer
And Payton Ford and I came back from the Glynn County
    slaughterhouse
With a bucket of entrails and blood. We tied one end of a hawser
To a spindling porch pillar and rowed straight out of the house
Three hundred yards into the vast front yard of windless blue water
The rope outslithering its coil   the two-gallon jug stoppered and
    sealed
With wax   and a ten-foot chain leader   a drop-forged shark hook
    nestling.
We cast our blood on the waters   the land blood easily passing
For sea blood   and we sat in it for a moment with the stain spreading
Out from the boat   sat in a new radiance   in the pond of blood in
    the sea
Waiting for fins   waiting to spill our guts also in the glowing water.
We dumped the bucket, and baited the hook with a run-over collie pup.
    The jug
Bobbed, trying to shake off the sun as a dog would shake off the sea.
We rowed to the house   feeling the same water lift the boat a new way,
All the time seeing where we lived rise and dip with the oars.
We tied up and sat down in rocking chairs, one eye or the other
    responding
To the blue-eye wink of the jug.   Payton got us a beer and we sat

All morning sat there with blood on our minds   the red mark out
In the harbor slowly failing us   then   the house groaned   the rope

Sprang out of the water   splinters flew   we leapt from our chairs
And grabbed the rope   hauled   did nothing   the house coming
     subtly
Apart   all around us   underfoot   boards beginning to sparkle
     like sand
With the glinting of the bright hidden parts of ten-year-old nails
Pulling out   the tarred poles we slept propped-up on   leaning to sea
As in land wind   crabs scuttling from under the floor   as we took
     turns about
Two more porch pillars   and looked out and saw   something
     a fish-flash
An almighty fin in trouble   a moiling of secret forces   a false start
Of water   a round wave growing: in the whole of Cumberland
     Sound   the one ripple.
Payton took off without a word   I could not hold him either

But clung to the rope anyway: it was the whole house bending
Its nails that held whatever it was   coming in a little and like a fool
I took up the slack on my wrist. The rope drew gently   jerked   I lifted
Clean off the porch and hit the water   the same water it was in
I felt in blue blazing terror at the bottom of the stairs and scrambled
Back up looking desperately into the human house as deeply as I
     could
Stopping my gaze before it went out the wire screen of the back door
Stopped it on the thistled rattan   the rugs I lay on and read
On my mother's sewing basket with next winter's socks spilling from it
The flimsy vacation furniture   a bucktoothed picture of myself.
Payton came back with three men from a filling station   and glanced
     at me
Dripping water   inexplicable   then we all grabbed hold like a
     tug-of-war.

We were gaining a little   from us a cry went up   from everywhere
People came running. Behind us the house filled with men and boys.
On the third step from the sea I took my place   looking down the rope
Going into the ocean, humming and shaking off drops. A houseful
Of people put their backs into it   going up the steps from me
Into the living room   through the kitchen   down the back stairs
Up and over a hill of sand   across a dust road   and onto a raised field
Of dunes   we were gaining   the rope in my hands began to be wet
With deeper water   all other haulers retreated through the house
But Payton and I on the stairs   drawing hand over hand on our blood
Drawing into existence by the nose   a huge body   becoming
A hammerhead   rolling in beery shallows   and I began to let up
But the rope still strained behind me   the town had gone
Pulling-mad in our house: far away in a field of sand they struggled

They had turned their backs on the sea   bent double   some on their
    knees
The rope over their shoulders like a bag of gold   they strove for the
    ideal
Esso station across the scorched meadow   with the distant fish
    coming up
The front stairs   the sagging boards   still coming in   up   taking
Another step   toward the empty house   where the rope stood
    straining
By itself through the rooms   in the middle of the air. "Pass the word,"
Payton said, and I screamed it: "Let up, good God, let up!"   to no one
    there.
The shark flopped on the porch, grating with salt-sand   driving
    back in
The nails he had pulled out   coughing chunks of his formless blood.
The screen door banged and tore off   he scrambled on his tail   slid
Curved   did a thing from another world   and was out of his
    element and in
Our vacation paradise   cutting all four legs from under the dinner
    table
With one deep-water move   he unwove the rugs in a moment
    throwing pints
Of blood over everything we owned   knocked the buck teeth out of
    my picture
His odd head full of crushed jelly-glass splinters and radio tubes
    thrashing
Among the pages of fan magazines   all the movie stars drenched in
    sea-blood.
Each time we thought he was dead   he struggled back and smashed
One more thing   in all coming back to die   three or four more
    times after death.
At last we got him out   log-rolling him   greasing his sandpaper skin
With lard to slide him   pulling on his chained lips as the tide came
Tumbled him down the steps as the first night wave went under the
    floor.
He drifted off   head back   belly white as the moon.   What could I
    do but buy
That house   for the one black mark still there   against death   a
    forehead-
toucher in the room he circles beneath   and has been invited to
    wreck?
Blood hard as iron on the wall   black with time   still bloodlike
Can be touched whenever the brow is drunk enough: all changes:
    Memory:
Something like three-dimensional dancing in the limbs   with age
Feeling more in two worlds than one   in all worlds the growing
    encounters.

The Sheep Child

Farm boys wild to couple
With anything   with soft-wooded trees
With mounds of earth   mounds
Of pinestraw   will keep themselves off
Animals by legends of their own:
In the hay-tunnel dark
And dung of barns, they will
Say   I have heard tell

That in a museum in Atlanta
Way back in a corner somewhere
There's this thing that's only half
Sheep   like a woolly baby
Pickled in alcohol   because
Those things can't live   his eyes
Are open   but you can't stand to look
I heard from somebody who . . .

But this is now almost all
Gone. The boys have taken
Their own true wives in the city,
The sheep are safe in the west hill
Pasture   but we who were born there
Still are not sure. Are we,
Because we remember, remembered
In the terrible dust of museums?

Merely with his eyes, the sheep-child may

Be saying   saying

> *I am here, in my father's house.*
> *I who am half of your world, came deeply*
> *To my mother in the long grass*
> *Of the west pasture, where she stood like moonlight*
> *Listening for foxes. It was something like love*
> *From another world that seized her*
> *From behind, and she gave, not lifting her head*
> *Out of dew, without ever looking, her best*
> *Self to that great need. Turned loose, she dipped her face*
> *Farther into the chill of the earth, and in a sound*
> *Of sobbing   of something stumbling*
> *Away, began, as she must do,*
> *To carry me. I woke, dying,*

In the summer sun of the hillside, with my eyes
Far more than human. I saw for a blazing moment
The great grassy world from both sides,
Man and beast in the round of their need,
And the hill wind stirred in my wool,
My hoof and my hand clasped each other,
I ate my one meal
Of milk, and died
Staring. From dark grass I came straight

To my father's house, whose dust
Whirls up in the halls for no reason
When no one comes   piling deep in a hellish mild corner,
And, through my immortal waters,
I meet the sun's grains eye
To eye, and they fail at my closet of glass.
Dead, I am most surely living
In the minds of farm boys: I am he who drives
Them like wolves from the hound bitch and calf
And from the chaste ewe in the wind.
They go into woods   into bean fields   they go
Deep into their known right hands. Dreaming of me,
They groan   they wait   they suffer
Themselves, they marry, they raise their kind.

Adultery

We have all been in rooms
We cannot die in, and they are odd places, and sad.
Often Indians are standing eagle-armed on hills

In the sunrise   open wide to the Great Spirit
Or gliding in canoes   or cattle are browsing on the walls
Far away   gazing down with the eyes of our children

Not far away   or there are men driving
The last railspike, which has turned
Gold in their hands.   Gigantic forepleasure lives

Among such scenes, and we are alone with it
At last.   There is always some weeping
Between us   and someone is always checking

A wristwatch by the bed to see how much
Longer we have left.   Nothing can come
Of this   nothing can come

Of us: of me with my grim techniques
Or you who have sealed your womb
With a ring of convulsive rubber:

Although we come together,
Nothing will come of us.   But we would not give
It up, for death is beaten

By praying Indians   by distant cows   historical
Hammers   by hazardous meetings that bridge
A continent.   One could never die here

Never die   never die
While crying.   My lover, my dear one
I will see you next week

When I'm in town.   I will call you
If I can.   Please get hold of   please don't
Oh God, Please don't any more I can't bear . . . Listen:

We have done it again   we are
Still living.   Sit up and smile,
God bless you.   Guilt is magical.

Falling

A 29-year-old stewardess fell . . . to her
death tonight when she was swept
through an emergency door that suddenly
sprang open . . . The body . . . was found
. . . three hours after the accident.

—New York Times

The states when they black out and lie there rolling   when they turn
To something transcontinental   move by   drawing moonlight out
     of the great
One-sided stone hung off the starboard wingtip   some sleeper next to
An engine is groaning for coffee   and there is faintly coming in
Somewhere the vast beast-whistle of space.   In the galley with its racks
Of trays   she rummages for a blanket   and moves in her slim tailored
Uniform to pin it over the cry at the top of the door.   As though she blew

The door down with a silent blast from her lungs   frozen   she is black
Out finding herself   with the plane nowhere and her body taking by the
     throat
The undying cry of the void   falling   living   beginning to be
     something
That no one has ever been and lived through   screaming without
     enough air
Still neat   lipsticked   stockinged   girdled by regulation   her hat
Still on   her arms and legs in no world   and yet spaced also strangely
With utter placid rightness on thin air   taking her time   she holds it
In many places   and now, still thousands of feet from her death
     she seems
To slow   she develops interest   she turns in her maneuverable body

To watch it. She is hung high up in the overwhelming middle of things
     in her
Self   in low body-whistling wrapped intensely   in all her dark
     dance-weight
Coming down from a marvellous leap   with the delaying,
     dumfounding ease
Of a dream of being drawn   like endless moonlight to the harvest soil
Of a central state of one's country   with a great gradual warmth
     coming
Over her   floating   finding more and more breath in what she has
     been using
For breath   as the levels become more human   seeing clouds placed
     honestly

Below her left and right   riding slowly toward them   she clasps it all
To her and can hang her hands and feet in it in peculiar ways   and
Her eyes opened wide by wind, can open her mouth as wide   wider
    and suck
All the heat from the cornfields   can go down on her back with a feeling
Of stupendous pillows stacked under her   and can turn   turn as
    to someone
In bed   smile, understood in darkness   can go away   slant   slide
Off tumbling   into the emblem of a bird with its wings half-spread
Or whirl madly on herself   in endless gymnastics in the growing warmth
Of wheatfields rising toward the harvest moon.   There is time to live
In superhuman health   seeing mortal unreachable lights far down
    seeing
An ultimate highway with one late priceless car probing it   arriving
In a square town and off her starboard arm the glitter of water catches
The moon by its one shaken side   scaled, roaming silver   My God
    it is good
And evil   lying in one after another of all the positions for love
Making   dancing   sleeping   and now cloud wisps at her no
Raincoat   no matter   all small towns brokenly brighter from inside
Cloud   she walks over them like rain   bursts out to behold a Greyhound
Bus shooting light through its sides   it is the signal to go straight
Down like a glorious diver   then feet first   her skirt stripped
    beautifully
Up   her face in fear-scented cloths   her legs deliriously bare   then
Arms out   she slow-rolls over   steadies out   waits for something
    great
To take control of her   trembles near feathers   planes head-down
The quick movements of bird-necks turning her head   gold eyes
    the insight-
eyesight of owls blazing into the hencoops   a taste for chicken
    overwhelming
Her   the long-range vision of hawks enlarging all human lights of cars
Freight trains   looped bridges   enlarging the moon racing slowly
Through all the curves of a river   all the darks of the midwest blazing
From above. A rabbit in a bush turns white   the smothering chickens
Huddle   for over them there is still time for something to live
With the streaming half-idea of a long stoop   a hurtling   a fall
That is controlled   that plummets as it wills   turns gravity
Into a new condition, showing its other side like a moon   shining
New Powers   there is still time to live on a breath made of nothing
But the whole night   time for her to remember to arrange her skirt
Like a diagram of a bat   tightly it guides her   she has this flying-skin
Made of garments   and there are also those sky-divers on TV   sailing
In sunlight   smiling under their goggles   swapping batons back
    and forth

And He who jumped without a chute and was handed one by a diving
Buddy. She looks for her grinning companion   white teeth   nowhere
She is screaming   singing hymns   her thin human wings spread out
From her neat shoulders   the air beast-crooning to her   warbling
And she can no longer behold the huge partial form of the world   now
She is watching her country lose its evoked master shape   watching
       it lose
And gain   get back its houses and peoples   watching it bring up
Its local lights   single homes   lamps on barn roofs   if she fell
Into water she might live   like a diver   cleaving   perfect   plunge

Into another   heavy silver   unbreathable   slowing   saving
Element: there is water   there is time to perfect all the fine
Points of diving   feet together   toes pointed   hands shaped right
To insert her into water like a needle   to come out healthily dripping
And be handed a Coca-Cola   there they are   there are the waters
Of life   the moon packed and coiled in a reservoir   so let me begin
To plane across the night air of Kansas   opening my eyes superhumanly
Bright   to the dammed moon   opening the natural wings of my jacket
By Don Loper   moving like a hunting owl toward the glitter of water
One cannot just fall   just tumble screaming all that time   one must use
It she is now through with all   through all   clouds   damp   hair
Straightened   the last wisp of fog pulled apart on her face like wool
       revealing
New darks   new progressions of headlight along dirt roads
       from chaos

And night   a gradual warming   a new-made, inevitable world of
       one's own
Country   a great stone of light in its waiting waters   hold   hold out
For water: who knows when what correct young woman must take up
       her body
And fly   and head for the moon-crazed inner eye of midwest imprisoned
Water   stored up for her for years   the arms of her jacket slipping
Air up her sleeves to go   all over her?   What final things can be said
Of one who starts out sheerly in her body in the high middle of night
Air   to track down water like a rabbit where it lies like life itself
Off to the right in Kansas?   She goes toward   the blazing-bare lake
Her skirts neat   her hands and face warmed more and more by the air
Rising from pastures of beans   and under her   under chenille
       bedspreads
The farm girls are feeling the goddess in them struggle and rise brooding
On the scratch-shining posts of the bed   dreaming of female signs
Of the moon   male blood like iron   of what is really said by the moan
Of airliners passing over them at dead of midwest midnight   passing
Over brush fires   burning out in silence on little hills   and will wake

To see the woman they should be   struggling on the rooftree to become
Stars: for her the ground is closer   water is nearer   she passes
It   then banks   turns   her sleeves fluttering differently as she rolls
Out to face the east, where the sun shall come up from wheatfields she must
Do something with water   fly to it   fall in it   drink it   rise
From it   but there is none left upon earth   the clouds have drunk
      it back
The plants have sucked it down   there are standing toward her only
The common fields of death   she comes back from flying to falling
Returns to a powerful cry   the silent scream with which she blew down
The coupled door of the airliner   nearly   nearly losing hold
Of what she has done   remembers   remembers the shape at the heart
Of cloud   fashionably swirling   remembers she still has time to die
Beyond explanation. Let her now take off her hat in summer air the
      contour
Of cornfields   and have enough time to kick off her one remaining
Shoe with the toes   of the other foot   to unhook her stockings
With calm fingers, noting how fatally easy it is to undress in midair
Near death   when the body will assume without effort any position
Except the one that will sustain it   enable it to rise   live
Not die   nine farms hover close   widen   eight of them separate,
      leaving
One in the middle   then the fields of that farm do the same   there
      is no
Way to back off   from her chosen ground   but she sheds the jacket
With its silver sad impotent wings   sheds the bat's guiding tailpiece
Of her skirt   the lightning-charged clinging of her blouse   the
      intimate
Inner flying-garment of her slip in which she rides like the holy ghost
Of a virgin   sheds the long windsocks of her stockings   absurd
Brassiere   then feels the girdle required by regulations squirming
Off her: no longer monobuttocked   she feels the girdle flutter   shake
In her hand   and float   upward   her clothes rising off her
      ascending
Into cloud   and fights away from her head the last sharp dangerous
      shoe
Like a dumb bird   and now will drop in   SOON   now will drop

In like this   the greatest thing that ever came to Kansas   down
      from all
Heights   all levels of American breath   layered in the lungs
      from the frail
Chill of space to the loam where extinction slumbers in corn tassels
      thickly
And breathes like rich farmers counting: will come among them after
Her last superhuman act   the last slow careful passing of her hands
All over her unharmed body   desired by every sleeper in his dream:

Boys finding for the first time their loins filled with heart's blood
Widowed farmers whose hands float under light covers to find themselves
Arisen at sunrise   the splendid position of blood unearthly drawn
Toward clouds   all feel something   pass over them as she passes
Her palms over *her* long legs   *her* small breasts   and deeply between
Her thighs   her hair shot loose from all pins   streaming in the wind
Of her body   let her come openly   trying at the last second to land
On her back   This is it   THIS
                                        All those who find her impressed
In the soft loam   gone down   driven well into the image of her body
The furrows for miles flowing in upon her where she lies very deep
In her mortal outline   in the earth as it is in cloud   can tell nothing
But that she is there   inexplicable   unquestionable   and remember
That something broke in them as well   and began to live and die more
When they walked for no reason into their fields to where the whole earth
Caught her   interrupted her maiden flight   told her how to lie
      she cannot
Turn   go away   cannot move   cannot slide off it and assume another
Position   no sky-diver with any grin could save her   hold her in
      his arms
Plummet with her   unfold above her his wedding silks   she can no
      longer
Mark the rain with whirling women that take the place of a dead wife
Or the goddess in Norwegian farm girls   or all the back-breaking whores
Of Wichita. All the known air above her is not giving up quite one
Breath   it is all gone   and yet not dead   not anywhere else
Quite   lying still in the field on her back   sensing the smells
Of incessant growth try to lift her   a little sight left in the corner
Of one eye   fading   seeing something wave   lies believing
That she could have made it   at the best part of her brief goddess
State   to water   gone in headfirst   come out smiling   invulnerable
Girl in a bathing-suit ad   but she is lying like a sunbather at the last
Of moonlight   half-buried in her impact on the earth   not far
From a railroad trestle   a water tank   she could see if she could
Raise her head from her modest hole   with her clothes beginning
To come down all over Kansas   into bushes   on the dewy sixth green
Of a golf course   one shoe   her girdle coming down fantastically
On a clothesline, where it belongs   her blouse on a lightning rod:

Lies in the fields   in *this* field   on her broken back as though on
A cloud she cannot drop through   while farmers sleepwalk without
Their women from houses   a walk like falling toward the far waters
Of life   in moonlight   toward the dreamed eternal meaning of
      their farms
Toward the flowering of the harvest in their hands   that tragic cost
Feels herself go   go toward   go outward   breathes at last fully
Not   and tries   less   once   tries   tries   AH, GOD—

False Youth: Autumn: Clothes of the Age

—for Susan Tuckerman Dickey—

Three red foxes on my head, come down
There last Christmas from Brooks Brothers
As a joke, I wander down Harden Street
In Columbia, South Carolina, fur-haired and bald,
Looking for impulse in camera stores and redneck greeting cards.
A pole is spinning
Colors I have little use for, but I go in
Anyway, and take off my fox hat and jacket
They have not seen from behind yet.   The barber does what he can
With what I have left, and I hear the end man say, as my own
Hair-cutter turns my face
To the floor, Jesus, if there's anything I hate
It's a middle-aged hippie.   Well, so do I, I swallow
Back: so do I   so do I
And to hell.   I get up, and somebody else says
When're you gonna put on that hat,
Buddy?   Right now.   Another says softly,
Goodbye, Fox.   I arm my denim jacket
On and walk to the door, stopping for the murmur of chairs.
And there it is
hand-stitched by the needles of the mother
Of my grandson   eagle riding on his claws with a banner
Outstretched as the wings of my shoulders,
Coming after me with his flag
Disintegrating, his one eye raveling
Out, filthy strings flying
From the white feathers, one wing nearly gone:
Blind eagle but flying
Where I walk, where I stop with my fox
Head at the glass to let the row of chairs spell it out
And get a lifetime look at my bird's
One word, raggedly blazing with extinction and soaring loose
In red threads burning up white until I am shot in the back
Through my wings   or ripped apart
For rags:

Poetry.

R.H.W. DILLARD

R.H.W. Dillard was born in Roanoke, Virginia in 1937. He teaches English at Hollins College, where he serves as chair of the creative writing program. He is the author of four books of poetry, most recently, *The Greeting: New & Selected Poems*. He has also published two novels and a collection of short fiction.

Photo Credit: Cathy Hankia

The Mullins Farm

The sun through the window
Is as warm as the smell of salt,
Of hams, the hum of bees
Where the smoke bellows lie
On the table by the netting,
The hat and the gloves.

My uncle hands you a turtle's heart,
Beating, beating in your open hand,
His head still hooked on the broom,
The hollow of his bones on the ground,
And his parts laid out by the fire,
The kettle made ready for soup.

The high horse, Mack, dappled white,
And the brown, too, slow and full,
The hill that falls off from the barn

Where the corn is husked in the dark,
And the hogs hanging to be split,
Filled with apples and corn and sweet slop.

By the branch out back and the small bridge,
In the damp concrete walls, the milk
Sits in spring water, and the squares
Of pressed butter, each with its bouquet
Of spring flowers, and on the bank,
An occasional frog or small snake.

The horseshoes must be bent on hot coals,
Red and white as new flowers, sprinkled
On the ground around the anvil, inviting
To your hand which must never touch,
And the shadows of the waiting horses,
The hot hammers, the hard men.

And the red hen in your arms is soft
And warm as the smell of feathers,
As the afternoon, while a small hawk
Watches from a crooked pine, watches
My grandfather in his clean tan clothes
Load his shotgun in the porch's shade.

And my grandmother rings the wood stove,
Takes the biscuits from the high warmer,
Calls her daughters to set the table,
And feeds the large family with squirrel
And green beans, squash and mashed potatoes
As a brace of dead crows hang from the fence.

The afternoon is unending and clear
As the branches in front of and behind
The white house, as you climb the hill
To the barn, smell the stacked hay,
Touch the smooth wood of the stalls,
And see the sun powdered by barn dust.

My grandfather has cut a log of green wood
And set it up in the fireplace
With dry props to light as the evening
Comes on, and you may sit in the dim room
With the shadows wrinkling your face,
Hear the fire living in the light's slow leak.

The hounds are asleep on the front porch,
Their flat brown ears and sharp ribs,
While the cats climb to eat on a fence post,
And the oaks rattle acorns in the grass
And on the tin roof of the porch,
And the corn stalks crack in the air.

Meditation for a Pickle Suite

Morning: the soft release
As you open a jar of pickles.
The sun through the window warm
And moving like light through brine,
The shadows of pickles swim the floor.
And in the tree, flowing down the chimney,
The songs of fresh birds clean as pickles.
Memories float through the day
Like pickles, perhaps sweet gherkins.
The past rises and falls
Like curious pickles in dark jars,
Your hands sure as pickles,
Opening dreams like albums,
Pale Polish pickles.
Your eyes grow sharp as pickles,
Thoughts as green, as shining
As rows of pickles, damp and fresh,
Placed out in the afternoon sun.

GEORGE GARRETT

George Garrett, born in Orlando, Florida in 1929, is the author of more than twenty books, including seven volumes of poetry. He has been awarded the Prix de Rome for Literature from the American Academy of Arts and Letters and holds a doctorate from Princeton. He teaches in the English Department at the University of Virginia and spends his summers with his wife, Susan, at their home in Maine.

The Magi

First they were stiff and gaudy,
three painted wooden figures on a table,
bowing in a manger without any walls
among bland clay beasts and shepherds
who huddled where my mother always put them
in a sweet ring around the Holy Child.
At that season and by candlelight
it was easy for a child to believe in them.

Later I became one. I brought gold,
ascended a platform in the Parish House
and muffed my lines, but left my gift
beside the cheap doll in its cradle,
knelt in my fancy costume trying to look wise
while the other two (my friends and rivals
for the girl who was chosen to be Mary)
never faltered with frankincense and myrrh.

Now that was a long time ago.
And now I know them for what they were,
moving across vague spaces on their camels,
visionaries, madmen, poor creatures possessed
by some slight deviation of the stars.
I know their gifts were shabby and symbolic.
Their wisdom was a thing of waking dreams.
Their robes were ragged and their breath was bad.

Still, I would dream them back.
Let them be wooden and absurd again
in all the painted glory that a child
could love. Let me be one of them.
Let me step forward once more awkwardly
and stammer and choke on a prepared speech.
Let me bring gold again and kneel
foolish and adoring in the dirty straw.

Revival

Now chaos has pitched a tent
in my pasture, a circus tent
like a huge toadstool
in the land of giants. Oh,
all night long the voices of
the damned and saved keep me
awake and, *basso*, the evangelist.
Fire and brimstone, thunder and lightning,
telegrams in the unknown tongue!
The bushes are crawling with couples.
I see one girl so leafy that
she might be Daphne herself.

I know there were giants once,
one-eyed wonders of the morning
world. Ponderous, they rode
dinosaurs like Shetland ponies,
timber for toothpicks, boulders for
baseballs, oceans for bathtubs,
whales for goldfish, Great God,
when they shook fists and roared,

stars fell down like snowflakes
under glass! Came then Christ
to climb the thorny beanstalk
and save us one and all.

ARE YOU SAVED?????
Rocks are painted, trees nailed
with signs, fences trampled.
Under the dome of the tent
falls salt of sweat and tears
enough to kill my grass at the roots.
Morning and I'll wake to find
the whole thing gone. Bright dew
and blessed silence. Nothing
to prove they camped here and tried
to raise a crop of hell except
that scar of dead space (where the tent was)
like a huge footprint.

Bubbles

Not like we used to with pipes
which combined the pleasure of
pretending we were smoking with
the chance of a mouthful of soap.

But nowadays with a sea-green liquid,
bottle, and a spoon-shaped eyelet
with a handle. You dip it
and in one wave you have

a room that's full of bubbles.
Round and rich they catch the light
in square small patches of color.
And they hover, float and fall

and pop. My children are
pleased and puzzled. It is new
to them. They snatch at globes
to find their hands are empty

and the bubble's gone.
Let some stern moralist take on
the task of making sense of this.
I never could explain why balloons

burst and playing-card towers fall.
I say they're beautiful to see,
however made, by pipe or wand,
and not to have.

Kings might have given ransom
to own an air so jeweled and clear,
so nothing-filled and handsome.
Children, there are no kings here.

Luck's Shining Child

Because I am broke again
I have the soles of my shoes repaired
one at a time.

From now on one will always be
fat and slick with new leather
while his sad twin,

lean and thin as a fallen leaf,
will hug a large hole like a wound.
When it rains

one sock and one foot get wet.
When I cross the gravel parking lot
one foot winces

and I have to hop along on the other.
My students believe I am trying
to prove something.

They think I'm being a symbol of
dichotomy, duality, double-dealing,
yin and yang.

I am hopping because it hurts.
Because there is a hole in my shoe.
Because I feel poor for keeps.

What I am trying not to do
is imagine how it will be in my coffin,
heels down, soles up,

all rouged and grinning above my polished shoes,
one or the other a respectable brother
and one or the other

that wild prodigal whom I love
as much or more than his sleek companion,
luck's shining child.

York Harbor Morning

Where clear air blew off the land,
wind turns around and the sky changes.
Where there was burning blue is pale gray now,
heavy and salty from cold open sea.
And the long groaning of the foghorn
saying *change . . . change . . . change*
like a sleeper dreaming and breathing.

Tide turning, too, with the weather.
The lobster boats swing about to pull
against their moorings like large dogs.
Gulls cry like hurt children and disappear.
And I think, surely it is a magician,
bitter and clever, who has pulled this trick.

That old magician is laughing in the fog.
And the cries of wounded children fade away
while the bellbuoy sounds *farewell . . . farewell . . .*
daring the dead to rise up from dreaming,
to hold their lives like water in their hands.

Buzzard

I've heard that holy madness is a state
not to be trifled with, not to be taken
lightly by jest or vow, by lover's token
or any green wreath for a public place. Flash
in the eyes of madmen precious fountains,
whose flesh is wholly thirst, insatiate.

I see this graceful bird begin to wheel,
glide in God's fingerprint, a whorl
of night, in light a thing burnt black,
unhurried. Somewhere something on its back
has caught his eye. Wide-winged he descends
like angels to the business of this world.

I've heard that saintly hermits, frail, obscene
in rags, slack-fleshed, eyes like jewels, kneel
in dry sand among the tortured mountains, feel
at last the tumult of their prayers take shape,
take wings, assume the brutal rush of grace.
This bird comes then and picks those thin bones clean.

MARGARET GIBSON

Margaret Gibson grew up in Richmond, Virginia, and was educated at Hollins College and the University of Virginia. She is Co-Writer in Residence at Phillips Academy/Andover and serves as co-editor of *Landscapes and Distance: Poets from Virginia*. Her second book of poems, *Long Walks in the Afternoon*, was awarded the Lamont Prize in 1982.

The Onion

Mornings when sky is white as dried gristle
and the air's unhealthy, coast
smothered, and you gone
                          I could stay in bed
and be the woman who aches for no reason, each day
a small death of love, cold rage for dinner,
coffee and continental indifference
at dawn.
                Or dream lazily a market day—
bins of fruit and celery, poultry strung up,
loops of garlic and peppers. I'd select one
yellow onion, fist-sized, test its sleek
hardness, haggle and settle a fair price.

Yesterday, a long day measured by shovel
and mattock, a wrestle with roots—
calm and dizzy when I bent over to loosen my shoes
at the finish—I thought
                     if there were splendors,

what few there were, knowledge of them
in me like fire in flint,
I would have them . . .

                  and now I'd say the onion,
I'd have that, too. The work it took,
the soup it flavors, the griefs
innocently it summons.

Invisible Work

Passionately joined to all things visible
she liked days
cold enough to see her breath.
Not to watch her hands in simple work
meant she would vanish.
She said even the woman
who put at an angle   here not there
her vase of reeds chose order,
was an artist.

Years after, I'll move a bowl of gourds
and think of her, wipe a sill of dust,
by canceling it make my mark . . .
place on the glass table
a glass bowl of leaves
almost leaving them in air.
A steep glide
begins.

Each poem I try to set right what last winter
tracking prints through snow I found:
a clean fled space
abruptly there
tracks vanished
as if complicity of hawk or wind had swept
up everything . . .

a miracle
though some would call it common
as a table spread white
with cloth.

Country Woman Elegy

With a hush in their voices
country people round here tell of the woman who walked
bareheaded in winter, keening aloud,
three days wandering with her seven-month child
dead inside her. She wouldn't be comforted,
and held her loss.

Telling this
the old men shake fear from their eyes as they might
shake rain from a hat or coat. Her madness they blame
on winter, the cold and closed-in weather.

I love that woman's fearless
mourning. The child dead, no help for that,
she had to wait until her wanting to love the child
died out in echo and outcry against bare stone.
She had to walk, nevermind the cold,
until she learned what she needed
to learn, letting go.

And I love those reticent men.
They know how most of us strain to ignore our dead,
the woman less fortunate to feel the weight of hers.
Who wants to admit death's there inside, more privy
to our secrets than any lover, and love
a kind of grief?

Therefore we dream.
Last night a wild, purple bougainvillea bloomed in sleep.
I thought to gather a handful, but the stalks broke
like straws, and the wind
took them

and drove them past that woman
bareheaded on the winter road, that woman whose cries
unwound and wouldn't be comforted by love or a lover's body,
by childhood or any piety.

R. S.
GWYNN

R. S. Gwynn, born in Eden, North Carolina in 1948, was educated at Davidson College and the University of Arkansas. He is the author of two poetry chapbooks, *Bearing and Distance* and *The Narcissiad*, both published by Cedar Rock Press. *The Drive-In* was published by the University of Missouri Press as winner of the Breakthrough Award. He is presently an Associate Professor of English at Lamar University in Beaumont, Texas.

Photo Credit: Joe Richard

1916

> . . . *some corner of a foreign field*
> *That is forever England.*
>
> —Rupert Brooke, "1914"

1.

Other Rank.　　　　"A" Company
　　　　　　　　　　1st Munster Grenadiers
　　　　　　　　　　Cape Helles
　　　　　　　　　　1 January

So thank Mum for the book of poetry
Which I've made use of, but to tell the truth
It's other than 'the red sweet wine of youth'
What's pouring by the pint of late from me.
Wasn't quite sure of catching what he means,
This bit about 'a richer dust concealed.'
The only rich spot in *this* foreign field
Is where we dug the regiment's latrines.

It's said we'll soon be off. Perhaps the Turk
Will rush down when the boats are out to sea
And stumble in. So if our dodges work
The *Times* can praise our 'artful strategy.'
As for the poems, say 'Send more!' to Mum—
Whatever's easiest on the bleedin' bum.

2.

Henry James. 21 Carlyle Mansions
         Cheyne Walk, S.W.
         Chelsea
         February 14

Of course, of course, his was a sacrifice;
Or, rather, as there seems small likelihood
Of compensation, or of *any* good
Resulting, one must label imprecise
The word he leans first toward, so dear the price
Exacted from us in the red sweet blood
Of our young men; thus, one is understood
To use the term (since no less will suffice
Than that which *must* be said) in conscious error
For which he makes apologies but never,
Questions of style aside, would wish revoked,
Such being the times: headlong, relentless terror
To which our destinies are tied, are yoked,
The day of bright young things now fled forever.

3.

Winston Churchill. 6th Royal Scots Fusiliers
            Somewhere in the Field
            March 15

My Dearest Puss: Have had great trouble sleeping.
Penance has been to dream-watch from a hill
While ranks of our lads, like blind swimmers leaping
Into nothingness, charge the far trench until
Not one remains. The Black Dog lingers still
To plague my waking thoughts. Dear Puss, it seems
These Ides of March bode your poor Caesar ill:
Miles Gloriosus laid low by his dreams!

At dawn the 5.9s caught our wiring teams
In no-man's land; all dead save a young chap
With shrapnel in both legs. Incessant screams
Led us to find him halfway down a sap.
He'd worked one piece out, and he *kissed it*, Clemmie:

O Beauty, wot a Blighty pass you've gi' me!

4.

Cathleen Nesbitt.   The Candler Theatre
                        New York City
                        April 1

This evening, in the wings, I missed my cue
And caused a crucial scene to be replayed,
Someone *was* there; I fancied it was you—
Sunny, alive, so dreadfully betrayed.
Our play is *Justice*. It is like most plays,
Cleverly fashioned, filled with complication,
Destined, one would assume, for ready praise.
I have allowed your letters' publication.

My April Fool, how much we missed the mark!
So much for me to learn, so much to teach you—
Our hearts knew what our bodies *should* have known.
Forgive me, dearest. I hold stage alone
And you have vanished in a house grown dark.
Beautiful History, I can't quite reach you.

5.

Subaltern, R.N.D.   Aboard the *Ajax*
                        Trebuki Bay, Skyros
                        23rd April

The grove is called Mesedhi. One's aware
Of spices in the seabreeze, thyme and sage,
As if the present met with some lost age
And many heroes congregated there.
It is precisely as Achilles said:
Rather I'd choose laboriously to bear
A weight of woes, and breathe the vital air
Than reign the sceptred monarch of the dead.

Is it a year? How soon one's imprints fade
Into the grain of anonymity.
The shepherd who is owner came to speak
Of keeping up the site, saying it made
Him proud the cross had borne some words in Greek.
He tried, but could not spell them out for me.

Among Philistines

The night before they meant to pluck his eyes
He caught his tale at six on *Action News*—
Some stylish moron blabbing the bald lies
The public swallowed as "Official Views."

After a word for snuff, Delilah made
A live appearance, and was interviewed.
Complaining what a pittance she was paid,
She plugged the film she starred in in the nude.

Unbearable, he thought, and flipped the switch,
Lay sleepless on the bed in the bright room
Where every thought brought back the pretty bitch
And all the Orient of her perfume,

Her perfect breasts, her hips and slender waist
Matchless among the centerfolds of Zion,
Which summoned to his tongue the mingled taste
Of honey oozing from the rotted lion;

For now his every mumble in the sack
(Bugged, of course, and not a whisper missed)
Would be revealed in lurid paperback
"As told to" Madame Sleaze, the columnist.

Beefcake aside, he was a man of thought
Who heretofore had kept to the strict law:
For all the cheap celebrity it brought
He honestly deplored that ass's jaw,

The glossy covers of their magazines
With taut chains popping on his greasy chest,
The ads for razor blades with the staged scenes
And captions: *Hebrew Hunk Says We Shave Best.*

Such were his thoughts; much more severe the dreams
That sped him through his sleep in a wild car:
Vistas of billboards where he lathered cream,
Gulped milk, chugged beer, or smoked a foul cigar,

And this last image, *this,* mile upon mile:
Delilah, naked, sucking on a pair
Of golden shears, winking her lewdest smile
Amid a monumental pile of hair

And headlines—*Meet the Babe Who Skinned the Yid!*
Starring in JUST A LITTLE OFF MY HEAD.
He noted how his locks demurely hid
Her monstrous tits. And how her lips were red,

Red as his eyes when he was roused at seven
To trace back to its source the splendid ray
Of sunlight streaming from the throat of Heaven
Commanding him to kneel and thus to pray:

"Lord God of Hosts, whose name cannot be used
Promotion-wise, whose face shall not adorn
A cornflake box, whose trust I have abused:
Return that strength of which I have been shorn,

That we might smite this tasteless *shiksa* land
With hemorrhoids and rats, with fire and sword.
Forgive my crime. Put forth thy fearsome hand
Against them and their gods, I pray you, Lord. . . ."

So, shorn and strengthless, led through Gaza Mall
Past shoeshop and boutique, Hallmark and Sears,
He held his head erect and smiled to all
And did not dignify the scene with tears,

Knowing that God could mercifully ordain,
For punishment, a blessing in disguise.
"Good riddance," he said, whispering to the pain
As, searing, the twin picks hissed in his eyes.

JIM
HALL

The author of four books of poetry, most recently *False Statements*, Jim Hall was born in Kentucky in 1947 and holds degrees from Eckerd College, Johns Hopkins, and the University of Utah. He has lived in Florida since 1973 and teaches at Florida International University.

Maybe Dats Your Pwoblem Too

All my pwoblems
who knows, maybe evwybody's pwoblems
is due to da fact, due to da awful twuth
dat I am SPIDERMAN.

I know, I know. All da dumb jokes:
No flies on you, ha ha,
and da ones about what do I do wit all
doze extwa legs in bed. Well, dat's funny yeah.
But you twy being
SPIDERMAN for a month or two. Go ahead.

You get doze cwazy calls fwom da
Gubbener askin you to twap some booglar who's
only twying to wip off color TV sets.
Now, what do I cawre about TV sets?
But I pull on da suit, da stinkin suit,
wit da sucker cups on da fingers,

and get my wopes and wittle bundle of
equipment and den I go flying like cwazy
acwoss da town fwom woof top to woof top.

Till der he is. Some poor dumb color TV slob
and I fall on him and we westle a widdle
until I get him all woped. So big deal.

You tink when you SPIDERMAN
der's sometin big going to happen to you.
Well, I tell you what. It don't happen dat way.
Nuttin happens. Gubbener calls, I go.
Bwing him to powice, Gubbener calls again,
like dat over and over.

I tink I twy sometin diffunt. I tink I twy
sometim excitin like wacing cawrs. Sometin to make
my heart beat at a difwent wate.
But den you just can't quit being sometin like
SPIDERMAN.
You SPIDERMAN for life. Fowever. I can't even
buin my suit. It won't buin. It's fwame wesistent.
So maybe dat's youwr pwoblem too, who knows.
Maybe dat's da whole pwoblem wif evwytin.
Nobody can buin der suits, dey all fwame wesistent.
Who knows?

White Trash

Now it's styrofoam pellets
that blow across the yard.
They settle in the new grass
like the eggs of Japanese toys.
It's a kind of modern snowing.

The boy next door opened a box,
took out the precious present
and shook these white spun plastic
droplets into the wind.
It's how his family thinks.

Hundreds of them. Shaped like
unlucky fetuses or the brains
of TV stars.
Now they burrow in the lawn,
defy the rake, wriggle like the toes
of the shallow buried.

They'll be there when we're gone.
Bright tumors, rooted in the dark.
Crowding the dirt. Nothing makes them
grow. But nothing kills them either.

Preposterous

At fifteen Jean Calvin made a list:
Best Legs, Sexiest Smile, Best Muscles,
all the rest. She had the right to judge us
since she was Most Buxom herself,
Most Dreamed About,
Most Discussed When Flesh Came Up.

I sat behind her in Civics that aromatic year
and whispered jokes and tried to breathe her hair.
For all that I won Wittiest. Wittiest.
And was runner-up for Best Legs on a Short Boy.

She posted it and overnight her picks
for All-round Sexiest, Perkiest Buns, Dreamiest,
drew flocks around their lockers.
And everything I said was suddenly preposterous
and clever. I could roll my eyes that June
and break up Biology.

It wasn't what I wanted, but I took it.
I wanted to be one of those who could whisper
in Jean Calvin's hair and make her wheel and slap
and turn back around with a secret smile.
I wanted a gift: Best Voice, Bedroomiest Eyes,
some arousing inherited trait. Not this,
this Wittiest, which makes me work so hard,
so everlastingly, to keep Jean Calvin entertained.

ANDREW — HUDGINS

Andrew Hudgins was born in Killeen, Texas, and raised in Alabama. He was educated at Huntingdon College, the University of Alabama, Syracuse University, and the University of Iowa. His first book, *Saints and Strangers*, was published in 1985. He teaches at the University of Cincinnati.

Around the Campfire

Around the campfire we sang hymns.
When asked I'd play my flute, and lay
a melody between night's
incessant cannonfire that boomed
irregularly, but with the depth
of kettle drums. Occasionally,
in lulls, we'd hear a fading snatch
of Yankee song sucked to us in
the backwash of their cannonballs.
These are, oddly enough, fond memories.

One night, a Texas boy sat down
and strummed a homemade banjo,
He'd bought it for a canteen full
of corn. He followed me around
and pestered me to teach him notes.
He loved that ragged box but, Lord,
he couldn't play it worth a damn.

Nobody could. I tried to tell him so.
"Hell, I know, Sid," he said. "If I
were any good, it would worry me
too much. This way I can just blame
the instrument."
                    And this, too, is
a fond instructive memory.

Boom BOOM. "Listen to that," he said.
Then silence once again as Yanks
swabbed out the cannonbarrel and rammed
another charge into the gun. They paused
a minute in their work. *Boom BOOM.*
Our cannon fired in answer to
in-coming shells. "Don't they," he asked
"sound like a giant limping through
the woods in search of us?" I laughed.
It was a peaceful night and we
were working on some liquid corn.
Boom BOOM. I filled my cup again
and said, "He's after us all right."
He laughed. *Boom BOOM.* I sloshed more in
his cup. A shell exploded to our right.
A piece of shrapnel nicked my ear,
and when the smoke had cleared, I saw
him sitting, looking for his cup
and for the hand he'd held it in.

From this, I didn't learn a thing.

Burial Detail

Between each layer of tattered, broken flesh
we spread, like frosting, a layer of lime,
and then we spread it extra thick on top
as though we were building a giant torte.
The lime has something to do with cholera
and aids, I think, the chemistry of decay
when slathered between the ranks of sour dead.
I know what we did; I'm not sure why.
The colonel had to ask us twice for volunteers;

the second time, I went. I don't know why.
Even in August heat I cannot sleep
unless I have a sheet across my shoulders.
I guess we owe our species something.
We stacked the flaccid meat all afternoon,
and then night fell so black and absolute
it was as if the day had never been,
was something impossible we'd made up
to comfort ourselves in our long work.
And even in the pitch-black, pointless dark
we stacked the men and spread the lime
as we had done all day. Though not as neat.

They were supposed to be checked thoroughly.
I didn't look; I didn't sift their pockets.
A lot of things got buried that shouldn't have been.
I tossed men unexamined in the trench.
But out of the corner of my eyes
I kept seeing faces I thought I knew.
At first they were the faces of anonymous men
I may have seen in camp or on the field.
Later, as I grew tired, exhausted, sick,
I saw they were my mother, father, kin
whom I had never seen but recognized
by features I knew in different combinations
on the shifting, similar faces of my cousins,
and even, once, a face that looked like mine.
But when I stopped to stare at them
I found the soft, unfocused eyes of strangers
and let them drop into the common grave.

Then, my knees gave. I dropped my shovel
and pitched, face first, into the half-filled trench.
I woke almost immediately, and stood
on someone's chest while tired hands pulled me out.
It's funny: standing there, I didn't feel
the mud-wet suck of death beneath my feet
as I had felt it often enough before
when we made forced marches through Virginia rain.
That is to say, the dead man's spongy chest
was firmer than the roads that led us—
and him—into the Wilderness.
For six or seven days I had to hear
a lot of stupid jokes about that faint:
folks are dying to get in, that sort of thing.
I wasn't the only one to faint.

You'd think I would have fainted for my father,
for some especially mutilated boy,
for Clifford or my mother. Not for myself.

In the hot inexhaustible work of the night
a good wind blowing from a distant storm
was heaven, more so because the bodies needed
to be wet, to ripen in moisture and lime,
to pitch and rock with tiny lives,
or whatever it takes to make them earth again.
Okay, I'm sorry for this, for getting worked up.
The thought that they might not decay
was enough to make my stomach heave.
Some men I've argued with seem to think
that they'll stay perfect, whole and sweet,
beneath the ground. It makes me shudder:
dead bodies in no way different from my own
except mine moves, and shudders in its moving.
I take great comfort in knowing I will rot
and that the chest I once stood on
is indistinguishable from other soil
and I will be indistinguishable from it.

But standing there, looking out of the grave,
eyes barely above the lip of earth, I saw
the most beautiful thing I've ever seen:
dawn on the field after the Wilderness.
The bodies, in dawn light, were simply forms;
the landscape seemed abstract, unreal.
It didn't look like corpses, trees, or sky,
but shapes on shapes against a field of gray
and in the distance a source of doubtful light,
itself still gray and close to darkness.
There were a thousand shades of gray,
with colors—some blue perhaps and maybe green—
trying to assert themselves against that gray.
In short, it looked like nothing human.
But the sun broke from the horizon soon enough
and we could see exactly what we'd done.

T.R. Hummer is the author of four collections of poetry, most recently *Lower-Class Heresy*, from the University of Illinois Press. A native of Noxubee County, Mississippi, where he was born in 1950, he was educated at the University of Southern Mississippi and the University of Utah. He is co-editor, with Bruce Weigl, of *The Imagination as Glory: On the Poetry of James Dickey* and teaches at Kenyon College.

Photo Credit: Marion Hummer

Inner Ear

Think of it this way, The doctor tells him,
A small sealed chamber with a fine dust inside.
He thinks of a country church, that tiny unused room
Where they keep old choir robes nobody ever wears.
He went there once with the girl who made a mistake

In Sunday School. "'Consider,'" she read aloud,
"'The lilies of the field. They do not sow,
Neither do they rape.'" The red she turned
When everybody laughed was a miracle.

The dust is always settling, always falling.
Your body knows. That's how it tells up from down.
Lying flat on his back in a hospital bed
He thinks it incredibly strange
That the spinning he feels in the world is not in the world

But in the dust inside his head.
It is true that the world is turning,
And its motionlessness is only apparent.
It is not true he feels it turning,

But maybe a doubling of illusions
Amounts to something like the truth.
That small room at the back of the church has a window in it.
When she grabs his hand and pulls him in,
They stand together in its hot shaft of light.

Have you ever kissed a girl, she whispers.
He doesn't answer, he just kisses her.
Sometimes it can be like that. It hits him
While he is driving. One minute everything is fine,

The next, everything turns upside down.
The nausea is indescribable. He goes so gray
His wife is certain it is his heart.
He sits there while she flags a passing car, his eyes shut,
His forehead jammed on top of the steering wheel

Which gives him no clues, being round.
In the hospital bed he lies carefully, not moving his head.
Everything that falls, he thinks, *falls*
Toward the center of some larger body.

Dust falls toward the center of the earth.
The girl is older than he is, almost sixteen.
She has to bend to kiss him.
He keeps his eyes open, sees how tight hers clench.
Her tongue darts in his mouth. She holds him hard.

Dustmotes rise around them in the sunlight,
Shimmering in a translucent eddy as if their bodies
Were an obstacle in some current.
Sometimes, the doctor says, *there'll be a disturbance.*

We don't know why it happens. But when it does,
The dust can't settle. And then your sense of direction
Goes haywire. You don't know which way is up.
His wife sits by the bed reading an article aloud:
I Am Joe's Inner Ear. "'The inner ear as a whole

Is referred to as *the labyrinth*. There are, in fact,
Two labyrinths, one inside the other.'"
"It's a hell of a clumsy way to do things,"
He says. "It's a crude piece of engineering."

"I thought it was your heart," she says. "I knew it was."
He stares at the ceiling, not turning to look at her.
"There's no connection," he says, "between the heart
And the inner ear." But he lies there holding on
To the bedrail's steel, believing he can feel

The pole tilt toward the solstice.
Bony labyrinth, he hears his wife murmur, *membranous labyrinth*.
An out-of-tune pedal organ in a distant room wheezes out
Rock of ages, cleft for me.

Listen, the girl whispers, *listen*,
But he stands straight and kisses her again and again.
There is only the rush of blood in his ears
And the voice that tells him *Really, we don't know much.*
It could happen any time. It may never happen again.

The Beating

Everybody knew Clifton Cockerell was not half bright,
But nobody knew his passion
Till we found him on the playground back of the junior high
Carving names on a tree. His poor secret
Stood no more chance of staying one

Once we had it, than Clifton did of knowing
Why we cared—but we couldn't let it rest
Till everybody heard it, especially the girl, who was pretty
And thought he was some brand of animal. We'd sing
Their names together every chance we got, impressed

With her way of changing color, like some
Exotic lizard trying to disappear,
And forgot about Clifton pretty much till he came on us
Sudden one afternoon, wrathful and dumb
And swinging a length of cable. It wasn't fear

That defeated us. It was surprise
That it mattered so much what we'd done.
How could we know? He'd been one of us all our lives,
So close it was hard to see how he'd beat us
This once: he was already man enough to think he loved a woman.

So he came down on us sudden, boys,
All of us, and he gave us a taste of the hurt
We'd live to know another way: how love
Can be wrong and still be the only joy
That's real: how, when we come to it,

We stand amazed but take the blow, transfigured, idiot.

Sorrow

When my grandmother was dying
She could forget
Everything she hated,
How my grandfather laid
His hard farmer's hands on her
And wrung out sons:
How she loved her sons,
But how bitter the act of love was,
Why she was a dark
And melancholy woman.

Maybe joy is a matter of losing
Your earthly connections,
Maybe only then can you love
Clean, without hatred or desire.
Once when I was a boy
I was walking in woods
I thought I knew, near dusk,
And suddenly everything went strange,
The light, the leaves on the ground:
Shadows pointed east
So I walked west, the way
I thought I had to go,
But nothing came clear,
Nothing but sunlight burning

Through oaks, blinding me
Until I found the shadow
Of one trunk to walk in:
I followed it, came
To a young tree, took it
In my hands
Like a woman's waist,
Forgot to be afraid, not caring
As long as I held on.

My mother told me this:
When my grandmother was dying,
She turned to a nurse
And asked *Are you my child?*
The nurse said *No.*
My grandmother took her hand,
Held on hard: whispered *Well*
It doesn't matter then.
It's all right.
Yes. All right.

Where You Go When She Sleeps

What is it when a woman sleeps, her head bright
In your lap, in your hands, her breath easy now as though it had never been
Anything else, and you know she is dreaming, her eyelids
Jerk, but she is not troubled, it is a dream
That does not include you, but you are not troubled either,
It is too good to hold her while she sleeps, her hair falling
Richly on your hands, shining like metal, a color
That when you think of it you cannot name, as though it has just
Come into existence, dragging you into the world in the wake
Of its creation, out of whatever vacuum you were in before,
And you are like the boy you heard of once who fell
Into a silo full of oats, the silo emptying from below, oats
At the top swirling in a gold whirlpool, a bright eddy of grain, the boy,
You imagine, leaning over the edge to see it, the noon sun breaking
Into the center of the circle he watches, hot on his back, burning
And he forgets his father's warning, stands on the edge, looks down,
The grain spinning, dizzy, and when he falls his arms go out, too thin
For wings, and he hears his father's cry somewhere, but is gone

Already, down in a gold sea, spun deep in the heart of the silo,
And when they find him, his mouth, his throat, his lungs
Full of the gold that took him, he lies still, not seeing the world
Through his body but through the deep rush of the grain
Where he has gone and can never come back, though they drag him
Out, his father's tears bright on both their faces, the farmhands
Standing by blank and amazed—you touch that unnamable
Color in her hair and you are gone into what is not fear or joy
But a whirling of sunlight and water and air full of shining dust
That takes you, a dream that is not of you but will let you
Into itself if you love enough, and will not, will never let you go.

What Shines in Winter Burns

December sun sits low over hedgerows, glitter
Of morning bright on cottonfield frost, on the dead
Stalks left brittle in rows to crumble
Under rain and cold-snap ice. The sun, silver
Over silver trees, is surely a star, scarcely

Too brilliant to look on through the window
Of the school bus bounding over washboard gravel
Roads, noisy as a tin can tied to the tail
Of a bird dog—bird dog weather,
This cold morning, when the smell

Of bob white hangs close to the ground, keen
To a dog's nose as alum—the scent of passion
A boy cannot know himself, but has to follow
Watching the quivering nose of the dog freeze
In a perfect point. Alone in the bus

With the driver, in the front seat, the first
Stop on the route, I am wanting so hard
To be walking those fields and hedgerows
With a dog, gunmetal cold in my hand,
That the thought of the gun speaking death

Into cold air is love, the covey breaking
Loud in the still morning, one bird black
Against that dim silver sun, the dark gun-barrel
Rising. In that dream I am a man
With power no boy ever learned

Anywhere a school bus might take him. I aim
My notebook out the windshield, sighting down
The spine of it, firing my desire
Over and over into the stiff dead stalks
The bus rattles through, not wondering whether love

Outlives the deaths we make for it:
I look for something, I pull the trigger, the gun
In my hand explodes, and I am a man about to say
Look, I am alive, I have touched the world
The way a man touches the body of the one

Woman he can never live without again.
But I do not say it, for suddenly I see
What I am aiming at: over the back of the notebook,
I am squinting at the body
Of a man half lost in dead silver cottonstalks,

Half in the road, a black man, frozen, silver,
Glinting with sunlight and frost. I shout,
But the driver knows, the bus squeals, stopping,
Quivering, hood pointing, tires
Not a foot from that shining head,

The driver saying *Stay here, stay here, don't look,*
As he goes out the door, but too late, I have seen already
The man's right hand frozen to the whiskey bottle,
The left hand clutching together the patched denim coat,
And his eyes, his dead eyes frozen open

Staring up at me, answering, *Boy, you will never*
Understand love until you lay your hand
Where mine is. Touch me. This is the body. I know.

RANDALL
JARRELL

Randall Jarrell was born in 1914 in Nashville, Tennessee, and studied at Vanderbilt University. From 1947 until his death in 1965, Jarrell taught at the Women's College of the University of North Carolina at Greensboro. His *Complete Poems* was published in 1969.

Photo Credit: Ted Russell

When I Was Home Last Christmas . . .

When I was home last Christmas
I called on your family,
Your aunts and your mother, your sister;
They were kind as ever to me.

They told me how well I was looking
And clearly admired my wife;
I drank tea, made conversation,
And played with my bread, or knife.

Your aunts seemed greyer; your mother's
Lame unexpecting smile
Wandered from doily to doily;
Your dead face still

Cast me, with parted lips,
Its tight-rope-walker's look. . . .
But who is there now to notice
If I look or do not look

At a photograph at your mother's?
There is no one left to care
For all we said, and did, and thought—
The world we were.

90 North

At home, in my flannel gown, like a bear to its floe,
I clambered to bed; up the globe's impossible sides
I sailed all night—till at last, with my black beard,
My furs and my dogs, I stood at the northern pole.

There in the childish night my companions lay frozen,
The stiff furs knocked at my starveling throat,
And I gave my great sigh: the flakes came huddling,
Were they really my end? In the darkness I turned to my rest.

—Here, the flag snaps in the glare and silence
Of the unbroken ice. I stand here,
The dogs bark, my beard is black, and I stare
At the North Pole . . .
                              And now what? Why, go back.

Turn as I please, my step is to the south.
The world—my world spins on this final point
Of cold and wretchedness: all lines, all winds
End in this whirlpool I at last discover.

And it is meaningless. In the child's bed
After the night's voyage, in that warm world
Where people work and suffer for the end
That crowns the pain—in that Cloud-Cuckoo-Land

I reached my North and it had meaning.
Here at the actual pole of my existence,
Where all that I have done is meaningless,
Where I die or live by accident alone—

Where, living or dying, I am still alone;
Here where North, the night, the berg of death
Crowd me out of the ignorant darkness,
I see at last that all the knowledge

I wrung from the darkness—that the darkness flung me—
Is worthless as ignorance: nothing comes from nothing,
The darkness from the darkness. Pain comes from the darkness
And we call it wisdom. It is pain.

The Death of the Ball Turret Gunner

From my mother's sleep I fell into the State,
And I hunched in its belly till my wet fur froze.
Six miles from earth, loosed from its dream of life,
I woke to black flak and the nightmare fighters.
When I died they washed me out of the turret with a hose.

The Player Piano

I ate pancakes one night in a Pancake House
Run by a lady my age. She was gay.
When I told her that I came from Pasadena
She laughed and said, "I lived in Pasadena
When Fatty Arbuckle drove the El Molino bus."

I felt that I had met someone from home.
No, not Pasadena, Fatty Arbuckle.
Who's that? Oh, something that we had in common
Like—like—the false armistice. Piano rolls.
She told me her house was the first Pancake House

East of the Mississippi, and I showed her
A picture of my grandson. Going home—
Home to the hotel—I began to hum,
"Smile a while, I bid you sad adieu,
When the clouds roll back I'll come to you."

Let's brush our hair before we go to bed,
I say to the old friend who lives in my mirror.
I remember how I'd brush my mother's hair
Before she bobbed it. How long has it been
Since I hit my funnybone? had a scab on my knee?

Here are Mother and Father in a photograph,
Father's holding me. . . . They both look so *young*.
I'm so much older than they are. Look at them,
Two babies with their baby. I don't blame you,
You weren't old enough to know any better;

If I could I'd go back, sit down by you both,
And sign our true armistice: you weren't to blame.
I shut my eyes and there's our living room.
The piano's playing something by Chopin,
and Mother and Father and their little girl

Listen. Look, the keys go down by themselves!
I go over, hold my hands out, play I play—
If only, somehow, I had learned to live!
The three of us sit watching, as my waltz
Plays itself out a half-inch from my fingers.

RODNEY JONES

Rodney Jones was born in Hartselle, Alabama in 1950 and educated at the University of Alabama and the University of North Carolina at Greensboro. *The Unborn* is his second volume of poems. He lives in Carbondale, Illinois, where he teaches at Southern Illinois University.

Sweep

The two Garnett brothers who run the Shell station here,
who are working separately just now,
one hunched under the rear axle of Skippy Smith's Peterbilt tractor,
the other humming as he loosens the clamps
to replace my ruptured heater hoses,
have aged twenty years since I saw them last
and want only to talk of high school
and who has died from each class.
Seamless gray sky, horns from the four-lane,
the lot's oil slicks rainbowing and dimpling with rain.
I have been home for three days, listening to an obituary.
The names of relatives met once,
of men from the plant where he works,
click like distant locks on my father's lips.
I know that it is death that obsesses him
more than football or weather
and that cancer is far too prevalent
in this green valley of herbicides and chemical factories.

Now Mike, the younger brother,
lifts from my engine compartment
a cluster of ruined hoses,
twisted and curled together like a nest of blacksnakes,
and whistles as he forages in the rack
for more. Slowly, the way things work down here,
while I wait and the rain plinks on the rims of overturned tires,
he and my father trade the names of the dead:
Bill Farrell for Albert Dotson,
Myles Hammond, the quick tackle of our football team,
for Don Appleton, the slow, redheaded one.
By the time the rack is exhausted
I'm thinking if I lived here all year I'd buy American,
I'd drive a truck, and I'm thinking
of football and my father's and Mike's words
staking out an absence I know I won't reclaim.
Because I don't get home much anymore,
I notice the smallest scintilla of change,
every burnt-out trailer and newly paved road,
and the larger, slower change
that is exponential,
that strangeness, like the unanticipated face
of my aunt, shrunken and perversely stylish
under the turban she wore after chemotherapy.
But mostly it's the wait, one wait after another,
and I'm dropping back deep in the secondary
under the chill and pipe smoke of a canceled October
while the sweep rolls toward me from the line of scrimmage,
and Myles Hammond, who will think too slowly
and turn his air-force jet into the Arizona desert,
and Don Appleton, who will drive out on a country road
for a shotgun in his mouth, are cut down,
and I'm shifting on the balls of my feet,
bobbing and saving one nearly hopeless feint,
one last plunge for the blockers
and the ballcarrier who follows the sweep,
and it comes, and comes on.

The Mosquito

I see the mosquito kneeling on the soft underside of my arm, kneeling
Like a fruitpicker, kneeling like an old woman
With the proboscis of her prayer buried in the idea of God,
And I know we shall not speak with the aliens
And that peace will not happen in my life, not unless
It is in the burnt oil spreading across the surfaces of ponds, in the dark
Egg rafts clotting and the wiggletails expiring like batteries.
Bring a little alcohol and a little balm
For these poppies planted by the Queen of Neptune.
In her photographs she is bearded and spurred, embellished
      five hundred times,
Her modular legs crouching, her insufferable head unlocking
To lower the razor-edge of its tubes, and she is there in the afternoon
When the wind gives up the spirit of cleanliness
And there rises from the sound the brackish oyster and squid smell
      of creation.
I lie down in the sleeping bag sodden with rain.
Nights with her, I am loved for myself, for the succulent
Flange of my upper lip, the twin bellies of my eyelids.
She adores the easy, the soft. She picks the tenderest blossoms of insomnia.
Mornings while the jackhammer rips the pavement outside my window,
While the sanitation workers bang the cans against the big truck and shout
      to each other over the motor,
I watch her strut like an udder with my blood,
Imagining the luminous pick descending into Trotsky's skull
      and the eleven days
I waited for the cold chill, nightmare, and nightsweat of malaria;
Imagining the mating call in the vibrations of her wings,
And imagining, in the simple knot of her ganglia,
How she thrills to my life, how she sings for the harvest.

The First Birth

I had not been there before where the vagina opens,
the petals of liver, each vein a delicate bush,
and where something clutches its way into the light
like a mummy tearing and fumbling from his shroud.
The heifer was too small, too young in the hips,
short-bodied with outriggers distending her sides,
and back in the house, in the blue *Giants of Science*
still open on my bed, Ptolemy was hurtling toward Einstein.
Marconi was inventing the wireless without me.
Da Vinci was secretly etching the forbidden anatomy
of the Dark Ages. I was trying to remember
Galen, his pen drawing, his inscrutable genius,
not the milk in the refrigerator, sour with bitterweed.
It came, cream-capped and hay-flecked, in silver pails.
At nights we licked onions to sweeten the taste.
All my life I had been around cows named after friends
and fated for slaughterhouses. I wanted to bring
Mendel and Rutherford into that pasture,
and bulb-headed Hippocrates, who would know what to do.
The green branch nearby reeked of crawfish.
The heavy horseflies orbited. A compass, telescope,
and protractor darted behind my eyes. When the sac
broke, the water soaked one thigh. The heifer lowed.
Enrico Fermi, how much time it takes, the spotted legs,
the wet black head and white blaze. The shoulders
lodged. The heifer walked with the calf wedged
in her pelvis, the head swaying behind her like a cut blossom.
Did I ever go back to science, or eat a hamburger
without that paralysis, that hour of the stuck calf
and the unconscionable bawling that must have been a prayer?
Now that I know a little it helps, except for birth
or dying, those slow pains, like the rigorous observation
of Darwin. Anyway, I had to take the thing, any way
I could, as my hands kept slipping, wherever it was,
under the chin, by tendony, china-delicate knees,
my foot against the hindquarters of the muley heifer,
to bring into this world, black and enormous,
wobbling to his feet, the dumb bull, Copernicus.

DONALD

JUSTICE

Donald Justice was born in Miami, Florida in 1925 and studied at the University of Miami, North Carolina, Stanford, and the University of Iowa. He has taught at several universities, including the University of Iowa, and is currently a professor of English at the University of Florida in Gainesville. His early work has been honored by a Lamont Poetry Award, and his *Selected Poems* was awarded the Pulitzer Prize in 1980.

Photo Credit: Joseph Levy

Sonnet: The Poet at Seven

And on the porch, across the upturned chair,
The boy would spread a dingy counterpane
Against the length and majesty of the rain,
And on all fours crawl under it like a bear
To lick his wounds in secret, in his lair:
And afterwards, in the windy yard again,
One hand cocked back, release his paper plane
Frail as a May fly to the faithless air.
And summer evenings he would whirl around
Faster and faster till the drunken ground
Rose up to meet him; sometimes he would squat
Among the bent weeds of the vacant lot,
Waiting for dusk and someone dear to come
and whip him down the street, but gently, home.

In Bertram's Garden

Jane looks down at her organdy skirt
As if *it* somehow were the thing disgraced,
For being there, on the floor, in the dirt,
And she catches it up about her waist,
Smooths it out along one hip,
And pulls it over the crumpled slip.

On the porch, green-shuttered, cool,
Asleep is Bertram, that bronze boy,
Who, having wound her around a spool,
Sends her spinning like a toy
Out to the garden, all alone,
To sit and weep on a bench of stone.

Soon the purple dark will bruise
Lily and bleeding heart and rose,
And the little Cupid lose
Eyes and ears and chin and nose,
And Jane lie down with others soon
Naked to the naked moon.

Heart

Heart, let us this once reason together.
Thou art a child no longer. Only think
What sport the neighbors have from us, not without cause.
These nightly sulks, these clamorous demonstrations!
Already they tell of thee a famous story.
An antique, balding spectacle such as thou art,
Affecting still that childish, engaging stammer
With all the seedy innocence of an overripe pomegranate!
Henceforth, let us conduct ourselves more becomingly!

And still I hear thee, beating thy little fist
Against the walls. My dear, have I not led thee,
Dawn after streaky dawn, besotted, home?
And still these threats to have off as before?
From thee, who wouldst lose thyself in the next street?
Go then, O my inseparable, this once more.
Afterwards we will take thought for our good name.

Men at Forty

Men at forty
Learn to close softly
The doors to rooms they will not be
Coming back to.

At rest on a stair landing,
They feel it
Moving beneath them now like the deck of a ship,
Though the swell is gentle.

And deep in mirrors
They rediscover
The face of the boy as he practices tying
His father's tie there in secret

And the face of that father,
Still warm with the mystery of lather.
They are more fathers than sons themselves now.
Something is filling them, something

That is like the twilight sound
Of the crickets, immense,
Filling the woods at the foot of the slope
Behind their mortgaged houses.

First Death

June 12, 1933

I saw my grandmother grow weak.
When she died, I kissed her cheek.

I remember the new taste—
Powder mixed with a drying paste.

Down the hallway, on its table,
Lay the family's great Bible.

In the dark, by lamplight stirred,
The Void grew pregnant with the Word.

In black ink they wrote it down.
The older ink was turning brown.

From the woods there came a cry—
The hoot owl asking who, not why.

The men sat silent on the porch,
Each lighted pipe a friendly torch

Against the unknown and the known.
But the child knew himself alone.

June 13, 1933

The morning sun rose up and stuck.
Sunflower strove with hollyhock.

I ran the worn path past the sty.
Nothing was hidden from God's eye.

The barn door creaked. I walked among
Chaff and wrinkled cakes of dung.

In the dim light I read the dates
On the dusty license plates

Nailed to the wall as souvenirs.
I breathed the dust in of the years.

I circled the abandoned Ford
Before I tried the running board.

At the wheel I felt the heat
Press upwards through the springless seat.

And when I touched the silent horn,
Small mice scattered through the corn.

June 14, 1933

I remember the soprano
Fanning herself at the piano,

And the preacher looming large
Above me in his dark blue serge.

My shoes brought in a smell of clay
To mingle with the faint sachet

Of flowers sweating in their vases.
A stranger showed us to our places.

The stiff fan stirred in mother's hand.
Air moved, but only when she fanned.

I wondered how could all her grief
Be squeezed into one small handkerchief.

There was a buzzing on the sill.
It stopped, and everything was still.

We bowed our heads, we closed our eyes
To the mercy of the flies.

Tremayne

I *The Mild Despair of Tremayne*

Snow melting and the dog
Barks lonely on his bottom from the yard.
    The ground is frozen but not hard.

The seasonal and vague
Despairs of February settle over
    Tremayne now like a light snow cover,

And he sits thinking; sits
Also not thinking for a while of much.
    So February turns to March.

Snow turns to rain; a hyacinth
Pokes up; doves returning moan and sing.
    Tremayne takes note of one more spring—

Mordancies of the armchair!—
And finds it hard not to be reconciled
    To a despair that seems so mild.

II *The Contentment of Tremayne*

Tremayne stands in the sunlight,
    Watering his lawn.
The sun seems not to move at all.
    Till it has moved on.

The twilight sounds commence then
    As those of water cease,
And he goes barefoot through the stir,
    Almost at peace.

Light leans in pale rectangles
    Out against the night.
Tremayne asks nothing more now. There's
    Just enough light,

Or when the street lamp catches
    There should be. He pauses:
How simple it all seems for once!—
    These sidewalks, these still houses.

III *The Insomnia of Tremayne*

The all-night stations—Tremayne pictures them
As towers that shoot great sparks off through the dark—
Fade out and drift among the drifted hours
Just now returning to his bedside clock;
And something starts all over, call it day.
He likes, he really likes the little hum,
Which is the last sound of all night-sounds to decay.

Call that the static of the spheres, a sound
Of pure in-betweenness, far, and choked, and thin.
As long as it lasts—a faint, celestial surf—
He feels no need to dial the weather in,
Or music, or the news, or anything.
    And it soothes him, like some night-murmuring nurse,
Murmuring nothing much, perhaps, but murmuring.

IV *Tremayne Autumnal*

Autumn, and a cold rain, and mist,
    In which the dark pine-shapes are drowned,
And taller pole-shapes, and the town lights masked—
A scene, oh, vaguely Post-Impressionist,
    Tremayne would tell us, if we asked.

Who with his glasses off, half blind,
    Accomplishes very much the same
Lovely effect of blurs and shimmerings—
Or else October evenings spill a kind
    Of Lethe-water over things.

'O season of half forgetfulness!'
    Tremayne, as usual, misquotes,
Recalling adolescence and old trees
In whose shade once he memorized that verse
    And something about 'late flowers for the bees . . .'

Thinking about the Past

Certain moments will never change, nor stop being—
My mother's face all smiles, all wrinkles soon;
The rock wall building, built, collapsed then, fallen;
Our upright loosening downward slowly out of tune—
All fixed into place now, all rhyming with each other.
That red-haired girl with wide mouth—Eleanor—
Forgotten thirty years—her freckled shoulders, hands.
The breast of Mary Something, freed from a white swimsuit,
Damp, sandy, warm; or Margery's, a small, caught bird—
Darkness they rise from, darkness they sink back toward.
O marvellous early cigarettes! O bitter smoke, Benton . . .
And Kenny in wartime whites, crisp, cocky,
Time a bow bent with his certain failure.
Dusks, dawns; waves; the ends of songs . . .

Variations on Southern Themes

> "But why do I write of the all unutterable and the
> all abysmal? Why does my pen not drop from my
> hand on approaching the infinite pity and tragedy
> of all the past? It does, poor helpless pen, with
> what it meets of the ineffable, what it meets of the
> cold Medusa-face of life, of all the life lived, on
> every side. Basta, basta!"
>
> —H. James, Notebooks

1: *At the Cemetery*

Above the fence-flowers, like a bloody thumb,
A hummingbird was throbbing . . . And some
Petals had taken motion from the wings
In hardly observable obscure quiverings.
The mother stood there, but so still her clothing
Seemed to have settled into stone, nothing
To animate her face, nothing to read there—
O plastic rose O clouds O still cedar!
She stood there for a long time while the sky
Pondered her with its great Medusa-eye;

Or in the son's memory she did.
                                  And then a
Slow blacksnake, lazy with long sunning, slid
Down from its slab, and through the thick grass, and hid
Somewhere among the purpling wild verbena.

2: *On the Farm*

The boy, missing the city intensely at that moment,
Moped and sulked at the window. There went the first owl, quite near,
But the sound hardly registered. And the kerosene lamp
Went on sputtering, giving off vague medicinal fumes
That made him think of sickrooms. He had been memorizing
"The Ballad of Reading Gaol," but the lamplight hurt his eyes;
And he was too bored to sleep, restless and bored. *Years later,*
Perhaps, he would recall the evenings, empty and vast, when,
Under the first stars, there by the back gate, secretly, he
Had relieved himself on the shamed and drooping hollyhocks.
Now he yawned; the old dream of being a changeling returned.
And the owl cried, and he felt himself like the owl—proud, strange,
Almost invisible—or like some hero in Homer
Protected by the cloud let down by the gods to save him.

3: *In the Train, Heading North Through Florida, Late*
at Night and Long Ago, and Ending with a Line
from Thomas Wolfe

Midnight or after, and the little lights
Glittered like lost beads from a broken necklace
Beyond smudged windows, lost and irretrievable—
Some promise of romance those Southern nights
Never entirely kept—unless, sleepless,
We should pass down dim corridors again
To stand, braced in a swaying vestibule,
Alone with the darkness and the wind—out there
Nothing but pines and one new road perhaps,
Straight and white, aimed at the distant gulf—
And hear, from the smoking-room, the sudden high-pitched
Whinny of laughter pass from throat to throat;
And the great wheels smash and pound beneath our feet.

American Scenes (1904)

—after Henry James

1. *Cambridge in winter*

Immense pale houses! The sunshine and the snow
Light up and pauperize the whole brave show—
Each fanlight, each veranda, each good address,
All a mere paint-and-pasteboard paltriness!

The winter sunsets are the one fine thing:
Blood on the snow, some last impassioned fling,
A wild frankness and sadness of surrender—
As if these cities ever could be tender!

2. *Railway junction south of Richmond, past midnight*

Indistinguishable engines hooting, red
Fires flaring, vanishing; a formless shed
Just straggling lifewards before sinking back
Into Dantean glooms beside the track,

All steam and smoke and earth—and even here,
Out of this little hell of spurts and hisses,
Come the first waftings of the Southern air,
Of open gates, of all-but-bland abysses.

3. *St. Michael's Cemetery, Charleston*

One can depend on these old cemeteries
To say the one charmed thing there is to say.
So here the silvery seaward outlook carries
Hints of another world beyond the bay,

The sun-warmed tombs, the flowers. Each faraway
Game-haunted inlet and reed-smothered isle
Speaks of lost Venices; and the South meanwhile
Has only to be tragic to beguile.

Epilogue: Henry James at the Pacific

—*Coronado Beach, California, March, 1905*

In a hotel room by the sea, the Master
Sits brooding on the continent he has crossed.
Not that he foresees immediate disaster,
Only a sort of freshness being lost.
Or should he go on calling it Innocence?
The sad-faced monsters of the plains are gone;
Wall Street controls the wilderness. There's an immense
Novel in all this waiting to be done,
But not, not—sadly enough—by him. His talents,
Such as they may be, want an older theme,
One rather more civilized than this, on balance.
For him now always the consoling dream
Is just the mild dear light of Lamb House falling
Beautifully down the pages of his calling.

ETHERIDGE KNIGHT

Etheridge Knight was born in Corinth, Mississippi in 1931. He began to write while serving eight years in the Indiana State Prison of a 10–25 year sentence for robbery and was released on parole shortly after the publication of *Poems from Prison* in 1968. *Born of a Woman: New and Selected Poems* appeared in 1980. He was poetry editor of *Motive* magazine and co-editor of *Black Box*.

He Sees Through Stone

He sees through stone
he has the secret
eyes this old black one
who under prison skies
sits pressed by the sun
against the western wall
his pipe between purple gums

the years fall
like overripe plums
bursting red flesh
on the dark earth

his time is not my time
but I have known him
in a time gone

he led me trembling cold
into the dark forest
taught me the secret rites
to take a woman
to be true to my brothers
to make my spear drink
the blood
of my enemies

now black cats circle him
flash white teeth
snarl at the air
mashing green grass beneath
shining muscles
ears peeling his words

he smiles
he knows
the hunt   the enemy
he has the secret eyes
he sees through stone

The Warden Said to Me the Other Day

The warden said to me the other day
(innocently, I think), "Say, etheridge,
why come the black boys don't run off
like the white boys do?"
I lowered my jaw and scratched my head
and said (innocently, I think), "Well, suh,
I ain't for sure, but I reckon it's cause
we ain't got no wheres to run to."

As You Leave Me

Shiny record albums scattered over
the livingroom floor, reflecting light
from the lamp, sharp reflections that hurt
my eyes as I watch you, squatting among the platters,
the beer foam making mustaches on your lips.

And, too,
the shadows on your cheeks from your long lashes
fascinate me—almost as much as the dimples:
in your cheeks, your arms and your legs:
dimples . . . dimples . . . dimples . . .

You
hum along with Mathis—how you love Mathis!
with his burnished hair and quicksilver voice that dances
among the stars and whirls through canyons
like windblown snow. sometimes I think that Mathis
could take you from me if you could be complete
without me. I glance at my watch. it is now time.

You rise,
silently, and to the bedroom and the paint:
on the lips red, on the eyes black,
and I lean in the doorway and smoke, and see you
grow old before my eyes, and smoke. why do you
chatter while you dress, and smile when you grab
your large leather purse? don't you know that when you
leave me I walk to the window and watch you? and light
a reefer as I watch you? and I die as I watch you
disappear in the dark streets
to whistle and to smile at the johns.

——— YUSEF ———
KOMUNYAKAA

Originally from Bogalusa, Louisi-
ana, where he was born in 1947,
Yusef Komunyakaa attended the
University of California where he
received an M.F.A. He is the au-
thor of *Copacetic* and *I Apologize
for the Eyes in My Head*, both pub-
lished by Wesleyan University
Press.

Photo Credit: Carolyne Wright

We Never Know

He was standing on the edge of us,
gazing at a photograph in his wallet,
when the bullet caught him
below the hairline.
He danced with the tall grass
for a moment, like he was swaying
to a woman's body. The air
spun red with her name.

Our gunbarrels glowed white hot.

When I got to him, a blue halo
of flies had already claimed him.
I pulled the crumbled photograph
from his fingers. There's no other way
to say this: I fell in love. The morning

cleared again, except for a distant mortar
& somewhere choppers taking off.
I slid the wallet into his pocket
& turned him over, so he wouldn't be

kissing the ground.

Ia Drang Valley

To sleep here, I play dead.
My mind takes me over the Pacific
to my best friend's wife nude
on their bed. I lean over & kiss her.
Sometimes the spleen decides
for the brain, what it takes
to bridge another night.
The picture dissolves into gray
& I fight in my sleep,
cursing the jump cut that pulls me back
to the man in a white tunic,
where I'm shoved against the wall
with the rest of the mute hostages.
The church spire hides under dusk
in the background, & my outflung arms
shadow bodies in the dirt.
I close my eyes but Goya's
Third of May holds steady,
growing sharper. I stand
before the bright rifles,
nailed to the moment.

Saigon Bar Girls, 1975

Where's Ho Xuan Huong
   among these Saigon
bar girls washing off their
   makeup & slipping into
     peasant clothes?

Where is she, that lotus
      queen of *chu nom* poetry?
I know she has a heavy story—air
   into ashes, a fist hidden
   in raw silk.

She couldn't be with those
     To Do Street whores
shedding their stateside miniskirts
   thinner than memories

denied, their French perfume
pale as history.
      Huong, you
          can speak now.
Those Top 40 hits
are forgotten, given to a gale
   moving toward the South
   China Sea.

Bar girls stand like Lot's wife
     at plaintive windows
or return to home villages
   as sleepwalkers. Is she
     among those disappearing

from off-limit doorways, leaving
   sloe gin glasses
   with lipstick prints?
   Years work like a search
   party behind masks.
   Unmirrored, she forgets

her lists of Mikes,
Bills, Joes, & Johns,
letting her clothes fall
into a hush
at her feet.

Facing It

My black face fades,
hiding inside the black granite.
I said I wouldn't,
dammit: No tears.
I'm stone. I'm flesh.
My clouded reflection eyes me
like a bird of prey, the profile of night
slanted against morning. I turn
this way—the stone lets me go.
I turn this way—I'm inside
the Viet Nam Veterans Memorial
again, depending on the light
to make a difference.
I go down the 58,022 names,
half-expecting to find
my own in letters like smoke.
I touch the name Andrew Johnson;
I see the booby trap's white flash.
Names shimmer on a woman's blouse
but when she walks away
the names stay on the wall.
Brushstrokes flash, a red bird's
wings cutting across my stare.
The sky. A plane in the sky.
A white vet's image floats
closer to me, then his pale eyes
look through mine. I'm a window.
He's lost his right arm
inside the stone. In the black mirror
a woman's trying to erase names:
No, she's brushing a boy's hair.

SUSAN
LUDVIGSON

Susan Ludvigson was born in 1942, and
has lived both in North and South Caro-
lina for more than fifteen years. The
winner of many awards and fellowships
for her poetry, Ms. Ludvigson teaches
presently at Winthrop College in South
Carolina.

Some Notes on Courage

Think of a child who goes out
into the new neighborhood,
cap at an angle, and offers to lend
a baseball glove. He knows
how many traps there are—
his accent or his clothes, the club
already formed.
Think of a pregnant woman
whose first child died—
her history of blood.
Or your friend whose father
locked her in basements, closets,
cars. Now when she speaks
to strangers, she must have
all the windows open.
She forces herself indoors each day,

sheer will makes her climb the stairs.
And love. Imagine it. After all
those years in the circus, that last
bad fall when the net didn't hold.
Think of the ladder to the wire,
spotlights moving as you move,
then how you used to see yourself
balanced on the shiny air.
Think of doing it again.

The Widow

A stranger arrives at her door
in a T-shirt, his truck
parked outside like a sign:
This is an honest repairman.
He wants directions, but she
does not know the street.
When he asks to use the phone,
she lets him into the kitchen
where the water has just begun
to boil, steaming the windows
like breath.

She remembers the novel
where a man holds a knife
to a child's small throat,
drawing a thin line of blood,
then takes the young mother
off in his truck to rape her.
She thinks where her knives are,
imagines throwing the water
straight from the stove
in his face.

He murmurs something
into the phone.
She has gone to another room
and can't make out the words,

the tone is too soft,
but she hears the water
boil over, spatter the gleaming
stainless steel of her range
like the hiss of firecrackers
before they explode.
He pulls the pan off the burner,
calls to her,
Lady? Lady?

She hides in the bathroom,
listens, even after she hears
the door open again, and close
like the click of a trigger.
When at last the truck
pulls away, she comes out,
spends the whole afternoon
drifting back and forth
to the window.

Making supper,
she burns her hand,
cries softly
long after the pain is gone.

The next morning, she's amazed
to see she'd forgotten
to lock the back door,
to turn off the lights
that burned all night
in the kitchen.

Man Arrested in Hacking Death Tells Police
He Mistook Mother-in-Law for Raccoon

Every morning she'd smear something brown
over her eyes, already bagged
and dark underneath, as if that would
get her sympathy. She never slept,
she said, but wandered like a phantom
through the yard. I knew it. Knew
how she knelt beneath our bedroom window too,
and listened to Janet and me.

One night when *again* Janet said No,
I called her a cow, said she might as well
be dead for all she was good to me.
The old lady had fur in her head
and in her ears,
at breakfast slipped and told us
she didn't think the cows would die.

Today when I caught her
in the garage at dawn, that dyed hair
growing out in stripes, eyes
like any animal surprised from sleep
or prowling where it shouldn't be,
I did think, for a minute,
she was the raider of the garden,
and the axe felt good, coming down
on a life like that.

The Punishment

Remember the tree, Charlie?
Where I tied you with ropes
wound from your shoulders
all the way down
to your skinny ankles
like a loose-wrapped mummy?
And then took the branches
lying on the ground
and stuffed them
between you and the ropes
like jail bars,
not to help hold you in,
but to scratch you?
Weeks earlier, Grandma told me
you went to the hospital
with a broken arm,
claiming I did it
because you tried to kiss me.
I would have,
but that's not how it happened
and I've always been a fiend
for truth.
You cried, but not enough,
so I took another leafy branch
and whipped you. And when
I finally turned you loose,
the welts blossoming
on your arm and legs
like roses,
your tears did not move me
at all. I could still see you
at the emergency room
grinning, arm in a sling,
selling stories to the nurses
that sent them out laughing,
repeating my innocent name.

Jeanne d'Arc

To be chosen—

my small body rejoices
at the words,
encases itself in silver
more lovely than silk.

Not to stay in the village
and marry the miller,
his babies heavy in my arms
as loaves of bread—

not to be God's bride
dressed in the long black robe
I've secretly named a shroud,
needing always to chasten myself
for my shimmering dreams—

but Christ's innocent mistress,
Lily of war!

Still, I can scarcely believe
how each time I speak
the sky brightens.

When the voice first came
from behind the dark trees
I sat for a long time, trembling.
Now my skin
burns, imagining how it will be,
the horse between my thighs,
a thousand men behind me
singing.

EVERETTE

MADDOX

A native of Alabama, Everette Maddox lives in New Orleans, where he has served as poet-in-the-schools and an assistant in the Louisiana Maritime Museum. For some years he has conducted a poetry reading series at the Maple Leaf Bar. He is the author of *The Everette Maddox Song Book*.

The Great Man's Death: An Anecdote

the famous poet Everette
Maddox had been advised
by a team of wrong-headed
specialists that one more
snort of the Devil's Brew
would turn his lights and
livers puce. Nonetheless,
he awoke one night in a
borrowed flat with
a surging boredom on—
his only love at a permanent
remove—and got up
and strode the 20 or 30
blocks to Tyler's Bar,
where he had "Four hundred
and seventy-two Margaritas,

straight up, on Bank
Americard. I think that's
the record," he said, and
dropped dead, into a biography.

Breakfast

Oh hush up
about the
Future: one

morning it
will appear,
right there on

your breakfast
plate, and you'll
yell "Take it

back," pounding
the table.
But there won't

be any
waiters.

1941

The clock gleams
down from on
top of the fan—
3:24 A.M.

What woke me up?

What low music
got me up
for this strange
moment,

out of the life
I'd passed out in
as if it were
a gutter?

Was it in my
head? or just
beyond the wall,
in the dusty
hallway?

is it 1941
out there? and are
my parents,
alive and young
and glamorous
again, bravely
dancing in the dark
to Artie Shaw?

Cleopatra Mathis has published two books of poetry, *Aerial View of Louisiana* and *The Bottom Land*, both from The Sheep Meadow Press. She was born in 1947 in Ruston, Louisiana, and attended Louisiana Tech, Tulane University, Southwest Texas State University, and Columbia. She teaches at Dartmouth.

Photo Credit: Vincent McGroary

Elegy for the Other

For Jimmy, killed November 1979.

1.

4 A.M. and still snowing,
far from the bottom land
where the creeks eddy and deepen to swamp.
Someone is crying down there and I call
Come back, but the body does not rise
or wave those arms which are limp and torn
in the mud. I cannot see the face
receding into black, only one
devastating mark, the stained forehead.

You are not here, not in the mottled light
of February. And this clean-iced pond
only reminds me of another, swollen by now
in the muddy rains. Across the lilac cold

I see you in the trees' black
against white, see you shrug and turn.
And if I run, clumsy in the crusted snow,
ragged breath rising, it will be to find
some child's sled upturned, a jacket swaying.

I wake and sleep in one long breath,
breath of rain that falls and falls.
You are a child again, my reflection
carrying a pail of berries,
black raspberries that never grow in the heat.
Smiling, you show me where they are hidden
on land no longer familiar to me. And the voice:
take them, we are alive. But when we enter
the knotted pine kitchen, I find the berries
furred in the bottom of the pail, impossible to save,
and cry out in my way: ruined,
see what you have ruined,
and in that smile see everything I have refused.

North and South again—through those months
the earth turns back and denies, I am still sister
calling brother. Come back, I say
as if to some change, not the bitter quiet of supper,
not the last wing of light
failing the path I search, vine and bramble
threading the marsh that circles the town.

2.

I expected more than a reed broken
in the rain. I thought you would rise up
with your fists, the pistol
radiant in your belt, badge of that country,
all the boys in their flannel shirts.
I would have dragged you out of there.
You, so good at turning your back,
knew full well what happens. Even when you'd quit
the dealing, the bar fights, the jails—
you called it *legacy.* The curse
is what we'll never know for sure, not without a body
to give us back its story—how they took you
out to some pecan grove or the endless pines
in November's first chill. This time

they emptied more than buckshot in you.
Them, with their deer rifles, wads of tobacco
and the spitting, every grudge
a smirk across the face. And the bastard
who tapped his gun on my wrist: *you won't ever
find him,* then waved over the line of trees that marks
the northern boundary of the endless bottoms.

When I can pray, this is my prayer:
that you went out with one pure breath,
the stroke of an arm reaching, as in flight
that unexpected beat when the long white
feathers of the nightjar open.
                              This prayer
against hatred, this prayer for grace:
that you were blind and deaf
so could not give them back themselves;
that with their touch, the intricate
cage of your body collapsed. Irrelevant,
the passing of flesh into those hands.

Night after night, I lie down cold
in that life again, where nothing has changed
in the opaque stillness, the dry sound of insects,
smell of swamp musk and lime.
If I could only let the darkness cover you,
a kind of coat but penetrable,
the way water is a garment
opening its arms to hold you
and hold you, until your face is the swamp's face
and there is nothing left to understand.

3.

The difference in our life
was how it stripped childhood bare.
How to endure the knock-upside-the-head,
hands tied under the table, the particular
taste of fist against teeth,
blanks fired behind you, blood against metal.
God knows I fought for any reason
except you, born the same
dead center of August, 1953:
your birth, our father's leaving.

Not so high above me, but unreachable
in the mimosa, that blossoming house.
And our sister with you, your secret
language I saw as denial. You hid
and were found: stepfather, the neighbor boy
with his ropes. Forgive my indifference,
forgive me my fear, which was how I lived.
If something in you closed
and never healed, I know what I didn't give,
not the cracked papershells in the pecan tree,
the rare hawthorne's mayhaw berry . . .
Maria remembers the afternoon the three of us
played in the house alone. She found a box in a drawer,
like some kind of gold and filled
with things. Held up to the sun
they were trinkets. But how we made them ours,
laughing; the give and take of light.

Forget it, you said: months of limping
and the Saturday morning I found you
stiff-legged, white. The year on your back
hole in the heart, you learned those things
we never thought to name in Tremont Bottoms—
lifespans of the water turtle, the white-tailed
deer who live out their flawed lives
prey to the hunters' misfire and every bodily affliction.
The last time I saw you, we drove out to the hill country
around D'Arbonne Swamp and its expensive
false lake. I took some deep velvet buds
from a friend's pasture and put them in your truck,
thinking I'd find some rare name.
Sumac, you said, brother to poison, but this one
called staghorn, for the bare antlers the branches make
rising out of winter.

4.

I am frightened of this sleep, the way it holds
and pulls under the child I carry,
the one I will abandon to save myself.
You walk, unreachable above water
and this time I am the one calling from below
until nothing will catch me
and the child too falls away,

growing smaller every time I dream.
My arms ache and release. I can't carry us both
I scream and you sink. Your eyes wide
and calm, you sink.

I powder the ugly leaves of mullein
and throw them on the water. The stunned fish rise,
your body rises. I collect the broken pieces
so the soul can reach
the forgetful region of sky.
All night I sift and pick, I separate
our skinny fingers, handfuls of our hair.
I count, I fit you together in a box.
What is flesh but silt? and what is nail?
Here's the softest bone,
box of water, box of air.

Give me back the face in the mirror,
the cup by my bed. I am not the eye of your mother,
the arm of your father. Don't come to me
wearing your face like an emptiness I must fill.
For the last time, I'll wrap you in my skin,
carry you home. I'll lay down
your bad heart, the ox-blood boots.
I'll bury my lack, my failure.

5.

We are staring with different eyes
into the maze of leaning cypress.
No longer children, we question
every detail, the tangle of snakes
jarring the surface,
the way our toes curl into the mucky ledge.
We are waiting to see
Audubon's snowy birds unfold
their ruffled feathers: pelican, egret, owl
lifting over the promise of water.

I can hear the sound of a clacking,
dry branch in the cedar, the snow
stripped away by wind; a louder
and louder creaking, as though every door
to this house has been broken. Then the wind

in the old tree subsides until it is
the sound of walking through the uncut field,
until it is night again
bringing another change in season.
If I stay up long enough, then you will come as well,
wearing the preoccupied mask of the dead,
that cast of light. I know you are dead
because your eyes reflect water,
because all water is the sound of crying.
Though I can't hold you, I lean into the white
wall of your body and you lull me,
somnambulant. You are the secret of sleep,
your face with its fine grasses and moss.

Out of the Northern spring
with its unmistakable signs of rain, of birds,
I come back.
Back through that religion of night sweat
and heat, the religion called South,
called family. Back through dark—
thin slice of swamp moon, sumac
and sweetgum turning, creek water,
whisky in the clear glass.
And in them all I find you. You
the master of disappearing, the artist
escaping burial, the trick of guilt.
And if I become more graceful,
it is that I am a shelter for your absence,
the smoothness imposed on rock
worn away from within, the force of water
in its essential movement. This is how I keep you
and this is how you break away,
leaving tear, blood, seed.

WALTER MCDONALD

Walter McDonald, a native of West Texas, serves as Director of Creative Writing at the Texas Tech University. The most recent of his several books of poetry is *The Flying Dutchman*.

Never in My Life

had I heard my father mention
love. By twelve I felt something
missing, a girlfriend, or millions
of rabbits I needed to murder.
By twenty I knew, but told myself
it did not matter. I had never told him,

either. By thirty, after years
of emergencies and two children,
I admitted to myself it did.
By forty, after a war and another child,
I resolved before we died
we would say it.
I returned from Southeast Asia

to hold my wife, each child,
to bless or to be blessed by father.
We shook hands. Months passed
the same. One night they rushed him
to the hospital. Drugged, for days
he lived by shots and tubes.
The night his hands moved

I lingered in the room,
the nurse waiting with crossed arms
while I studied this man
who fought in Flanders.
Bending down
louder than I meant
I called his name.

The dim eyes opened,
tried focusing
without glasses.
Up past the failing heart,
he mumbled Humm?
I touched the blue vein
of our blood that throbbed

beneath his head's pale skin, slowly,
slowly pulsing. I brushed his sparse
white wisps of hair back into place,
held my hand on his cool skull
and spoke the words.
His breathing stopped.
I thought *I've killed him.*

At last his dry lips closed.
He breathed again. Somewhere
far back of the blur in his eyes
I imagined electrons flashing,
decoding this dim disturbing news
for his numbed brain.
Squinting, his eyes sank far away,

away from me and from the ceiling,
down maybe to his childhood
and his own dead father's doors.
The empty eyes jerked back
and focused on my face.
Fiercely I focused too
and kept the contact tight.

Then the drugs drowned him again
in sleep. It was enough,
was all I could receive or ever give
to him. Even in that glaze
that stared toward death,
I had seen him take me in,
been blessed by what I needed all my life.

Hauling over Wolf Creek Pass in Winter

If I make it over the pass
I park the rig, crawl back to the bunk
and try to sleep, the pigs swaying
like a steep grade, like the last curve
Johnson took too fast and burned.
But that was summer. His fire
spread to the next county.

It doesn't worry me.
I take the east climb no sweat
and the rest is a long coasting
down to the pens in Pagosa Springs.
It's the wolves I wait for.
We never see them any other way,
not in this business.
Sometimes five, six hauls before
propped on one arm, smoking,
I see them slink from the dark pines
toward the truck. They drive the pigs
crazy, squealing
as if a legion of demons had them.
Later, when I start up and go,
the pigs keep plunging,
trying to drive us over the cliff.

I let them squeal, their pig hearts
exploding like grenades.
The wolves are dark and silent.
Kneeling, I watch them split up
like sappers, some in the tree lines,
some gliding from shadow to shadow,

red eyes flashing in moonlight,
some farther off, guarding the flanks.
Each time, they know they have me.

I take my time, knowing I can crawl
over the seat, light up,
sip from the steaming thermos.
I crank the diesel,
release the air brakes
like a rocket launcher.
Wolves run in circles. I hit the lights.
Wolves plunge through deep snow
to the trees, the whole pack starving.
Revving up, the truck rolls down the highway
faster, the last flight out of Da Nang.
I shove into third gear, fourth,
the herd of pigs screaming, the load
lurching and banging on every turn,
almost delivered, almost airborne.

Starting a Pasture

This far out in the country no one is talking,
no rescue squads row by in boats to prairie land
so dry the Ogallala water table drops
three feet every year. The digger rams down
through dirt no plow has turned. In the heat
I let my mind run wild. For days I've thought
the world is ending, the red oaks turning red
again, the last geese there could be
stampeding from the north, surviving
to show us the only hope, the tips of their
arrow formations pointing the way. So many birds,
if the world doesn't end this will be for Canada
the year of the locust. I shake my head
at my schemes, and sweat flies: cattle
on cottonland. The market for beef
is weak, the need for cotton constant.

I might as well raise goats and sheep as cows,
or trap for bounty the wolves and coyotes
that claim my fields at night. I might as well
rent a steam shovel and dig a lake deep as an ark,
empty my last irrigation well to fill it green enough
for geese on the flyway both seasons. I could
raise trout and channel cat, horses and bees
like the pastures of heaven, gazelles and impala
imported from other deserts, two of each kind
of animals in a dying world.

                      Sun going down,
the last hole dug, the last post dropped
and tamped tight enough to hold three strands of wire,
I toss the digger in the pickup between bales
of barbed wire ready for stringing, the calves
I bought last week already overdue, the feedbill
mounting. My father used to say a man could lift
a bull if he'd practice on a calf each day.
Pulling my gloves back on, I lift the first bale
out and nail the end, uncoil the wire and nail it
tight to the posts. And as it turns dark
I go on stretching and nailing until I don't care
how many neighbors drive by with their lights on,
honking, sticking their heads out the windows and laughing.

HEATHER ROSS MILLER

Heather Ross Miller was born in 1939 in Albermarle, North Carolina. She is a graduate of the University of North Carolina at Greensboro, where she studied with Randall Jarrell. The author of eight published books, Miller is a professor of English in the M.F.A. Program in Creative Writing at the University of Arkansas. Her most recent work has appeared in *Redbook* and *American Scholar*.

Minor Things

You are here,
inside plain folded paper, along its blue lines
ready for your tongued-out letters, ABC,
and you call me eloquently.

Your hair spills again, tangles,
and upsets the morning, circling your finger,
then mine. I cut off this hair,
and folded it away twenty-two years ago
against the day you sat
listening to the blade flash.

Alone this morning,
listening myself to the flashy mockingbird
outside insisting any child I ever had,
had got herself grown-up and gone,

I've fumbled apart this paper,
disturbing your quiet trash:
golden bone and fingernail,
a handful of curly stuff.
I am amazed these seeds still sprout.
You glow in the dark, rising from my hand,
despite me. Such minor things
bring back myself to myself.

Buried under and brushed back
twenty-two blond years, silent and accurate
as Magellan's maps,
you evolve a real woman.
I have this paper-folded hair.
I have what died and left itself inside,
put away by me for me:
your terrifying seed,
your minor gold. You mystify me.
I am too old, a child's darkening history.

Girl, Prince, Lizard

The little girl knew,
locked up and mute,
her hair growing day and night,
the resplendent hair of the dead,
she knew she had better things to do.

"Turn on the TV, study your Bible,"
lisped the old lizard,
sensing strange power
invade the child's tower.
She knew, too.

And the prince knew more than they,
stumbling along the highway,
soft eager boy,
without a chance in hell.

But through torrents, darkness,
acres and acres of badly marked maps,
through tight mountain passes,
slippery with moonlight,
he kept toward them.

And years later,
the old lizard dead, the girl's hair
cut off and sold,
the stubborn prince, sick of visions,
kicked in the cold door,
and engineered remission.

JIM WAYNE MILLER

Jim Wayne Miller, born in North Caro-
lina in 1936, holds degrees from Berea
College and Vanderbilt University. He
has published several books of poetry,
most recently *Nostalgia for 70*. He
teaches at Western Kentucky University.

Closing the House

While rumbling trunks pushed down the hall upstairs
boom like the scudding thunderstorm just passed,
we bear out cardboard boxes, tables, and chairs
stripped from rooms grown hollow, strange and vast.
We plod, as humdrum over such a deep
as veteran thieves lifting petty loot,
too dried-sweat stiff to feel the sweep
of grief that rolls the floor from underfoot.
Mule-footed plundering done, the rooms all sacked,
now only the furrowed shell that stops the door
remains, impounding the roaring foaming fact
all the years. I pick it off the floor.
It murmurs in my ear, floods my breath,
and drowns me in the sea-sound of your death.

Hanging Burley

I'm straddling the top tier, my wet shirt clinging;
under this hot tin roof sweat balls and rolls.
Smothered in gummy green, my seared eyes stinging,
I'm hanging burley tobacco on peeled tier poles.
A funeral mood below me on the ground:
a blank-faced filing past the loaded sled;
a coming with a solemn, swishing sound;
tobacco borne as if it were the dead.
Even the children, shadowed by our grief,
hang broken leaves and ape the studied pace.
—Let burley come, and save each frog-eyed leaf,
till every wilted stick is hung in place,
till gazing on the naked, empty field,
we see, row after row, your death revealed.

Squirrel Stand

Now burley's curing in the high-tiered barn
and yellow leaves ride out on slow black water.
Cold wind moving in the rows of corn
rattles the blades like an old man pulling fodder.
Down from the mountain pastures overnight,
cattle stand by the yellow salt block bawling.
Now it's September in the world; fine rain is falling.

—When gray squirrels had grown fat on hickory nuts,
my gun in the crook of my arm, once I went stepping
through yellow leaves and fine rain falling.
Resting on a ridge above our tents,
I heard what raincrows off in the mist were calling:
my days were growing full, sliding, dropping
like waterbeads along the barbed-wire fence.

The Hungry Dead

I think the dead lie hungry in the dark,
below the living teeming in the light.
I've fished nights in a graveyard cove
of drowned trees, my jonboat tethered
to topmost limbs, dead fingers still
reaching up. In the yellow ring of rocking
lantern light minnows swarmed, turning
like silver undersides of willow leaves.
Moving from dark slips between drowned
limbs, crossing deepest shafts of quivering
light, rising, slow black shadows gulped
small fish and fell, shadows into the dark,
just as the hungry dead, rising to light,
devour the living and sink back again.

VASSAR
MILLER

Vassar Miller has lived all her life in Houston, Texas, where she was born in 1924. Recent books of poetry include *Selected and New Poems* and *Struggling to Swim on Concrete*.

Photo Credit: Maud Lipscomb

Adam's Footprint

Once as a child I loved to hop
On round plump bugs and make them stop
Before they crossed a certain crack.
My bantam brawn could turn them back,
My crooked step wrenched straight to kill
Live pods that then screwed tight and still.

Small sinner, stripping boughs of pears,
Shinnied past sweet and wholesome airs,
How could a tree be so unclean?
Nobody knows but Augustine.
He nuzzled pears for dam-sin's dugs—
And I scrunched roly-poly bugs.

No wolf's imprint or tiger's trace
Does Christ hunt down to catch with grace
In nets of love the devious preys
Whose feet go softly all their days:
The foot of Adam leaves the mark
Of some child scrabbling in the dark.

Reciprocity

You who would sorrow even for a token
Of hurt in me no less than you would grieve
For seeing me with my whole body broken
And long no less to solace and relieve;
You who, as though you wished me mere Good Morning,
Would smash your heart upon the hardest stones
Of my distress as when you once, unscorning,
Would sleep upon the margin of my moans—
I yield my want, this house of gutted portals,
All to your want, I yield this ravaged stack,
In testimony that between two mortals
No gift may be except a giving back.
What present could I make you from what skill
When your one need is me to need you still?

Beside a Deathbed

Her spirit hiding among skin and bones
In willingness and wariness waits death
Like hares that peer from corners of their pens
Lured by a curiosity, yet loath.
Her eyes meet bed, chair, face, but do not focus,
As if these objects, heretofore mere shade,
Have caught up with their shadows. Things that wake us
Upon her eyelids heap a heavy load.
As straws pierce rock, our words reach where she lies,
Heedless of our cheerfulness or condolence.
Uncaring how our chatter ebbs or flows,
She catches the first syllable of silence.
So true the craftsman, memory, in lying
She will be less a stranger dead than dying.

Bout with Burning

I have tossed hours upon the tides of fever,
Upon the billows of my blood have ridden,
Where fish of fancy teem as neither river
Nor ocean spawns from India to Sweden.
Here while my boat of body burnt has drifted
Along her sides crawled tentacles of crabs
Sliming her timbers; on the waves upwafted
Crept water rats to gnaw her ropes and ribs.
Crashing, she has dived, her portholes choking
With weed and ooze, the swirls of black and green
Gulping her inch by inch, the seagulls' shrieking
Sieved depth through depth to silence. Till blast-blown,
I in my wreck beyond storm's charge and churning
Have waked marooned upon the coasts of morning.

from Love's Bitten Tongue

1

Lord, hush this ego as one stops a bell
Clanging, cupping it softly in the palm.
Should it make music, silence it as well,
For there's no difference when one wants calm
Of silence from the ego's loud tinnitus
Buzzing in spirit's ear with no relief,
With every reverence a false hiatus
Which brings those moments I name prayer to grief,
Tempts me to think I better honor them
By turning away from prayer as I did once.
So my thoughts, snared by their own strategem,
Like balls that children toss aside, all bounce
In my head back and forth until despair
Of praying may, in mercy, become prayer.

2

Of praying may (in mercy become prayer)
My backward journey be—Christ, teach me this!
This trek begun and left when, hope to spare
I saw ahead a new metropolis
All burnished brightly with an innocence
Now peeled the same as paint from ancient houses,
Its steel now buckled like a picket fence,
And found, that built for worship or carouses,
Buildings will suffer tediums of age,
As buildings must, as mine must too too soon.
So, may I never mind if I engage
The winks and titters from the ones who've known
Me from my wanderer's days and wisely nod
As His old daughter toddles home to God.

WILLIAM MILLS

Born in Hattiesburg, Mississippi in 1935, William Mills was educated in Louisiana and now lives in Baton Rouge. He has published eight books, three of which are poetry, and directed the Oklahoma State University graduate poetry workshops for two years, at the same time serving as poetry editor of the *Cimarron Review*.

Photo Credit: M. K. Wegmann

Pity

She asked me twice
Didn't I kill the
Catfish
Before I took the pliers
And stripped his hide.
I said no,
You'd have to break his neck.
I, now uneasy,
Blood bright on my fingers
Saw her wince,
The whiskered fish
Twisting.
Looks like torture that way,
She said,
And I said look
If you ask that question
It leads to another.
This is the way it's done.

Motel

This motel room
On Interstate 40 West
Has one copy of a blue bird,
One lamp, one chair.

Events have fallen out
That no one knows
I am lying here
Watching the major league
In this single bed.

For some reason
(Maybe the color blue)
I remember another scene—
This one on a box of salt,
The one with the girl
Who shields herself from the rain
And salts the ground behind her
With salt from a box with a girl
Who shields herself from the rain
And salts the ground behind,
And on and on,
Laying waste to the land
None of them looking back.

Rituals Along the Arkansas

for Robert Lowery

By the first hour we knew the day's luck
Would leave us time to think about each fish.
Not a day when even the unskilled
Pulls fish after fish into a thoughtless boat.

Mindful, we worked the rock jetties
Dragging our baits through the waters
Of a fast Arkansas.
Sometimes it was a rock bass,
Sometimes a white.

But it was the final fish
We held out for—the black,
His barrel of a mouth
Waiting like a mine.
We moved to the pools at the river's edge,
Full of tangle, full of food.
We knew he waited to eat there
Or be eaten.

The priests of do, we sat patiently,
Working our rods with solemnity
And form and always hope,
The idea of Fish large in our minds
Awaiting its marriage to fish.

We brought only water to keep it simple,
The beer was for another time.
Lowery caught the biggest and should have.
His study has been longer.
This black seemed not to want to leave his world below.
But he rose up and danced the bottom of the boat.
That brought the morning to a proper end.

We lay each glistening bass,
Rock, white and black,
On the cleaning board at the boat's side
And prepared their bodies for our use.
First the great heads with their lidless eyes
Were slipped overboard, and then the skin and the bones,
Set to drift through the live waters
Feeding the underworld.

There on the wooden board I poured water
Over the mound of luminous white meat.
As I laid my hands on the meat
To pack it away Lowery looked up river.
"Looks like Canadians flying."
The sight of the big birds
Lining toward us made me forget my duty.
As they drew nearer we knew
We had read the signs wrong.
"Pelicans, white pelicans," he cried.

The line turned into a great spiral of birds
Riding thermals above us:
The utterly no sound, no bird cry,
Only whisper of their outstretched wings
Above our boat, above the Arkansas.
There in the high summer sun
Their great helix of white
Drew fish and man with them.
We are wedded to what we use,
What we love, what we find beautiful.

The Necessity of Falling

We sat before an October fire
In the hardwoods.
The wind blessed us by not blowing.
A half-moon pearled the fields;
Our tent stood in the woods.
Something fell and should have:
An acorn, a limb, a star.
We understood the fire as it settled.

——— ROBERT ———
MORGAN

Robert Morgan was born in 1944 in Hendersonville, North Carolina, and grew up on a farm in nearby Zirconia. He attended Emory, North Carolina State, the University of North Carolina at Chapel Hill, and received an M.F.A. from the University of North Carolina at Greensboro. His most recent work includes *At the Edge of the Orchard Country*. He teaches at Cornell University.

Photo Credit: Dorothy Alexander

The Hollow

First travelers to the coves of the Blue Ridge
up near the headsprings,
found no trails between
the cabin clearings. Each bit
of acreage along its branch
opened like an island inside the wilderness,
with paths to water and to the turnip patch
always stopping at the margin where
a groundhog sunned its gob of fur.
The children chewed tobacco or drank corn,
when someone picked his way
out through the thickets to obtain some.
Their best diversion of all, their most
accomplished: watching the mountain haze, the blue
haunt overhead that cooled
and lulled even the August sun

and lay out along the slopes like
a smoke of silence, an incense of their
lifelong vigil between the unstoned graves
and the wormy appletree, a screen
sent up from the oaks and hickories
to keep them hidden from disease
and god and government, and even time.

Mountain Bride

They say Revis found a flatrock
on the ridge just
perfect for a natural hearth,
and built his cabin with a stick

and clay chimney right over it.
On their wedding night he lit
the fireplace to dry away the mountain
chill of late spring, and flung on

applewood to dye
the room with molten color while
he and Martha that was a Parrish
warmed the sheets between the tick

stuffed with leaves and its feather
cover. Under that wide hearth
a nest of rattlers,
they'll knot a hundred together,

had wintered and were coming awake.
The warming rock
flushed them out early.
It was she

who wakened to their singing near
the embers and roused him to go look.
Before he reached the fire
more than a dozen struck

and he died yelling her to stay
on the big four-poster.
Her uncle coming up the hollow
with a gift bearham two days later

found her shivering there
marooned above a pool
of hungry snakes,
and the body beginning to swell.

Death Crown

In the old days back when
one especially worthy lay dying
for months, they
say the feathers in the pillow would
knit themselves into a crown
that those attending felt in perfect
fit around the honored head.
The feather band they took to be
certain sign of another crown,
the saints and elders of the church,
the Deep Water Baptists said.
I've seen one unwrapped from its
cloth in the attic, the down
woven perfect and tight for
over a century, shiny but
soft and light almost as light.

Walnutry

When walnuts grew in stands like oak
or hickory in some mountain coves
and the timber market lay
over trails and feisty creeks,
some cut their big nut groves the same
as pine, and sawed out planks for
porches, barns, even hogpens.
With never stain nor varnish they
took the weather for a century,
growing stronger, like cement.
The seasoning took twenty years.
They didn't need the meat as
long as there were chestnuts.
Where the cows had rubbed
their stalls shone like mirrors.

Rainy Sundays in late fall my father
took the egg basket out to the walnut
in the chicken lot and gathered
half a bushel. The hull ink
tanned his palms.
Inside he set them on the hearth
and peeled the sooty rinds off
into the fire. They
censed the house with raw
fumes. He sat there all afternoon
on the warm rock cracking with
his mason's hammer, holding the shells
on end so they split clean,
working careful as a sculptor
to get the little figures of meat
intact from their molds,
and dealt the pieces to Sister
and me for hours while rain
flared on the windows and burst in the fire
compacting brighter on the diet
of shells. That night I'd throw up
the oily seeds gluttoned all evening,
and remember again the ground
under the big walnut
purged bare by the drip
and dissolution of
the tree's powerful bile.

Passenger Pigeons

Remembering the descriptions by Wilson
and Bartram, the Audubon and other
early travelers to the interior, of the sky
clouded with the movements of winged pilgrims
wide as the Mississippi, wide as the Gulf
Stream, hundred-mile epics of equidistant wings
horizon to horizon, how their droppings
splashed the lakes and rivers, how
where they roosted whole forests broke down
worse than from ice storms, and the woods floor
was paved with their lime, how the settlers
got them with ax and gun and broom
for hogs, how when a hawk attacked
the endless steam bulged away
and kept the shift long after
the raptor was gone, and having read how
the skies of America became silent, the fletched
oceans forgotten, how can I replace
the hosts of the sky, the warmblooded jetstreams?
To echo the birdstorms of those early
sunsets, what high river of electron, cell and star?

The Gift of Tongues

The whole church got hot and vivid
with the rush of unhuman chatter
above the congregation,
and I saw my father looking at
the altar as though electrocuted.
It was a voice I'd never heard
but knew as from other centuries.
It was the voice of awful fire.
"What's he saying?" Ronald hissed
and jabbed my arm. "Probably Hebrew."
The preacher called out another
hymn, and the glissade came again,
high syllables not from my father's
lips but elsewhere, the flare of
higher language, sentences of light.
And we sang and sang again, but
no one rose as if from sleep to
be interpreter, explain the writing
on the air that still shone there like
blindness. None volunteered a gloss
or translation or receiver
of the message. My hands hurt
when pulled from the pew's varnish
they'd gripped and sweated so. Later,
standing under the high and plain-
singing pines on the mountain I clenched
my jaws like pliers, holding in
and savoring the gift of silence.

NAOMI SHIHAB NYE

Naomi Shihab Nye was born in St. Louis in 1952 and lived in Jerusalem before moving to Texas in 1967. She graduated from Trinity University at San Antonio and served for ten years as a poet-in-the-schools throughout Texas. *Hugging the Jukebox* appeared in 1982.

Photo Credit: Michael Nye

New Year

Maybe the street is tired of being a street.
They tell how it used to be called Bois d'Arc,
now called Main, how boys in short pants
caught crawdads for supper at a stone acequia
now covered over.
Sometimes the street-sweeper stops his machine
and covers his eyes.

Think of the jobs people have.
The girl weighing citron in the basement
of H. L. Green's, for a man who says
he can't wait to make fruitcake
and she says, What is this stuff anyway
before it looks like this? and he leaves
on his cane, slowly, clutching the bag.
Then she weighs garlics for a trucker.

Think of the streams of headlights
on the Houston freeway all headed somewhere
and where they will be headed after that.
After so long, even jets might be tired of acceleration,
slow-down, touching-ground-again,
as a child is so tired of his notebook
he pastes dinosaurs on it to render it extinct.
Or the teacher, tired of questions,
hearing the anthem *How long does it have to be?*
play itself over and over in her sleep
and she just doesn't know. As long as you want it.

What was this world? Where things you never did
felt more real than what happened.
Your friend's dish-towel strung over her faucet
was a sentence which could be diagrammed
while your tumbled life, that basket of phrases,
had too many ways it might fit together.

Where a street might just as easily have been
a hair-ribbon in a girl's ponytail
her first day of dance class, teacher in mauve leotard
rising to say, We have much ahead of us,
and the little girls following, kick, kick, kick,
thinking what a proud sleek person she was,
how they wanted to be like her someday,
while she stared outside the window at the high wires
strung with ice, the voices inside them opening out
to every future which was not hers.

Sure

Today you rain on me from every corner of the sky.
Softly vanishing hair, a tiny tea-set from Mexico
perched on a shelf with the life-size cups.

I remember knotting my braid on your bed,
ten months into your silence.
Someone said you were unreachable,
we could chatter and you wouldn't know.
You raised yourself on magnificent dying elbows
to speak one line,
"Don't—be—so—sure."
The room was stunned.
Lying back on your pillow, you smiled at me.
No one else saw it.
Later they even denied they heard.

All your life, never mind.
It hurts, but never mind.
You fed me corn from cans, stirring busily.
I lined up the salt shakers on your table.
We were proud of each other for nothing.
You, because I finished my meal.
Me, because you wore a flowered dress.
Life was a tablet of small reasons.
"That's that," you'd say, pushing back your chair.
"And now let's go see if the bakery has a cake."

Today, kneeling to spell a word for a little boy,
it was your old floor under me,
cool sections of black and white tile,
I'd lie on my belly tracing their sides.
St. Louis, movies sold popcorn,
baby lions born in zoos,
the newspapers would never find us.

One moth lighting on the sink
in a dark apartment years ago.
You point, should I catch it?
Oh, never mind.
A million motions later, I open my hand,
and it is there.

The Traveling Onion

*It is believed that the onion originally came
from India. In Egypt it was an object of worship—
why I haven't been able to find out. From Egypt
the onion entered Greece and on to Italy, thence
into all of Europe.*

—Better Living Cookbook

When I think how far the onion has traveled
just to enter my stew today, I could kneel and praise
all small forgotten miracles,
crackly paper peeling on the drainboard,
pearly layers in smooth agreement,
the way knife enters onion, straight,
and onion falls apart on the chopping block,
a history revealed.

And I would never scold the onion
for causing tears.
It is right that tears fall
for something small and forgotten.
How at meal, we sit to eat,
commenting on texture of meat or herbal aroma
but never on the translucence of onion,
now limp, now divided,
or its traditionally honorable career:
For the sake of others,
disappear.

Hello

Some nights
the rat with pointed teeth
makes his long way back
to the bowl of peaches.
He stands on the dining room table
sinking his tooth
drinking the pulp
of each fruity turned-up face
knowing you will read
this message and scream.
It is his only text,
to take and take in darkness,
to be gone before you awaken
and your giant feet
start creaking the floor.

Where is the mother of the rat?
The father, the shredded nest,
which breath were we taking
when the rat was born,
when he lifted his shivering snout
to rafter and rivet and stone?
I gave him the names of the devil,
seared and screeching names,
I would not enter those rooms
without a stick to guide me,
I leaned on the light, shuddering,
and the moist earth under the house,
the gray trailing tails of clouds,
said he was in the closet,
the drawer of candles,
his nose was a wick.

How would we live together
with our sad shoes and hide-outs,
our lock on the door
and his delicate fingered paws
that could clutch and grip,
his blank slate of fur
and the pillow where we press our faces
saying No in the night?

The bed that was a boat is sinking.
And the shores of morning loom up
lined with little shadows,
things we never wanted to be, or meet,
and all the rats are waving hello.

Going for Peaches, Fredericksburg, Texas

Those with experience look for a special kind.
Red globe, the skin slips off like a fine silk camisole.
Boy breaks one open with his hands. Yes, it's good,
my old relatives say, but we'll look around.
They want me to stop at every peach stand
between Stonewall and Fredericksburg,
leave the air conditioner running,
jump out and ask the price.

Coming up here they talked about
the best ways to die. One favors a plane crash,
but not over a city. The other wants to make sure
her grass is watered when she goes.
Ladies, ladies! This peach is fine,
it blushes on both sides.
But they want to keep driving.

In Fredericksburg the houses are stone,
they remind me of wristwatches, glass polished,
years ticking by in each wall.
I don't like stone, says one. What if it fell?
I don't like Fredericksburg, says the other.
Too many Germans driving too slow.
She herself is German as Stuttgart.
The day presses forward, wearing complaints
like charms on its bony wrist.

Actually ladies (I can't resist),
I don't think you wanted peaches after all,
you just wanted a nip of scenery,
some hills to tuck behind your heads.

The buying starts immediately, from a scarfed woman who says
I gave up teachin' for peachin'.
She has us sign the guest book.
One aunt insists on re-loading into her own box,
so she can see the fruit on the bottom.
One rejects any slight bruise.
But Ma'am, the seller insists, nature isn't perfect.
Her hands are spotted, like a peach.

On the road, cars weave loose patterns between lanes.
We will float in flowery peach-smell
back to our separate kettles, our private tables and knives,
and line up the bounty,
deciding which ones go where.
A canned peach, says one aunt, lasts ten years.
She was 87 last week. But a frozen peach
tastes better on ice cream.
Everything we have learned so far,
the stages of ripening alive in our skins,
on a day that was real to us, that was summer,
motion going out and memory coming in.

BRENDA MARIE OSBEY

A native of New Orleans, Brenda Marie Osbey was born in 1957. She attended Dillard University, Université Paul Valéry at Montpélliér, France, and the University of Kentucky at Lexington. She has taught at Dillard University, and was Curator and Researcher at the Louisiana Division of the New Orleans Public Library, specializing in Louisiana Black and Creole History and French and Créole translations. She is the author of *Ceremony for Minneconjoux*.

The Wastrel-Woman Poem

she goes out in the night again
wastreling about
her thin-woman blues
slung over one shoulder
an empty satchel
one carries out of habit.

the first time you see her
you think her body
opens some new forbidden zone
you think she has something to do with you.
she never does.
at least not the way you mean.
not here
not any more.
lives ago perhaps
she would have been
your second cousin

a lover who murdered you
a woman who passed you on market-day
threw bones to the ground
or stepped over you
as though you were dust or air
some spirit she knew of
but did not counsel.

the first time you see her
a story begins
that has nothing to do with you:

a woman uncle feather knew
and never told you of
you were so young
and one day he lost the connection
between your question
and her name.

her name could have been anything
but you never would know
she would pass
and look into your eyes
directly
as if you were not there
as if she knew it
and would not tell.

tak-o-me-la
tak-o-me-la

something you hear when she passes
sounds from another living
but there she is
wastreling about you

someone calls to you
you watch your thin-woman move
between baskets of fish
and date-wine bottles

you turn to answer

heart like a brick
down between your knees.

"In These Houses of Swift Easy Women"

In the room the women come and go talking of Michaelangelo
—T.S. Eliot, "The Love Song of J. Alfred Prufrock"

in these houses
of swift easy women
drapes and the thin panels between them
hug to the walls—
some promise of remembering,
litanies of minor
pleasures and comforts.

these women know subtlety
sleight of hand
cane liquor
island songs
the poetry of soundlessness.

a man could get lost
in such a house as this
could lose his way
his grasp of the world
between the front room
and the crepe myrtle trees out back.

Portrait

i sit for my portrait on the veranda.
this was once a family house
the landlady describes
how it must have looked:
double parlors
and of course,
this veranda.

almost without malice
i say
we call them galleries.

she looks out onto the avenue
horses in her flat blue eyes
skin like unleavened bread
brittle
and without variation.

2.

i sit for my portrait on the veranda.
the photographer pushes his lips together
explaining how tiring this will be
how he wants this perfect
does not want me
to look too dark.

3.

his name is lejamn
a burly big-waisted man
sooty colored

he takes two yellow-stained
gunmetal fingers
pushes my forehead back
tells me not to look so stern.

4.

big burly gunmetal black lejamn
fourth generation photographer

how did his grandfather make a living then?
taking pictures of smooth-skinned nieces
of lady-friends from paillet-land?
too proud perhaps to work in the city
selling dry goods to the white folk
or vegetables to the black?
no rag-man
tin-man

old-gold-and-diamond man
these so many lives later
to push young writer women on the forehead
and tell them not to look so black.

5.

jamaica
he says for no reason
you look just like jamaica

in my head i make a dance in jamaica

he says it again:

just like jamaica to me

what can i say?
i am only
the material he works in
given over entirely
to technique.

6.

when I come there was no street sign
only dirt roads
dirt roads and a vegetable man
give me a ride,
a soft alligator pear,
and taken me home to his aunt sue lee.

they sent me to school in the city
him selling vegetables on the weekday
all the time taking pictures
sue lee taking in shirts from the uptown whites
talking at them through me

tell them I said
tell them I will

taking in shirts from the whites
and teaching little colored girls
to speak bon francais

no one stopping to question
a little tan woman
with hollow cinnamon eyes

would white children die if they looked at her?
they looked past her narrow waist instead
mouthing instructions
saying
miz suzy
too ill-bred to know
they were taking nothing from her.

sue lee sitting on the gallery of an afternoon
talking at them through me
in english when she wanted to
to show she could pronounce
the flat dead words

waving them out of sight
the screen door standing open
them running down the front walk
and sue lee never rising
until they were past her field of vision

i stood counting out the pieces
or the money when they had come to pay
counting the silver once
twice
slowly enough to please sue lee.

7.

i sit for my portrait on the veranda.
i, named evangeline eva marie
christened by sue lee st. clementh
and her nephew august anthony peter le jamn.

i sit completely still
on the three-quarter gallery
of the house where i was raised

by a sand-faced vegetable-man photographer
and his bon francais aunt.

i stare in the face of the lies i have heard,
i stare into the camera's far-sighted eye.
he asks me only once:

what is your name?

evangeline, i say
evangeline eva marie clementh

he wipes a white handkerchief across his mouth
only the camera gives its click
and again:
click.

THOMAS
RABBITT

Thomas Rabbitt was born in 1943 and lives on a farm in Cottondale, Alabama, where he raises and trains quarter horses. Since 1972 he has taught at the University of Alabama. *The Booth Interstate*, his second collection, was published by Knopf in 1981.

Gargoyle

He looks down to watch the river twist
Like a dead vein into the suburbs.
From his height it is all flat, stone-grey
And ugly. He knows he himself is hideous,
Sterile, the artist's pleasantry set up
To scare off devils. He knows nothing.
He is stunning in his pure impossibility.
Enough cherry trees blossom along the river.
Enough paired lovers gaze through the pink air.
Drab birds, disguised as money, sing prettily
And the sun blinds itself in the water.
He hears laughter. He knows nothing.
When the lovers glance up, they take him in.
Their looks are incidental, monumental, sweeping.

The Old Sipsey Valley Road

Booths knew nothing either. They built themselves in.
They owned pines, tin houses, some collapsing barns.
They *owned* them. Fields, gullies taking the fields,
And a pocked blacktop curving out of sight
Downhill into Coker and a brown lake
And the brick houses that needed to make
Head or tail of the face hidden in the hill.
The first Booth fell out of the sky one day,
Without a mule or pickup, nothing his,
Belonging to a fear who had devised him,
Who had sent him to the hill to claim
He could clear the brush from the fields for free
If he could have the wood. Someone said, Yes,
And that was it and then the scrub pine closed in.

Coon Hunt

Dell's hounds leap like the damned around the trunk
Of a water oak, biggest in my swamp.
Our flashlights flood the stage, the coon our star
Dimmed by the floating shadows of the leaves.
Later we move to dry ground to get drunk.
Home is close; still we call the hillside camp.
We build a fire, stare through the light it weaves
And make up lies about the Asian war
We fought. Dell struggles to take off his boot.
There's a puckered stump where his toes should go.
He calls up Tay Ninh and a jungle mine
Cong soldiers set for him. Truth is, he shot
Himself one night at home. I say I know
Chinese, that I have shrapnel in my spine.

BIN
RAMKE

Bin Ranke was born in 1947 in Port Neches, Texas, where he spent his childhood. He attended L.S.U., the University of New Orleans, and Ohio University, where he received the Ph.D. Ramke's first volume of poetry was a recipient of the Yale Series of Younger Poets Award. He is on the writing faculty at the University of Denver.

Nostalgia

I did not grow up among paintings.
We had calendars on the kitchen wall
And a portrait of poor Jesus, but I remember
A picture, a calendar above my bed,
October, I suppose, a picture of trees
Turned gold in autumn. I was a schoolboy
Home sick; I stared for hours through
Long afternoons while mother cleaned
Around me or cooked beans and chicken;
I entered it as she listened to the radio's
Romance of Helen Trent. I walked
Myself down a trail littered with gold,
I felt the crispness of cold like you
Feel the crushed ice of daiquiris
Against the tongue. You understand I was
A small boy in south Texas who knew nothing
Of autumn leaves, of winter, or of art.

Victory Drive, Near Fort Benning, Georgia

I hold a rattlesnake in my hand, gently:
even a bird does not have bones so fragile.
He is, in his way, humiliated, and makes
his rattle, his only poem. You can see him
any day, a lonely exhibit in a bar
where soldiers go to dream of jungles,
of chances lost.

Georgia

What bones? What bones? Stones instead.

I see a lamp hanging from a pickup truck,
two eager dogs, and men resting on stiff legs;

this state is filled with hunters, and frantic game
leaps fences, logs, the trees the roads the houses.

yet only little violence, and mostly quiet: the shot
is seldom fired. The deer more likely dies

of scurrilous disease. The men wither dryly
as the corn in fall, then drift

over red horizons, become
the stone heart's surviving children,

remembered, boneless ghosts.

Paula Rankin grew up in Newport
News, Virginia, where she was born in
1945. She holds graduate degrees from
William and Mary College and Vander-
bilt University. Her three volumes of po-
etry include *Augers* and *To The House
Ghost*.

Photo Credit: Michael Purswell

Hot Bath in an Old Hotel

Asleep, you turn
on the knots in your neck
though I spent an hour
ironing your back with my knuckles.
We stiffen with travel.
I take off my clothes
and sit on the cold porcelain bottom
of the tub. I want it like this,
my spine slabbed and chilled
as a column of ice cubes.
Look, I can take it, I hiss
through my teeth, through the door.

I turn the handle
and lie back as water
scalds its way up like memories.
With each inch I lose a sadness.
By the time it reaches my neck,
I have forgotten who we are.

Middle Age

The groundhog we dumped in the woods
is back in the yard
where he lies with his head in a cloud
of lice, an aura of flies,
a pale apple-green shimmering.

You say the dogs bring him back,
wanting praise, claiming credit.
At first I thought him but one more proof
of Spring, like wasps in vents,
ticks in children. All I know is he's there
when I walk to the mailbox,
when I lie in the sun,
when I look up at the stars
to say we're all nearer
to each other than we are.

He's a message from my father,
refusing to settle with the dead,
warning me I lack the skills
to keep them buried. Something's trying
to keep me from grief, but I'm not fooled:
love doesn't come back
like this, nor second chance.

Children gather to poke the remains,
then go fishing. I'm left
where the dead and the young
would keep me, cleaning up the mess.
What a mess they leave.

PATTIANN
ROGERS

Born in Missouri in 1940, Pattiann Rogers moved to Texas in 1969. She received her M.A. from the University of Houston. Her works include *The Expectations of Light* and *The Tattoed Lady in the Garden*. She lives in Stafford, Texas.

A Giant Has Swallowed the Earth

What will it do for him, to have internalized
The many slender stems of riverlets and funnels,
The blunt toes of the pine cone fallen, to have ingested
Lakes in gold slabs at dawn and the peaked branches
Of the fir under snow? He has taken into himself
The mist of the hazelnut, the white hairs of the moth,
And the mole's velvet snout. He remembers, by inner
Voice alone, fogs over frozen grey marshes, fine
Salt on the blunt of the cliff.

What will it mean to him to perceive things
First from within—the mushroom's fold, the martin's
Tongue, the spotted orange of the wallaby's ear,
To become the object himself before he comprehends it.
Putting into perfect concept without experience
The din of the green gully in spring mosses?

And when he stretches on his bed and closes his eyes,
What patterns will appear to him naturally—the schematic
Tracings of the Vanessa butterfly in migration, tacks
And red strings marking the path of each mouse
In the field, nucleic chromosomes aligning their cylinders
In purple before their separation? The wind must settle
All that it carries behind his face and rise again
In his vision like morning.

A giant has swallowed the earth,
And when he sleeps now, o when he sleeps,
How his eyelids murmur, how we envy his dream.

Achieving Perspective

Straight up away from this road,
Away from the fitted particles of frost
Coating the hull of each chick-pea,
And the stiff archer bug making its way
In the morning dark, toe hair by toe hair,
Up the stem of the trillium,
Straight up through the sky above this road right now,
The galaxies of the Cygnus A cluster
Are colliding with each other in a massive swarm
Of interpenetrating and exploding catastrophes.
I try to remember that.

And even in the gold and purple pretense
Of evening, I make myself remember
That it would take 40,000 years full of gathering
Into leaf and dropping, full of pulp splitting
And the hard wrinkling of seed, of the rising up
Of wood fibers and the disintegration of forests,
Of this lake disappearing completely in the bodies
Of toad slush and duckweed rock,
40,000 years and the fastest thing we own,
To reach the one star nearest to us.

And when you speak to me like this,
I try to remember that the wood and cement walls
Of this room are being swept away now

Molecule by molecule, in a slow and steady wind,
And nothing at all separates our bodies
From the vast emptiness expanding, and I know
We are sitting in our chairs
Discoursing in the middle of the blackness of space.
And when you look at me
I try to recall that at this moment
Somewhere millions of miles beyond the dimness
Of the sun, the comet Biela, speeding
In its rocks and ices, is just beginning to enter
The widest arc of its elliptical turn.

Suppose Your Father Was a Redbird

Suppose his body was the meticulous layering
Of graduated down which you studied early,
Rows of feathers increasing in size to the hard-splayed
Wine-gloss tips of his outer edges.

Suppose, before you could speak, you watched
The slow spread of his wing over and over,
The appearance of that invisible appendage,
The unfolding transformation of his body to the airborne.
And you followed his departure again and again,
Learning to distinguish the red microbe of his being
Far into the line of the horizon.

Then today you might be the only one able to see
The breast of a single red bloom
Five miles away across an open field.
The modification of your eye might have enabled you
To spot a red moth hanging on an oak branch
In the exact center of the Aurorean Forest.
And you could define for us, "hearing red in the air,"
As you predict the day pollen from the poppy
Will blow in from the valley.

Naturally you would picture your faith arranged
In filamented principles moving from pink
To crimson at the final quill. And the red tremble

Of your dream you might explain as the shimmer
Of his back lost over the sea at dawn.
Your sudden visions you might interpret as the uncreasing
Of heaven, the bones of the sky spread,
The conceptualized wing of the mind untangling.

Imagine the intensity of your revelation
The night the entire body of a star turns red
And you watch it as it rushes in flames
Across the black, down into the hills.

If your father was a redbird,
Then you would be obligated to try to understand
What it is you recognize in the sun
As you study it again this evening
Pulling itself and the sky in dark red
Over the ege of the earth.

Concepts and Their Bodies
(The Boy in the Field Alone)

Staring at the mud turtle's eye
Long enough, he sees *concentricity* there
For the first time, as if it possessed
Pupil and iris and oracular lid,
As if it grew, forcing its own gene of circularity.
The concept is definitely
The cellular arrangement of sight.

The five amber grasses maintaining their seedheads
In the breeze against the sky
Have borne *latitude* from the beginning,
Secure *civility* like leaves in their folds.
He discovers *persistence* in the mouth
Of the caterpillar in the same way
As he discovers clear syrup
On the broken end of the dayflower,
Exactly as he comes accidentally upon
The mud crown of the crawfish.

The spotted length of the bullfrog leaping
Lakeward just before the footstep
Is not bullfrog, spread and sailing,
But the body of *initiative* with white glossy belly.
Departure is the wing let loose
By the dandelion, and it does possess
A sparse down and will not be thought of,
Even years later, even in the station
At midnight among the confusing lights,
As separate from that white twist
Of filament drifting.

Nothing is sharp enough to disengage
The butterfly's path from *erraticism.*
And *freedom* is this September field
Covered this far by tree shadows
Through which this child chooses to run
Until he chooses to stop,
And it will be so hereafter.

The Possible Salvation of Continuous Motion

adapted from a love letter written by E. Lotter (1872–1930)

If we could be taken alone together in a driverless
Sleigh pulled by horses with blinders over endless
Uninhabited acres of snow; if the particles
Of our transgression could be left behind us
Scattered across the woodlands and frozen lakes
Like pieces of light scattered over the flashing snow;

If the initiation and the accomplishment of our act
In that sleigh could be separated by miles
Of forest—the careful parting begun
Under the ice-covered cedars, the widening and entering
Accomplished in swirls of frost racing along the hills,
The removal and revelation coming beside the see-saw shifting
Of grassheads rustling in the snowy ditches; all the elements
Of our interaction left in a thousand different places—
Thigh against thigh with the drowsy owlets in the trees
Overhead, your face caught for an instant above mine
In one eye of the snow hare;

If the horses could go fast enough across the ice
So that no one would ever be able to say, "Sin
Was committed *here*," our sin being as diffuse
As broken bells sounding in molecules of ringing
Clear across the countryside;

And under the blanket beside you in the sleigh
If I could watch the night above the flying heads
Of the horses, if I could see our love exploded
Like stars cast in a black sky over the glassy plains
So that nothing, not even the mind of an angel,
Could ever reassemble that deed;

Well, I would go with you right now,
Dearest, immediately, while the horses
Are still biting and strapping in their reins.

Discovering Your Subject

Painting a picture of the same shrimp boat
Every day of your life might not be so boring.
For a while you could paint only in the mornings,
Each one different, the boat gold in the new sun
On your left, or the boat in pre-dawn fog, condensing
Mist. You might have to wait years, rising early
Over and over, to catch that one winter morning when frost
Becomes a boat. You could attempt to capture
The fragile potential inherent in that event.

You might want to depict the easy half-circle
Movements of the boat's shadows crossing over themselves
Through the day. You could examine every line
At every moment—the tangle of nets caught
In the orange turning of evening, the drape of the ropes
Over the rising moon.

You could spend considerable time just concentrating
On boat and birds—Boat with Birds Perched on Bow,
Boat with Birds Overhead, Shadows of Birds Covering
Hull and Deck, or Boat the Size of a Bird,
Bird in the Heart of the Boat, Boat with Wings,
Boat in Flight. Any endeavor pursued long enough
Assumes a momentum and direction all its own.

Or you might decide to lie down one day behind a clump
Of marsh rosemary on the beach, to see the boat embedded
In leaves. You might picture the boat cut into pieces
By the blades of the saltwort or show how strangely
The stalk of the clotbur can rise higher than the mast.
Boat Caught Like a Flower in the Crotch of the Sand Verbena.

After picturing the boat among stars, after discovering
The boat as revealed by rain, you might try painting
The boat in the eye of the gull or the boat in the eye
Of the sun or the boat in the eye of a storm
Or the eye trapped in the window of the boat.
You could begin a series of self-portraits—The Boat
In the Eye of the Remorseful Painter, The Boat in the Eye
Of the Blissful Painter, The Boat in the Eye of the Blind Painter,
The Boat in the Lazy Painter Forgetting his Eye.

Finally one day when the boat's lines are drawn in completely,
It will begin to move away, gradually changing its size,
Enlarging the ocean, requiring less sky, and suddenly it might seem
That you are the one moving. You are the one altering space,
Gliding easily over rough surfaces toward the mark
Between the ocean and the sky. You might see clearly,
For the first time, the boat inside the painter inside the boat
Inside the eye watching the painter moving beyond himself.
You must remember for us the exact color and design of that.

Finding the Tattooed Lady in the Garden

Circus runaway, tattooed from head to toe in yellow
Petals and grape buds, rigid bark and dust-streaked
Patterns of summer, she lives naked among the hedges
And bordered paths of the garden. She hardly
Has boundaries there, so definite is her place.

Sometimes the golden flesh of the butterfly,
Quiet and needled in the spot of sun on her shoulder,
Can be seen and sometimes the wide blue wing
Of her raised hand before the maple and sometimes
The criss-crossed thicket, honeysuckle and fireweed,
Of her face. As she poses perfectly, her legs apart,

Some people can find the gentian-smooth meadow-skin showing
Through the distant hickory groves painted up her thighs
And the warm white windows of open sky appearing
Among the rose blossoms and vines of her breasts.

Shadow upon tattooed shadow upon real shadow,
She is there in the petaled skin of the iris
And the actual violet scents overlapping
At the bend of her arm, beneath and beyond
The initial act announcing the stems
Of the afternoon leaved and spread
In spires of green along her ribs, the bronze
Lizard basking at her navel.

Some call her searched-for presence the being
Of being, the essential garden of the garden.
And some call the continuing postulation
Of her location the only underlying structure,
The single form of flux, the final proof
And presence of crafted synonymy.
And whether the shadows of the sweetgum branches
Above her shift in the breeze across her breasts
Or whether she herself sways slightly
Beneath the still star-shaped leaves of the quiet
Forest overhead or whether the sweetgum shadows
Tattooed on her torso swell and linger
As the branches above are stirred by her breath,
The images possessed by the seekers are one
And the same when they know them as such.

And in the dark of late evening,
Isn't it beautiful the way they watch for her
To turn slowly, displaying the constellations
Penned in light among the black leaves
And blossoms of her back, the North Star
In its only coordinates shining at the base
Of her neck, the way they study the first glowing
Rim of the moon rising by its own shape
From the silvered curve of her brilliant hip?

GIBBONS RUARK

Gibbons Ruark, born in North Carolina in 1941, holds degrees from the Universities of North Carolina and Massachusetts. His books include *A Program for Survival, Reeds, Keeping Company,* and *Small Rain.* He teaches English at the University of Delaware.

The Visitor

Holding the arm of his helper, the blind
Piano tuner comes to our piano.
He hesitates at first, but once he finds
The keyboard, his hands glide over the slow
Keys, ringing changes finer than the eye
Can see. The dusty wires he touches, row
On row, quiver like bowstrings as he
Twists them one notch tighter. He runs his
Finger along a wire, touches the dry
Rust to his tongue, breaks into a pure bliss
And tells us, "One year more of damp weather
Would have done you in, but I've saved it this
Time. Would one of you play now, please? I hear
It better at a distance." My wife plays
Stardust. The blind man stands and smiles in her
Direction, then disappears into the blaze

Of new October. Now the afternoon,
The long afternoon that blurs in a haze
Of music . . . Chopin nocturnes, *Clair de Lune,*
All the old familiar, unfamiliar
Music-lesson pieces, *Papa Haydn's*
Dead and gone, gently down the stream . . . Hours later,
After the latest car has doused its beams,
Has cooled down and stopped its ticking, I hear
Our cat, with the grace of animals free
To move in darkness, strike one key only,
And a single lucid drop of water stars my dream.

The Muse's Answer

I ask the muse about this drifting
Far from my body,
About my song dissolving in this wilderness of water
Running in my head.
Should I set sail,
Leaving the blood behind,
Opening my skin like wings to the ocean wind?
And the muse answers,
"When you lean by a moving river,
You must cup your hands to drink,
And if the face of the Lord should appear
On the face of the river,
You have a choice.
You can keep your hands on sweet water,
Or let the water fall,
Or let the water fall like glory,
Praising the Lord in a widening of arms."

Sleeping Out with My Father

Sweet smell of earth and easy rain on
Canvas, small breath fogging up the lantern
Glass, and sleep sifting my bones, drifting me
Far from hide-and-seek in tangled hedges,
The chicken dinner with its hills of rice
And gravy and its endless prayers for peace,
Old ladies high above me creaking in the choir loft,
And then the dream of bombs breaks up my sleep,
The long planes screaming down the midnight
Till the whistles peel my skin back, the bombs
Shake up the night in a sea of lightning
And stench and spitting shrapnel and children
Broken in the grass, and I am running
Running with my father through the hedges
Down the flaming streets to fields of darkness,
To sleep in sweat and wake to news of war.

Lament

What I regret is many things
in my future.

—Melina Mercouri

One sore thing is the way
Our only friends will die
With nothing more to say
Than a long goodbye

Or no goodbye at all.
Another thing's the work
Shutting down to a small
Eye batting in the dark.

Then come the gay daughters
Gone from their wedding clothes.
Where you heard their laughter,
Hang a drained garden hose.

Write down dry veins, the hug
Of pain in every kiss.
Soon any catalogue
Of woe must come to this:

My body breaking down
Beside your body
Till one of us is gone
And the sheets are bloody,

And I am your lover
Taken by the darkness
Or a blank light forever
Where your lovely head was.

Lost Letter to James Wright, With Thanks for a Map of Fano

Breathing his last music, Mozart is supposed
To have said something heartbreaking which escapes me
For the quick moment of your bending to a dime

Blinking up from York Avenue, the last chill evening
I ever saw you, laughter rising with the steam
From your scarred throat, long-remembering laughter,

"Well, the old *eye* is still some good, anyway."
I thought of your silent master Samuel Johnson
Folding the fingers of drowsing vagrant children

Secret as wings over the coppers he left in their palms
Against the London cold and tomorrow's hunger.
You could not eat, I think you could scarcely swallow,

And yet that afternoon of your sleep and waking
To speak with us, you read me a fugitive passage
From a book beside your chair, something I lose all track of

Now, in this dim hour, about the late driftwood letters
Of writers and how little they finally matter.
You wrote to me last from Sirmione (of all things,

Sirmione had turned gray that morning), and it mattered.
We were together when the gray December dusk
Came down on snapshots of the view from Sirmione,

Sunlight ghosting your beard on the beach at Fano.
I had thought to write you a letter from Fano,
A letter which could have taken years to reach you

On the slow river ways of the Italian mails,
And now I write before we even come to leave.
We are going to Fano, where we may unfold this map

At a strange street corner under a window box
Of thyme gone to flower, and catch our breath remembering
Mozart breathing his last music, managing

Somehow to say in time, "And now I must go,
When I have only just learned to live quietly."
Last time I saw you, walking a little westward

From tugboats in the harbor, your voice was already breaking,
You were speaking quietly but the one plume of your breath
Was clouding and drifting west and away from Fano

Toward the river ferry taking sounding after sounding.

For a Suicide, a Little Early Morning Music

Most of the mornings here, when we awaken,
She and I can see what's left of the stars together,
And so we can this morning, even though lonely,

Imagining you. You were alight with elegance,
You were nervously and splendidly intelligent,
You loved the cities and you loved the shores,

You wanted to awaken with somebody.
Now, in this early morning, gathering
The last star's sunlight in a large warm bed,

We can see it clearly rising, rippling
A few temporary clouds with color
Over the water, and in the carved surf

A man of sixty, lean beneath his years,
Is swimming closely with a slender woman.
They must have awakened early together,

And then they thought of something they could do.
Sunlit in a place you loved, I can see you
Sunlit in another, you and I together

Down to our shirtsleeves in the brilliant streets,
Our neckties riffling as we round the corners
To Hester Street for veal and some wine from Verona,

Mulberry Street for pasta to carry home.
We were late for the train, and you were happy,
For you liked nothing better than wearing

A light suit, walking the streets in a hurry,
Packages under your arm for somebody lovely.
In Florence once, we saw the dark cool David

Of Verrocchio, and did not have the wit
To think of you running bareback through the summer.
From Rome we sent you a picture of Augustus

Looking under thirty in extreme old age,
But what we looked at longest was the beautiful
Bronze boy patiently and tenderly pulling

A thorn from his foot for several thousand years.

Postscript to an Elegy

What I forgot to mention was the desultory
Unremarkable tremor of the phone ringing
Late in the day, to say you were stopping by,
The door slung open on your breezy arrival,
Muffled car horns jamming in the neighborhood,

Our talk of nothing particular, nothing of note,
The flare of laughter in a tilted wineglass.
Or we would be watching a tavern softball game
And you would come short-cutting by, your last hard mile

Dissolving in chatter and beer on the sidelines.
How did that Yankee third baseman put it, tossing
His empty glove in the air, his old friend
Sheared off halfway home in an air crash? "I thought
I'd be talking to him for the rest of my life."

Talk as I may of quickness and charm, easy laughter,
The forms of love, the sudden glint off silverware
At midnight will get in my eyes again,
And when it goes the air will be redolent still

With garlic, a high note from Armstrong, little shards
That will not gather into anything,
Those nearly invisible flecks of marble
Stinging the bare soles of the curious
Long after the statue is polished and crated away.

Basil

There in Fiesole it was always fresh
In the laneway where the spry grandfather
Tipped you his smile in the earliest wash
Of sunlight, piling strawberries high and higher
In a fragile pyramid of edible air.
Light down the years, the same sun rinses your dark
Hair over and over with brightness where
You kneel to stir the earth among thyme and chard,
Rosemary and the gathering of mints,
The rough leaf picked for tea this summer noon,
The smooth one saved for *pesto* in the winter,
For the cold will come, though you turn to me soon,
Your eyes going serious green from hazel,
Your quick hand on my face the scent of basil.

LARRY RUBIN

Larry Rubin was born in New Jersey but grew up in Florida. He holds degrees from Emory University, and is a professor of English at Georgia Institute of Technology. He has published three collections of poetry, most recently *All My Mirrors Lie*.

The Manual

I found it in the bottom drawer
Under her wedding linen
And reading it was like eating the wild apples
That grew in my grandfather's orchard
Till I was sick with ferment and love
And ran for relief, racing the rain in my bowels
But now my canals were thick with the freight of their fourteen years
And the dreams came thick and heavy
At the point where dew descends
At the moment of belief in those printed words
When the diagrams exploded in my dreams

And I was putting the book back in the drawer
Under her wedding linen
When she came in and saw me
And asked if I understood.
Smoothing the folds in something she'd bought as a bride
I saw the bewilderment in my mother's eyes
And quietly closed the drawer, and lied

The Brother-in-Law

Haunt him, Mona! Haunt him, demon sister!
He who filled your bed for twenty years,
Inflating placentas, till you withered in
His bursting gifts, and burrowed into safer
Ground, he will betray those nights; he's found
A woman newer in the flesh, and has pushed
Your grave below his bed.
                                    They will wed,
But I who was your lover first, before
I knew what women hid—by the manhood
I had then, I conjure you to wall
Their nights, and lie between their straining parts.
Haunt him in his massive hour—
                                    child, I call.

Dinner at the Mongoloid's

She sat by me and eyed me craftily
Through eyes squeezed tight, two broken ovals,
While her mother went to wash the dishes, leaving
Us to get acquainted on the sofa.
My adult silence hung in empty air,
While she sat prettily, scrubbed and ribboned,
Smelling of soap, and waited for a question,
For visitors knew the rules. But I was dumb,
Feeling my words fall hollow through the ovals
Of her eyes, and she moved closer, turning
Her dented features toward my face, and said,
'I think you're very handsome.' I smiled, truncated,
Faceless, afraid of mirrors, chromosomes.

JAMES SEAY

James Seay is the author of two volumes of poetry, *Let Not Your Hart* and *Water Tables*, as well as limited editions by Deerfield/Gallery and Palaemon Press Limited. Born in Mississippi in 1939, he teaches at the University of North Carolina at Chapel Hill.

Photo Credit: Josh Seay

It All Comes Together Outside the Restroom in Hogansville

It was the hole for looking in
only I looked out
in daylight that broadened
as I brought my eye closer.
First there was a '55 Chevy
shaved and decked like old times
but waiting on high-jacker shocks.
Then a sign that said J.D. Hines Garage.
In J.D.'s door was an empty Plymouth
with the windows down and the radio on.
A black woman was singing in Detroit
in a voice that brushed against the face
like the scarf
turning up in the wrong suitcase
long ago after everything came to grief.
What was inside we can only imagine—

men I guess trying to figure what would make it
work again. Beyond them
beyond the cracked engine blocks and thrown pistons
beyond that failed restroom
etched with our acids beyond that American Oil Station
beyond the oil on the ground
the mobile homes all over Hogansville
beyond our longing
all Georgia was green.
I'd had two for the road
a cheap enough thrill
and I wanted to think
I could take only what aroused me.
The interstate to Atlanta was wide open.
I wanted a different life.
So did J.D. Hines. So did the voice on the radio.
So did the man or woman
who made the hole in the window.
The way it works is this:
we devote ourselves to an image
we can't live with and try to kill
anything that suggests it could be otherwise.

When Our Voices Broke Off

From the porch, if they hold to what there is
no need to imagine, they can color the hedge,
the sound, the lighthouse with its pattern of black
and white lozenges, or the air over the island
and anything lofted in its translations.
My sons turn their brushes instead to the chronic
bad dreams of the race, fixing them at random
in the watercolors of flame or collision.
They are old hands at apostrophe.
The shrimper's son from across the road tries a few circles
and then begins the outline of a boat.

Last night from this porch I looked up
with my wife and friends to our share
of the galaxy, whorled pure and free of mainland lights.

I felt our voices drawn out into the dark
and it seemed to me the round island was a stone
turning beneath us, grinding our voices with the shells
of shrimp in the kitchen pail, the quilts by the door,
the hyphens in the names of boats at anchor—all of it drawn
and turning under the stone—the drums of paint
for the lighthouse diamonds, the bright water that breaks
on shoals and jetties, whatever yields to silence, ground
with our voices and spread like grist across the spaces.

One of the Dippers brought us out of silence
and we began working our way through the known.
For the constellations we could not name
we imagined *Cricket's Knee, Bill & Doris' Blown Electric Range,*
Anne's New Rod & Reel, Tommy's Measles, and so on
until we all were found.
We called it The Myth of the New Understanding.
It was a way of turning from the silence beyond the porch
railing, the silence in the hedge along the road
and out across the sound to the lighthouse.
It was a way of understanding the lights
burning their codes through darkness.

The boat is colored yellow and the water blue.
It is headed to the left of the paper,
under what appears clear weather.
Toward dawn we saw his father make fast the mooring
and load his catch into a skiff.
I do not know if he looks up at the stars at sea
and wonders what is at the farthest reach of darkness
or if he dwells on whether the shrimp are vanishing.
I do not know if he has told his son of the silent migrations.
He declined the beer.
We bought the shrimp still moiling in the bucket.

Clouds over Islands

First there was a dream not wholly mine.

I told my friends the dream
comes with the bed, its source a cloud
accumulated in the air surrounding sleep.

Just off the plane, I had dozed on their bed
as they swam in the screened pool, promising
I would like the crabs at Joe's Stone Crabs,
the daughter would be off the phone in my room
shortly, she was in love. The migrant dream
settled around me as the rhythm of the laps they swam
defined the rhythm of my breathing.

When I woke it took their voices
from beside the pool for me to know
I had breathed the dream
from the cloud above their private island of sleep.

The dream itself does not matter,
in its particulars,
not even to my friends.
Nor could I have told it clearly, its cloud
so tropic and brief in my life.

I told them of a family I knew in Ohio
who bought the childhood furniture
of a famous astronaut, his little bed and mattress,
the strange vast air
in which the family's daughter began to dream.

Then together we remembered confusions
in the expired air over beds we had held
in hotels, hospitals, the compartments of trains,
or rooms of senility where our grandfathers called back
the gifts they had given us,
how sometimes still we rise from sleep in beds
where no friends have breathed dreams
we can enter without fear,
how we stumble to our belongings,
trying to make sure of what we left there.

DAVE

SMITH

Dave Smith, born in Portsmouth, Virginia, in 1942, was educated at the University of Virginia, Southern Illinois University, and Ohio University. The author of thirteen collections of poetry, including *The Roundhouse Voices: Selected and New Poems,* he is Professor of English at Virginia Commonwealth University.

Photo Credit: Maurice Duke

Mending Crab Pots

The boy had run all the way home
from school to tell the old man
about a book he'd found which put
the whole thing in a new light:
'The beautiful sea, grandfather,
in a poem you might have written,
out there always to be touched
or swum in, or worked, or just
looked at, the way you told me.'

The old man gave the wire trap
one extra twist, like a chicken's
neck, relit his dead cigar, said
he heard the slovenly bitch still
ranted around, couldn't be got
rid of, or lived with. He slit
the head from a blowfish, stuffed
it in the mouth of the pot, grinned.
'Them poets, goddam 'em, always
in school with their white hands.'

Sailing the Back River

Tonight no one takes fish. Tattered pennants
of T-shirts flap, their shadows riding wave crests,
among the hulls half-ashore and wholly sunken.
Always I am the waterman snagging nets on keels
in the graveyard of boats, the pale sailor who
glides with the music of nails through plank rot
and oil scum to sit in the toy wheelhouse of fathers.

I do not ask you to come with me or even to watch
the pennants signaling the drift of the winds.
Nothing I could do would raise one body bound
under these mud-struck beams, but I mean to do
what I can to save my own water-logged life and here
is the best place I know to beg. I throw out love
like an anchor and wait where the long houselights
of strangers tickle the river's back. I go alone

as a creaky-boned woman goes to the far bench
at the heart of her garden where the rose suffers.
There will be time for you to hold in your palm
what each has held here, the sudden canting of gulls,
a room with one back-broken chair, the pot-belly
sputtering as it answers the wind, the soft knock
waters make at the fair skin of roots. I come here
to stop up my lying words: your life was always bad.

Isn't it right to drag the rivers for the bodies
not even the nets could catch? I won't lie, I want
you to lie with me on the tumbling surface of love.
This is the place to honor crab song, reed's aria,
where every hour the mussel sighs *begin again.* Say
I am water and learn what I hold as river, creek,
lake, ditch or sewer. I am equal with fire and ice.
We are one body sailing or nothing. My life, yours,
what are they but hulls homing, moving the sand?

Rain Forest

The green mothering of moss knits shadow and light,
silence and call of each least bird where
we walk and find there are only a few words
we want to say: water, root, light, and love,
like the names of time. Stunned from ourselves,
we are at tour's tail end, our guide long gone,
dawdling deep in what cannot be by any human
invented, a few square miles of the concentric
universe intricate as the whorls of fingertips.
The frailest twigs puff and flag in the giantism
of this elaborate grotto, and we are the dream,
before we know better, of an old grotesque
stonecutter who squats under a brow of sweat,
the afternoon a long glowing stalk of marble.
We have entered the huge inward drift behind
his eyes and wait to become ourselves. We stare
through limpid eyes into the vapor-lit past
where breath, wordlessly, like a near river
seams up, seams in and out and around darkness.
Somewhere far back in the hunch of shadows,
we stood by this wall of vines, and he, angry,
froze us in our tracks and the blade of belief.
That tree there bore the same long slithering
of light from a sky he owned. Disfigured now,
its trunk rises thick and black as a monument
that rings when struck. Here the hiking path,
a crease, stops, then spirals around into stumps.
Our party has gone that way, stumbling quietly.
From time to time, someone calls out but we know
only the words whispered from the wall of leaves:
water, root, light, and love. We stand silent
in the earliest air remembered, hearing at last
the distant and precise taps of the mallet
until our clothes, as if rotted, fall away
and the feckless light fixes us on the column
of our spines. Without warning, we begin to dance,
a bird cries, and another. Our feet seem to spark
on the hard dirt as we go round the black tree
and for no reason we know we see ourselves
throwing our heads back to laugh, our gums
and teeth shiny as cut wood, our eyes marbled,
straining to see where it comes from, that
hoarse rasp of joy, that clapping of hands
before which we may not speak or sing or ever stop.

The Roundhouse Voices

In full glare of sunlight I came here, man-tall but thin
as a pinstripe, and stood outside the rusted fence
with its crown of iron thorns while
the soot cut into our lungs with tiny diamonds.
I walked through houses with my grain-lovely slugger
from Louisville that my uncle bought and stood
in the sun that made its glove soft on my hand
until I saw my chance to crawl under and get past
anyone who would demand a badge and a name.

The guard hollered that I could get the hell from there quick
when I popped in his face like a thief. All I ever wanted
to steal was life and you can't get that easy
in the grind of a railyard. *You can't catch me
lardass, I can go left or right good as the Mick,*
I hummed to him, holding my slugger by the neck
for a bunt laid smooth where the coal cars
jerked and let me pass between tracks
until, in a slide on ash, I fell safe and heard
the wheeze of his words: *Who the hell are you, kid?*

I hear them again tonight Uncle, hard as big brakeshoes,
when I lean over your face in the box of silk. The years
you spent hobbling from room to room alone crawl
up my legs and turn this house to another
house, round and black as defeat, where slugging
comes easy when you whip the gray softball over
the glass diesel globe. Footsteps thump on the stairs
like that fat ball against bricks and when I miss
I hear you warn me to watch the timing, to keep
my eyes on your hand and forget the fence,

hearing also that other voice that keeps me out and away
from you on a day worth playing good ball. Hearing
Who the hell . . . I see myself, like a burning speck
of cinder come down the hill and through a tunnel
of porches like stands, running on deep ash,
and I give him the finger, whose face still gleams
clear as a B & O headlight, just to make him get up
and chase me into a dream of scoring at your feet.
At Christmas that guard staggered home sobbing,
the thing in his chest tight as a torque wrench.

In the summer I did not have to run and now
who is the one who dreams of a drink as he leans over
tools you kept bright as a first-girl's promise? I
have no one to run from or to, nobody to give
my finger to as I steal his peace. Uncle, the light
bleeds on your gray face like the high barbed wire
shadows I had to get through and maybe you don't remember
you said to come back, to wait and you'd show me
the right way to take a hard pitch
in the sun that shudders on the ready man. I'm here

though this is a day I did not want to see. In the roundhouse
the rasp and heel-click of compressors is still,
soot lies deep in every greasy fingerprint.
I called you from the pits and you did not come up
and I felt the fear when I stood on the tracks
that are like stars which never led us
into any kind of light and I don't know who'll
tell me now when the guard sticks his blind snoot
between us: take off and beat the bastard out.
Can you hear him over the yard, grabbing his chest,
cry out *Who the goddamn hell are you, kid?*

I gave him every name in the book, Uncle, but he caught us
and what good did all those hours of coaching do?
You lie on your back, eyeless forever, and I think
how once I climbed to the top of a diesel and stared
into that gray roundhouse glass where, in anger,
you threw up the ball and made a star
to swear at greater than the Mick ever dreamed.
It has been years but now I know what followed there
every morning the sun came up, not light
but the puffing bad-bellied light of words.

All day I have held your hand, trying to say back that life,
to get under that fence with words I lined
and linked up and steamed into a cold room
where the illusion of hope means skin torn in boxes
of tools. The footsteps come pounding into words
and even the finger I give death is words
that won't let us be what we wanted, each one
chasing and being chased by dreams in a dark place.
Words are all we ever were and they did us
no damn good. Do you hear that?

Do you hear the words that, in oiled gravel, you gave me
when you set my feet in the right stance to swing?
They are coal-hard and they come in wings
and loops like despair not even the Mick
could knock out of this room, words softer
than the centers of hearts in guards or uncles,
words skinned and numbed by too many bricks.
I have had enough of them and bring them back here
where the tick and creak of everything dies
in your tiny starlight and I stand down
on my knees to cry, *Who the hell are you, kid?*

An Antipastoral Memory of One Summer

It is written that a single hurricane holds the power
to run our whole country for one year. Imagine
lights in Minnesota chicken coops, firebells
ringing every borough of New York, dock pumps
spewing the bilge from Louisiana shrimpers,
the pulse that sends a voice from San Francisco
to Nagasaki where a woman wakes, folds, and refolds
the American edition of news already forgotten.

Yet even in the dark silos of our countrymen who
practice graceful moves at the missile's panel
that is like a piano with the amazing, unplayed
notes not even Beethoven could hear into fusion,
no one dreams how to harness the storm for good.
That is why I think of two people at a bulkhead,
an old woman desperately pushing down the hem
of her flowered dress, holding a boy's small hand
where the waves they have come to see blossom

one after another, sluicing over their driven hair,
the salt sting so strong their eyes begin to swell,
until they fall back across the elegant Boulevard,
and even there the unexpected crescendos boom in
laces and strings of water radiant as new light.
The noise is unforgettable and deafening, the sea
keeps orchestrating, as if it means to address
all our preparations, the boarded windows, the dead

cars with their rain-blistered glass, the sidewalk
clotted now with seaweed like abandoned bodies.
That suddenly, then, the calm eye stalls on them,
a stillness like a lock with no key, a hand
hovering at a switch, waiting for music unheard,
and see—the woman turns, drags the boy brutally
past oaks older than them both, leaves this fall
blinking like lights, trembling, limbs like spears,
two entering a powerless house to huddle, to pray
to the still God, though they call it hurricane.

Frank Stanford was born in Mississippi in 1948. He grew up in Tennessee and later Arkansas, where he attended high school at Subiaco, a Benedictine monastery. The author of nine collections of poetry, Stanford died of self-inflicted gunshot wounds in 1978.

Photo Credit: Fred Killman

The Intruder

after Jean Follain

In the evenings they listen to the same
tunes nobody could call happy
somebody turns up at the edge of town
the roses bloom
and an old dinner bell rings once more
under the thunder clouds
In front of the porch posts of the store
a man seated on a soda water case
turns around and spits and says
to everybody
in his new set of clothes
holding up his hands
as long as I live nobody
touches my dogs my friends

Inventory

A man came into the store
Told mother he was looking for a good knife
She took him behind the counter
And let him look a spell under the glass

You could smell his new clothes
What a beautiful shirt
He had on my mother told him

It was blackwatch plaid

We all got one after that
Mother ordered one
They sent forty-nine

What kind of knife are you needing she asked
I'm needing one that'll touch bottom

IIe looked over his shoulder when he said that
And a man buying shoelaces nodded

He said a man don't want to go shallow
You know how it is
I'd hate to come short on a critter

That's the one I want the man in the new clothes said
It's from Sweden and it'll set you back she told him

Lady I don't care

Right then I heard a car on the ridge
Hit the bedrock
It was going pretty fast

Now how's about a nice stone
To go along with the knife said she
The man looked over his shoulder again
This time out the window

O.Z. was hoeing weeds around the monuments
We sold on the side

I mean a whetstone
Just for the steel she smiled

He swallowed like it was dark medicine
He didn't laugh
Just so it'll cut once lady
Is all I care
He told her trying it out on the sole
Of his new issue boot

Midnight or so I was down in the storm cellar
Stealing a little jam
By God if I didn't hear someone
Hit the bedrock again

Place on a Grave

It's not hard to forget what they ate
Every winter, when the father
And oldest brother went back to do time,
Cowpeas and smoked goat, all winter
The same muddy supper, their voices
Thick as pan bread, the hollering
At dawn when the mother went out
To the pens in cowboy boots
With a bucket of feed and a roll
Of toilet paper, finding a swatch
Of her daughter's nightgown
Fluttering on the barbed-wire,
The hollering and calling
The rest of them did when they
Raised up from their cold beds
And went out searching at first light
For their crippled sister, who dreamed
Walking over the mountains
In the dead of winter, the smell
Of cooking in her hair, believing
She was gone from there, dignified
Like a wooden figure on the prow
Of a ship with no horizon.

Allegory of Death and Night

When he comes home from work
He washes his hands
And sits down at the dinner table
And eats. He doesn't say much,
He drinks from an old bottle.
What he doesn't eat, the dog does.
And while the hound is licking
The man is snoring at the table.
The woman slaps the oil cloth
With a fly swatter, and he comes to.
A milksnake is crawling
Along a rafter in the barn
And a storm is making in the east.
There is a bird flying high
And the shadow of smoke
From the last fires in the moonlight.
He's laying crossways over the bed
On his belly. She's taken off
His pants and unlaced his boots.
Whatever he dreams he keeps to himself,
Like a prayer sent up for rain.
When he's dead to the world
She reaches into the pocket
Of his trousers for a white pouch.
She rolls a cigarette with one hand.
She smokes in the dark. Clouds
Go by, turning under the soil.
She turns a flashlight on
The man's body, looking for seed
Ticks that have been there since dawn.

Between Love and Death

I watched the woman in the room.
She moved in her misery
Like a pine in the wind.
I could hear the woman sweeping her floors,
Boiling roots, and drinking milk.
I could watch the woman
Turning the tap of her bath
Through the hole in the wall.
On the summer nights I whistled,
Wanting her to hear me.
She would look my way, sometimes,
With an apple core in her mouth.
Working late, overhauling her truck,
She would drink coffee and hum,
Go to sleep with grease on her fingers.
God I was crazy for not
Going to her door,
Tapping on her window,
Following her to the river
Where her dory grew wet like the moon.
A bird sick of its tree, I despair.
Leaves without wind, I lay
Damp and quiet on the earth.
She bled through the walls
Into my side of the house,
And they came with their lights
Asking did I know the woman,
And I said no, not I.

Island Funeral

Mama Julinda is let down into a hole
Her sons have to dig minutes ahead
Of time or the water will rise up
And make a channel around her,
And then it would be like having
Bad dreams, standing in a circle on the bank,
Throwing shovels of dirt at a boat.
The oldest is wearing a new blue suit.
It shines for night, like a fish.
The white gloves he had to cut the arms from
Are a tad soiled, like gardenias
After you touch them, and there's dust
Glowing on his long-toed shoes.
He's breaking the seal
On the bottle, breaking the law,
Drinking untaxed whiskey, the oldest
Son taking a deep, stiff drink,
And the grease on his head runs down
His temple, and everybody is going
To the glove compartments of their cars,
Like acolytes for their pints,
While the goat is turned and burned,
Deep in the moon of the delta,
An island funeral
Where days passed like a barge,
Around us many stars sinking in their light.

JAMES
STILL

James Still was born in 1906 in Alabama. Since 1939, he has lived in a two-story log house between Dead Mare Branch and Wolfpen, on Little Carr Creek in Knott County, Kentucky. *The Wolfpen Poems* was published in 1986.

Spring

Not all of us were warm, not all of us.
We are winter-lean, our faces are sharp with cold
And there is a smell of wood smoke in our clothes;
Not all of us were warm, though we hugged the fire
Through the long chilled nights.

                      We have come out
Into the sun again, we have untied our knot
Of flesh: We are no thinner than a hound or mare,
Or an unleaved poplar. We have come through
To the grass, to the cows calving in the lot.

On Double Creek

I was born on Double Creek, on a forty-acre hill.
North was the Buckalew Ridge, south at our land's end
The county poor farm with hungry fields
And furrows as crooked as an adder's track.

Across the creek I saw the paupers plowing.
I can remember their plodding in the furrows,
Their palsied hands, the worn flesh of their faces,
And their odd shapelessness, and their tired cries.
I can remember the dark swift martins in their eyes.

Ballad

They were a man's words, a ballad of an old time
Sung among green blades, whistled atop a hill.
They were words lost to any page, tender and fierce,
And quiet and final, and quartered in a rhyme.

This was a man's song, a ballad of ridge and hound,
Of love and loss. The words blossomed in the throat.
This was a man's singing alone behind his plow
With a bird's excellence, a man's shagbark sound.

Wolfpen Creek

How it was in that place, how light hung in a bright pool
Of air like water, in an eddy of cloud and sky,
I will long remember. I will long recall
The maples blossoming wings, the oaks proud with rule,
The spiders deep in silk, the squirrels fat on mast,
The fields and draws and coves where quail and peewees call.
Earth loved more than any earth, stand firm, hold fast;
Trees burdened with leaf and bird, root deep, grow tall.

LEON
STOKESBURY

Leon Stokesbury was born in Oklahoma
in 1945, and at the age of seven moved
to Southeast Texas, where he was
raised. He holds degrees from Lamar
University, the University of Arkansas,
and Florida State University, and is the
author of two books of poetry, most re-
cently *The Drifting Away*. He has taught
literature and creative writing at univer-
sities in several southern states.

The Luncheon of the Boating Party

Under the red-and-white striped awning
extended over the restaurant porch,
the eyelids of these fourteen sundry revelers

seem to sag a bit, and that is because
by now they are all just a little drunk.
The party is as parties are. The people

are talking. Laughing. But in the upper
left-hand corner, a man wearing
a saffron straw hat, tilted jauntily down

over his brow, stands slightly apart
and silent against the thin balustrade.
This man stands with his back arched,

his chest out, and the large muscles
in his bare arms self-consciously flexed.
Certainly, he cannot be at ease, but then those

who desperately hope to be loved rarely are.
I say this because if one follows
the man's gaze across the top of the canvas,

across the party, to the upper right-hand corner,
one sees that he is, I believe, staring
at a young woman who has raised her hands

to adjust her hat or her hair, or to cover her ears
so as not to hear what the two men talking
to her are saying. The two men are smiling,

and one has taken the liberty of slipping
his arm round her waist. The young woman
is the only person in the boating party being

physically touched, and though she seems
oblivious to it, the man in the saffron hat
is not, and is not much amused by it either.

Then, as the eye roams over the rest
of the festive scene, the quiet joke of the artist
begins to emerge. For, although a half dozen

conversations continue on, half of these people
are not even seeing the person looking at them.
They are looking at somebody else. It is a sort

of visual quadrille, the theme of five hundred
French farces, except in this case the painter
must care very much for them all, for he has soothed

their wants and aches in a wash of softness.
I think he must have been a little drunk too.
But it is the eyes, these misty, wine-dark eyes

of the three women in the center of the painting,
that draw a viewer back again and again.
The women are looking at men. They are looking

that way women sometimes look
when they have had a little wine, and when
they are listening to someone in whose presence

they see no reason to be other than who they are,
someone to whom, as a matter of fact,
they wish to communicate how simple and gentle

life can sometimes be, how amniotic even,
as it seems to them now. It is not clear
if the men of the boating party perceive this,

or anything. To be honest, they seem selfish and vain.
But the artist sees it. And this is his gift,
this warm afternoon, his funny story to tell again

and again: a day of blue grapes and black wine, of tricks
of the eye, of the flow and lulls of time, and everything,
everything soaked in the light of sex and love and the sun.

Day Begins at Governor's Square Mall

Here, newness is all. Or almost all. And like
a platterful of pope's noses at a White House dinner,
I exist apart. But these trees now—
how do you suppose they grow this high in here?
They look a little like the trees I sat beneath in 1959
waiting with my cheesecloth net for butterflies.
It was August and it was hot. Late summer,
yes, but already the leaves in trees were
flecked with ochers and the umbers of the dead.
I sweated there for hours, so driven,
so immersed in the forest's shimmering life,
that I could will my anxious self not move
for half a day—just on the imagined chance
of making some slight part of it my own.
Then they came. One perfect pair of just-hatched
black-and-white striped butterflies. The white
lemon-tipped with light, in shade
then out, meandering. Zebra swallowtails,
floating, drunk in the sun, so rare to find

their narrow, fragile, two-inch tails intact.
At that moment I could only drop my net and stare.
The last of August. 1959. But these trees, now,
climb up through air and concrete never hot or cold.
And I suspect the last lepidoptera that found
themselves in here were sprayed then swept away.
Everyone is waiting though, as before a storm—
anticipating something. Do these leaves never fall?

Now, and with a mild surprise, faint
music falls. But no shop breaks open yet.
The people, like myself, range aimlessly;
the air seems thick and still. Then, lights blink on;
the escalators jerk and hum. And in the center, at
the exact center of the mall, a jet of water spurts
twenty feet straight up, then drops and spatters
in a shallow pool where signs announce that none
may ever go. O bright communion! O new cathedral!
where the appetitious, the impure, the old, the young,
the bored, the lost, the dumb, with wide dilated eyes
advance with offerings to be absolved and be made clean.
Now, the lime-lit chainlink fronts from over one hundred
pleasant and convenient stalls and stores are rolled away.
Now, odors of frying won tons come wafting up from
Lucy Ho's Bamboo Garden. And this music, always
everywhere, yet also somehow strangely played as if
not to be heard, pours its soft harangue down now.
The people wander forward now. And the world begins.

Adventures in Bronze

At the Waldron Court Apartments
a young mother takes her toddler
into the living room to play,
then returns to the kitchen
to iron, and listen
to *Stella Dallas* on the radio.

Now the little one pushes at the front screen door,
finds it open, so stumbles out into the sun
where seven slightly older kids

come along, allowing him
to follow them
down the walk, down the road
to the old abandoned junior high
and the enormous, sunken, concrete storm drain there—
concrete smooth and cool,
concrete in the shade,
dark concrete the color
of Robert Oppenheimer's eyes
at any given moment in 1945.

The children climb down, scream, run around,
and so, with help, does the toddler too.
But then the older kids
climb out and run away,
climb out and leave the toddler alone.

The tips of his fingers can almost touch
the dead yellow grass
at the ground level top of the drain.

Soon enough he sees
there is nothing to do
except sit down on concrete and cry.

Soon enough he feels
there is nothing on earth
for him but this gray
and that blue rectangular swatch of sky.

From far far down the black tube of time
a man studies this scene in bronze.

A bronzed toddler is crying,
then looks up, seeing
first the head, then shoulders,
then the bronzed pedalpushers
of a bronzed mother there.

The man does not remember
the arms reaching up, or the arms reaching down,
just the distant sensation—
mendicant
supplicant—
that he is risen,
that he inherits the air.

To Laura Phelan: 1880–1906

for James Whitehead

Drunk I have been. And drunk I was that night
I lugged your stone across the other graves,
to set you up a hundred yards away.
Flowers I found, then. Drunk I have been.
And am, standing here with no moon to spill
on the letters of your name; my loud fingers
feeling them out. The stone is mossed over.
And why must I bring myself in the dark
to stand here among the sour grasses
that stain my white jeans? Drunk I have been.
See, the thick dew slides on the trees, wet weeds,
wetness smears the air; and a vague surf
of wildflowers pushes my feet, slipping
close to my legs. When the thought comes at last
that people fall apart, that the things we do
will not do. Ends. Then, we come to scenes
like this. This scene of you. You apart:
this is not you; and yet, this is where I stand
and close my eyes, and feel the ragged wind
blow red and maul my hair. In the night somewhere,
dandelions foam. This is not you. Drunk
I have been. Across this graveyard, that
is where you are. Yet I stand here. Would ask
things of your name. Would wish. Would not be told
of the stink in the skull, the eye's collapse.
Would be told something new, something unknown.—
A mosquito bites my hand. The only sound
is the rough wind. Drunk I have been,
here, at the loam's maw, before this stone
of yours, which is not you. Which is.

JOHN —
STONE

John Stone attended Millsaps College in Jackson, Mississippi, where he was born in 1936. He received his M.D. from Washington University, with postgraduate work at the University of Rochester and Emory, where he is now Professor of Medicine. He has published three collections of poetry, including *In All This Rain* and *Renaming the Streets*.

Photo Credit: Stephen Cord

The Girl in the Hall

with the Mickey Mouse
watch tells me the time

without knowing

that I have come up
the stairs
from a crushed leg
scared eyes

and the stump
blood   bandages

the bones of the stretcher

he is gradually getting used to

the fact of no leg
below the knee
no toes to wiggle
though they move still
in his mind's foot

which remembers now only
the crane coming down on it.

She glances at her wrist.

In his head's watch
in the middle of morphine
he clutches the giant hands
like Harold Lloyd holding on
at half past five
while the cars line up
below him.

The expressway roars outside.

She asks.
I say I'm fine.

She has her clocks.
He, his.
I, mine.

Death

I have seen   come on
slowly as rust
sand

or suddenly   as when
someone leaving
a room

finds the doorknob
come loose in his hand

After Love

which is what
she has not been making
there will be time for thought
about keeping and taking

for recalling, one night older,
all she was told to fear:
same lunging shoulder
and breathing in her ear.

Early Sunday Morning

Somewhere in the next block
someone may be practicing the flute
but not here

where the entrances
to four stores are dark
the awnings rolled in

nothing open for business
Across the second story
ten faceless windows

In the foreground
a barber pole, a fire hydrant
as if there could ever again

be hair to cut
fire to burn
And far off, still low

in the imagined East
the sun that is again
right on time

adding to the Chinese red
of the building
despite which color

I do not believe
the day
is going to be hot

It was I think
on just such a day
it is on just such a morning

that every Edward Hopper
finishes, puts down his brush
as if to say

As important
as what is
happening

is what is not.

DABNEY

STUART

Dabney Stuart is the author of seven volumes of poetry, including *Rockbridge Poems* and *Common Ground*. Born in 1937 in Richmond, Virginia, he has taught at Middlebury College, Ohio University, the University of Virginia, and is currently on the faculty of Washington and Lee University.

Photo Credit: Bill Giduz

The Soup Jar

Its metal top refused my father's twisting;
He tried warm water, a dishcloth, the heel of a shoe,
But he couldn't budge its stubborn *status quo*.
It had stood its ground, longer than he, rusting.

I had to help. Gripped the jar while he cursed
Into place the tricky gadget guaranteed
To open anything, then gave it all he had.
I jerked my hand, and a hunk of glass, back when it burst.

Someone else tied my tourniquet. He paled
And had to sit down. Seven stitches later
We cleaned the floor and had another dish for supper.
Alone, he got nothing. It took us both to fail.

Weeks after, my world spun around that jar
And I saw it, and him, through angry tears.
Now it seems, recalled through these shattered years,
So small a thing—some broken glass, a scar.

The Ballad of the Frozen Field

This is the true end of desire:
The closed ground deflecting sleet;
All seasons tend to this season
And the world is flat.

This is the true end of exploration
Over the low and the high seas;
Whoever fares may try lightly
All edges but these.

This is the true end of language,
That Way of ways:
All sound shaped to the one sound,
Ice echoing ice.

Mining in Killdeer Alley

for Nathan

One, and then another, they settled before me like flakes of air,
Halfway up the hill, their splayed toes sketching
Shadows, the grass tufts, gravel, merging;
They came down from their marvelous fluency
To wobble on dumb stilts
Like earthbound creatures, hindered by strangeness.
The shadows were blue and voluminous, and their toes lost,
And the pronouns confused, and they shied and took flight
Again as I drove the rest of the way up the hill.
When I entered the house
And called my wife to the window they were back,
                                                settled,
Settled into the dark; and in the Blue Ridge morning
They parted, again, for my descent.
                                    They were there
Every day the last seven months before the gift,
Feathering my passage
Like wings, their angled wings, her shoulder blades
As she bent awkwardly before the sink, mornings,
In the ninth month.

So that my father, who we thought was dying,
Could see him, we carried his newborn grandson
Up the back stairs of the hospital. The light was broken
All over the blanket, and our child swam in his glasses
With pieces of that broken light.
                                        Their russet throats,
The sun shattered in the gravel,
                                        the gray veins
Of his impeccable wrist,
                              Lord, for the life of me.

When we brought him home they had flown away.

─── HENRY ───
TAYLOR

Henry Taylor lives in Lincoln, Virginia, where he was born in 1942. His four collections include *The Flying Change*, which was awarded the Pulitzer Prize in Poetry for 1985. Taylor holds degrees from the University of Virginia and Hollins College, and is Professor of Literature at The American University in Washington, D.C.

Photo Credit: Sandra Ehrenkranz

Taking to the Woods

    Clearing brush away
is the mean part of working up firewood from these
   cut-off treetops—a chaotic souvenir
of the doubtful covenant I made the day
     I marked a dozen white oak trees
     and sold them for veneer.

    There might be more in this
of character or courage if it were need that drove
   my weekly trials in this little wood,
   but this is amateur thrift, a middle-class
     labor as much for solitude
     as for a well-stocked stove.

    For more than safety's sake,
therefore, I take a break to light up and daydream,
   and as the chainsaw ticks and cools, I smoke

my way back to an hour spent years ago,
   when I knelt above a shallow stream—
     the scanty overflow

    from the springhouse at my back.
The ache of holding still dwindled away to less
   than the absent-minded effort that has carved
   these grooves between my eyebrows; on the surface
    oarlocked water-striders swerved
     above the scribbled black

    shadows minnows made
on rippled mud below their bright formations,
   and a dragonfly, the green-eyed snakedoctor
   with wings out of old histories of aviation,
    backed and filled down a stair of nectar-
     scent toward a jewelweed

    and struck a brittle stillness
like the spell the wood boss broke when he touched my hand
   as I stood absorbed in the loggers' technique:
   "Have you ever seen a big tree fall?" "Yes."
    "Good." Not the graceful faint we make
     of tall trees in the mind,

    but swift and shattering.
I counted the growth rings—one hundred sixty-four—
   and found where, fifty years ago, the wood
   drew in against the drought one narrow ring;
    I touched the band that marked the year
     when I was born, then stood

    and let them drop the rest.
This is everyday danger, mundane spectacle,
   spectacular and dangerous all the same.
   I hover between hope that it is practical
    to give young trees more light, and shame
     at laying old trees waste,

    then yank the starting cord
and turn to dropping stovewood from this chest-high limb,
   my touch light, leaving real work to the saw,
   my concentration thorough and ignored
    at once, lest the blade take on a whim
     of its own; and I think how

our small towns have collected
in legend the curious deaths of ordinary men—
    as once, on a siding up the road from here,
    Jim Kaylor, if that was his name, directed
        the coupling of a single freight car
        to the middle of a train—

    an intricacy he knew
as most of us know how to shave, say, or shift gears.
    That day, he managed to be caught somehow,
    and the couplings clicked inside him, just below
        the ribcage, and he hung between cars
        in odd silence as the crew

    swarmed from the depot,
told each other to stand back, give him air, send
    for the doctor, and he asked for a cigarette,
    received it with steady fingers, smoked, and saw—
        well, what could he have seen? The end
        of a boxcar, the set

    of a face in disbelief,
or something, in smoke shapes before him, that he kept
    when he finished the cigarette, flicked it aside,
    nodded, and, as the boxcars were slipped
        apart, dropped with a sound of relief
        to the crossties, and died.

    Now I think hard for men
mangled by tractors and bulls, or crushed under trees
    that fall to ax or chainsaw in their season,
    and for myself, who for no particular reason
        so far survive, to watch the woodlot ease
        under the dark again,

    withdraw into the mist
of my unfocused eyes, into my waiting stare
    across bare trees that lift toward landscapes
    through which snakedoctors may still wheel to rest,
        then to walk home, behind the shapes
        my breath ghosts in sharp air.

The Way It Sometimes Is

At times it is like watching a face you have just met,
trying to decide who it reminds you of—
no one, surely, whom you ever hated or loved,
but yes, somebody, somebody. You watch the face

as it turns and nods, showing you, at certain angles,
a curve of the lips or a lift of the eyebrow
that is exactly right, and still the lost face
eludes you. Now this face is talking, and you hear

a sound in the voice, the accent on certain words—
yes! a phrase . . . you barely recall sitting outside,
by a pool or a campfire, remarking
a peculiar, recurring expression. Two syllables,

wasn't it? Doorknob? Bathroom? Shawcross? What the hell
kind of word is shawcross? A name; not the right one.
A couple of syllables that could possibly be
a little like something you may once have heard.

So the talk drifts, and you drift, sneaking glances,
pounding your brain. Days later a face occurs to you,
and yes, there is a resemblance. That odd word, though,
or phrase, is gone. It must have been somebody else.

Yes, it's like that, at times; something is, maybe;
and there are days when you can almost say what it is.

Artichoke

*If poetry did not exist, would you
have had the wit to invent it?*

—Howard Nemerov

He had studied in private years ago
the way to eat these things, and was prepared
when she set the clipped green globe before him.
He only wondered (as he always did
when he plucked from the base the first thick leaf,
dipped it into the sauce and caught her eye
as he deftly set the velvet curve against
the inside edges of his lower teeth
and drew the tender pulp toward his tongue
while she made some predictable remark
about the sensuality of this act
then sheared away the spines and ate the heart)
what mind, what hunger, first saw this as food.

As on a Darkling Plain

The years pile up, but there rides with you still,
across old fields to which you have come back
to invent your home and cultivate the knack
of dying slowly, to contest your will
toward getting death behind you, to find a hill
where you can stop and let the reins go slack
and parse the dark swerve of the zodiac,
a face whose eyes find ways to hold you still.

They hold you now. You turn the chestnut mare
toward the next hill darkening to the west
and stop again. The eyes will sometimes change,
but they ride with you, glimmering and vast
as the sweet country you lost once, somewhere
between the Blue Ridge and the Wasatch Range.

At the Swings

Midafternoon in Norfolk,
late July. I am taking our two sons for a walk
away from their grandparents' house; we have
directions to a miniature playground,
and I have plans to wear them down
toward a nap at five.

when my wife and I
will leave them awhile with her father. A few blocks
south of here, my wife's mother drifts from us
beneath hospital sheets, her small strength bent
to the poisons and the rays they use
against a spreading cancer.

In their house now, deep love
is studying to live with deepening impatience
as each day gives our hopes a different form
and household tasks rise like a powdery mist
of restless fatigue. Still, at five
my wife and I will dress

and take the boulevard
across the river to a church where two dear friends
will marry; rings will be blessed, promises kept
and made, and while our sons lie down to sleep,
the groom's niece, as the flower girl,
will almost steal the show.

But here the boys have made
an endless procession on the sides, shrieking down
slick steel almost too hot to touch; and now
they charge the swings. I push them from the front,
one with each hand, until at last
the rhythm, and the sunlight

that splashes through live oak
and crape myrtle, dappling dead leaves on the ground,
lull me away from this world toward a state
still and remote as an old photograph
in which I am standing somewhere
I may have been before:

there was this air, this light,
a day of thorough and forgetful happiness;
where was it, or how long ago? I try
to place it, but it has gone for good,
to leave me gazing at these swings,
thinking of something else

I may have recognized—
an irrecoverable certainty that now,
and now, this perfect afternoon, while friends
are struggling to put on their cutaways
or bridal gowns, and my wife's mother,
dearer still, is dozing

after her medicine,
or turning a small thing in her mind, like someone
worrying a ring of keys to make small sounds
against great silence, and while these two boys
swing back and forth against my hand,
time's crosshairs quarter me

no matter where I turn.
Now it is time to go. The boys are tired enough,
and my wife and I must dress and go to church.
Because I love our friends, and ceremony,
the usual words will make me weep:
hearing the human prayers

for holy permanence
will remind me that a life is much to ask
of anyone, yet not too much to give
to love. And once or twice, as I stand there,
that dappled moment at the swings
will rise between the lines,

when I beheld our sons
as, in the ways of things, they will not be again,
though even years from now their hair may lift
a little in the breeze, as if they stood
somewhere along their way from us,
poised for a steep return.

RICHARD TILLINGHAST

Richard Tillinghast holds degrees from the University of the South and Harvard. He has published three books of poetry, including *Our Flag Was Still There*. Originally from Memphis, Tennessee, where he was born in 1940, Tillinghast teaches in the creative writing program at the University of Michigan.

Photo Credit: Chase Twichell

Summer Rain

Summer rain, and the voices of children
     from another room.
Old friends from summers past,
we drink old whiskey and talk about ghosts.
The rain ebbs, rattles the summer cottage roof,
   soaks the perished leaves in wooden gutters,
then gusts and
     drowns our fond talk.
It's really coming down, we chatter,
   as though rain sometimes rose.
The power fails.
We sit under darkness, under the heavy storm.
Our children—frightened, laughing—
   run in to be beside us.

The weak lights surge on.
We see each other's children newly.
How they've grown! we prose

with conventional smiles, acceptingly commonplace,
    as they go back to playing.
Yet growing is what a child does.

And ourselves?
You haven't changed a bit,
    we not exactly lie,
meaning the shock is not so great
        as we'd expected.
It's the tired look around the eyes,
the flesh a little loose on the jaw . . .

Your oldest daughter's a senior at Yale.
We're like our grandparents and our parents now,
        shocked by the present:
A buggy without a horse to pull it?
                        A man on the moon?
            Girls at Yale?
We say goodnight. I can hardly lift
        my young son anymore
as I carry him to the car asleep.

The rain comes down, comes down, comes down.
One would think it would wear the earth away.
You told us about a skeleton
        you awoke seeing—
the dawn light on the bone.
It wakes me this morning early.
But I'm sure it wasn't a ghost, you said
        in your sensible way,
It was just my terrible fear of death.

Rain roars on the broad oak leaves
    and wears away the limestone.
I smell the mildewed bindings
    of books I bought as a student.
How shabby, how pathetic they look now
    as they stand there on their shelves unread!
Children are all that matters, you said
    last night, and I agreed.
The children's play-song—repetitive, inane—
    keeps sounding in my head.
I get up—last night's spirits alive
    this morning in my blood—
and write these perishing words down
in the voice of summer rain.

The Knife

What was it I wonder?
   in my favorite weather   in the driving rain
      that drew me like a living hand
What was it
   like a living hand
that spun me off the freeway
     and stopped me
on a sidestreet in California
with the rain pelting slick leaves down my windshield

to see the words of my brother's poem
    afloat on the bright air,
   and the knife I almost lost
     falling end over end through twenty years
        to the depths of Spring River—

the knife I had used to cut a fish open,
       caught in time
  the instant where it falls
     through a green flame of living water.

My one brother,
   who saw more in the river than water
  who understood what the fathers knew,
    dove from the Old Town canoe
  plunged and found his place
    in the unstoppable live water

seeing with opened eyes
    the green glow on the rocks
       and the willows running underwater—
   like leaves over clear glass in the rain—

While the long-jawed, predatory fish
  the alligator gar
watched out of prehistory
   schooled in the water like shadows
   unmoved in the current,
  watched unwondering.

    The cold raw-boned, white-skinned boy
curls off his dive in deep water

and sees on the slab-rock
filling more space than the space it fills:

     the lost thing   *the knife*
  current swift all around it

and fishblood denser than our blood
  still stuck to the pike-jaw knifeblade
which carries a shape like the strife of brothers
      —old as blood—
  the staghorn handle smooth as time.

    Now I call to him
    and now I see
David burst into the upper air
gasping as he brings to the surface our grandfather's knife
    shaped now, for as long as these words last,
     like all things saved from time.

  I see in its steel
    the worn gold on my father's hand
     the light in those trees
the look on my son's face   a moment old

    like the river   old like rain
  older than anything that dies can be.

Envoi

Go little book, *par avion.*
Wing, verses, toward your targets:
Where faces cool and harden behind bars,
Where an idea straps on a pistol,

Where the people eat their right to vote,
Where machine guns and TV cameras
Look from the tops of glass buildings.
Go, little peregrine.

Fly as I taught you
With bombs tucked under your wings,
In a V of attack, low to the ground,
Underneath the enemy's lazy radar. . . .

It's too much though—isn't it, little friend?
You glide over cool marble floors
Out into the womanly moonlight.
A rosevine encircles you, you bleed on the thorns.

Your throat opens to a harmony of seasons.
You sing of the nest, of unruffled June mornings,
Of leaving the nest, of building it again;
Of its perfect circle.

You would have me kill, you whose life is a breath?
I pity you, yes I pity you, you warble,
And take off into the distance
As if you thought you would live forever.

I stand in the predawn field, boots drenched,
The big glove covering my wrist and hand,
And watch you soar, a speck now,
Into the rainy future.

ELLEN BRYANT VOIGT

Ellen Bryant Voigt is the author of two volumes of poetry, including *The Forces of Plenty*. She received degrees from Converse College and the University of Iowa, and teaches in the M.F.A. Program for Writers at Warren Wilson College in North Carolina.

Photo Credit: Jane Dennison Myers

Farm Wife

Dark as the spring river, the earth
opens each damp row as the farmer
swings the far side of the field.
The blackbirds flash their red
wing patches and wheel in his wake,
down to the black dirt; the windmill
grinds in its chain rig and tower.

In the kitchen, his wife is baking.
She stands in the door in her long white
gloves of flour. She cocks her head and
tries to remember, turns like the moon
toward the sea-black field. Her belly
is rising, her apron fills like a sail.
She is gliding now, the windmill churns
beneath her, she passes the farmer,
the fine map of the furrows.
The neighbors point to the bone-white
spot in the sky.

Let her float
like a fat gull that swoops and circles,
before her husband comes in for supper,
before her children grow up and leave her,
before the pulley cranks her down
the dark shaft, and the church blesses
her stone bed, and the earth seals
its black mouth like a scar.

Jug Brook

Beyond the stone wall,
the deer should be emerging from their yard.
Lank, exhausted, they scrape at the ground
where roots and bulbs will send forth
new definitions. The creek swells in its ditch;
the field puts on a green glove.
Deep in the woods, the dead ripen,
and the lesser creatures turn to their commission.

Why grieve for the lost deer,
for the fish that clutter the brook,
the kingdoms of midge that cloud its surface,
the flocks of birds that come to feed.
The earth does not grieve.
It rushes toward the season of waste—

On the porch the weather shifts,
the cat dispatches
another expendable animal from the field.
Soon she will go inside to cull her litter,
addressing each with a diagnostic tongue.
Have I learned nothing? God,
into whose deep pocket our cries are swept,
it is you I look for
in the slate face of the water.

Daughter

There is one grief worse than any other.

When your small feverish throat clogged, and quit,
I knelt beside the chair on the green rug
and shook you and shook you,
but the only sound was mine shouting you back,
the delicate curls at your temples,
the blue wool blanket,
your face blue,
your jaw clamped against remedy—

how could I put a knife to that white neck?
With you in my lap,
my hands fluttering like flags,
I bend instead over your dead weight
to administer a kiss so urgent, so ruthless,
pumping breath into your stilled body,
counting out the rhythm for how long until
the second birth, the second cry
oh Jesus that sudden noisy musical inhalation
that leaves me stunned
by your survival.

Sweet Everlasting

Swarming over the damp ground with pocket lenses
that discover and distort like an insect's
compound eye, the second grade
slows, stops at the barrier on the path.
They straddle the horizontal trunk, down for months;
rub the rough track of the saw, then focus
on the new shoots at the other end—
residual, suggestive.
I follow the children into open land
above the orchard, its small clouds tethered
to the grass, where we gather
samples of the plentiful white bud
that stipples the high pasture, and name it

by the book: wooly stem, pale lanceolate leaves;
the one called Everlasting. The punishment for doubt
is doubt—my father's death has taught me that.
Last week, he surfaced in a dream as promised,
as, at night, the logic of earth subsides
and stars appear to substantiate
what we could not see. But when I woke,
I remembered nothing that could tell me
which among those distant pulsing inconclusive signs
were active, which extinguished—
remembered, that is,
nothing that could save him.

Landscape, Dense with Trees

When you move away, you see how much depends
on the pace of the days—how much
depended on the haze we waded through
each summer, visible heat, wavy and discursive
as the lazy track of the snake in the dusty road;
and on the habit in town of porches thatched in vines,
and in the country long dense promenades, the way
we sacrificed the yards to shade.
It was partly the heat that made my father
plant so many trees—two maples marking the site
for the house, two elms on either side when it was done;
mimosa by the fence, and as it failed, fast-growing chestnuts,
loblolly pines; and dogwood, redbud, ornamental crab.
On the farm, everything else he grew
something could eat, but this
would be a permanent mark of his industry,
a glade established in the open field. Or so it seemed.
Looking back at the empty house from across the hill,
I see how well the house is camouflaged, see how
that porous fence of saplings, their later
scrim of foliage, thickened around it,
and still he chinked and mortared, planting more.
Last summer, although he'd lost all tolerance for heat,
he backed the truck in at the family grave
and stood in the truckbed all afternoon, pruning
the landmark oak, repairing recent damage by a wind;

then he came home and hung a swing in one
of the horse-chestnuts for my visit.
The heat was a hand at his throat,
a fist to his weak heart. But it made a triumph
of the cooler air inside, in the bedroom,
in the maple bedstead where he slept,
in the brick house nearly swamped by leaves.

The Lotus Flowers

The surface of the pond was mostly green—
bright green algae reaching out from the banks,
then the mass of water lilies, their broad round leaves
rim to rim, each white flower spreading
from the center of a green saucer.
We teased and argued, choosing the largest,
the sweetest bloom, but when the rowboat
lumbered through and rearranged them
we found the plants were anchored, the separate
muscular stems descending in the dense water—
only the most determined put her hand
into that frog-slimed pond
to wrestle with a flower. Back and forth
we pumped across the water, in twos and threes,
full of brave adventure. On the marshy shore,
the others hollered for their turns,
or at the hem of where we pitched the tents
gathered firewood—
                    this was wilderness,
although the pond was less than half an acre
and we could still see the grand magnolias
in the village cemetery, their waxy,
white conical blossoms gleaming in the foliage.
A dozen girls, the oldest only twelve, two sisters
with their long braids, my shy neighbor,
someone squealing without interruption—
all we didn't know about the world buoyed us
as the frightful water sustained and moved the flowers
tethered at a depth we couldn't see.

In the late afternoon, before they'd folded
into candles on the dark water,
I went to fill the bucket at the spring.
Deep in the pines, exposed tree roots
formed a natural arch, a cave of black loam.
I raked off the skin of leaves and needles,
leaving a pool so clear and shallow
I could count the pebbles
on the studded floor. The sudden cold
splashing up from the bucket to my hands
made me want to plunge my hand in—
and I held it under, feeling the shock that wakes
and deadens, watching first my fingers,
then the ledge beyond me,
the snake submerged and motionless,
the head propped in its coils the way a girl
crosses her arms before her on the sill
and rests her chin there.
              Lugging the bucket
back to the noisy clearing, I found nothing changed,
the boat still rocked across the pond,
the fire straggled and cracked as we fed it
branches and debris into the night,
leaning back on our pallets—
spokes in a wheel—learning the names of the many
constellations, learning how each fixed
cluster took its name:
not from the strongest light, but from the pattern
made by stars of lesser magnitude,
so like the smaller stars we rowed among.

The Farmer

In the still-blistering late afternoon,
like currying a horse the rake
circled the meadow, the cut grass ridging
behind it. This summer, if the weather held,
he'd risk a second harvest after years
of reinvesting, leaving fallow.
These fields were why he farmed—
he walked the fenceline like a man in love.

The animals were merely what he needed: cattle
and pigs; chickens for a while; a drayhorse,
saddle horses he was paid to pasture—
an endless stupid round
of animals, one of them always hungry, sick, lost,
calving or farrowing, or waiting slaughter.

When the field began dissolving in the dusk,
he carried feed down to the knoll,
its clump of pines, gate, trough, lick, chute
and two gray hives; leaned into the Jersey's side
as the galvanized bucket filled with milk;
released the cow and turned to the bees.
He'd taken honey before without protection.
This time, they could smell something
in his sweat—fatigue? impatience,
although he was a stubborn, patient man?
Suddenly, like flame, they were swarming over him.
He rolled in the dirt, manure and stiff hoof-prints,
started back up the path, rolled in the fresh hay—
refused to run, which would have pumped
the venom through him faster—passed the oaks
at the yard's edge, rolled in the yard, reached
the kitchen, and when he tore off his clothes
crushed bees dropped from him like scabs.

For a week he lay in the darkened bedroom.
The doctor stopped by twice a day—
the hundred stings "enough to kill an ox,
enough to kill a younger man." What saved him
were the years of smaller doses—
like minor disappointments,
instructive poison, something he could use.

The Last Class

Put this in your notebooks:
All verse is occasional verse.
In March, trying to get home, distracted
and impatient at Gate 5 in the Greyhound station,
I saw a drunk man bothering a woman.

A poem depends on its detail
but the woman had her back to me,
and the man was just another drunk,
black in this case, familiar, dirty.
I moved past them both, got on the bus.

There is no further action to report.
The man is not a symbol. If what he said to her
touches us, we are touched by a narrative
we supply. What he said was, "I'm sorry,
"I'm sorry," over and over, "I'm sorry,"
but you must understand he frightened the woman,
he meant to rob her of those few quiet
solitary moments sitting down,
waiting for the bus, before she headed home
and probably got supper for her family,
perhaps in a room in Framingham,
perhaps her child was sick.

My bus pulled out, made its usual turns
and parted the formal gardens from the Common,
both of them camouflaged by snow.
And as it threaded its way to open road,
leaving the city, leaving our sullen classroom,
I postponed my satchel of your poems
and wondered who I am to teach the young,
having come so far from honest love of the world;
I tried to recall how it felt
to live without grief; and then I wrote down
a few tentative lines about the drunk,
because of an old compulsion to record,
or sudden resolve not to be self-absorbed
and full of dread—
                I wanted to salvage
something from my life, to fix
some truth beyond all change, the way
photographers of war, miles from the front,
lift print after print into the light,
each one further cropped and amplified,
pruning whatever baffles or obscures,
until the small figures are restored
as young men sleeping.

ALICE
WALKER

Alice Walker, primarily known as a novelist and writer of short stories, has published several books of poetry. A graduate of Sarah Lawrence College, she was born in Eatontown, Georgia in 1944. Her novel, *The Color Purple,* was awarded the Pulitzer Prize for fiction.

Photo Credit: Robert Allen

My Husband Says

My husband says
this shortness of breath
and feeling of falling down a well
I suffer
in the half-life I share
with my lover
will soon cease to plague me.
That love, like war,
escalates
each side raising its demands
for what it wants
as emotions rise
higher and higher
and what was unthought of in the beginning
becomes the inevitable result.

"Soon you will write
you can not live without him
no matter that he has a wife.
He will tell you
the 1,000 miles separating you
is crushing to his soul.
As for me,
I love no one now
except you.
But if I am ever asked
in your presence
if this is true,
please don't take offense
at the vehemence
of my negative
reply."

Your Soul Shines

Your soul shines
like the sides of a fish.
My tears are salty
my grief is deep.
Come live in me again.
Each day I walk along the edges
of the tall rocks.

Even As I Hold You

Even as I hold you
I think of you as someone gone
far, far away. Your eyes the color
of pennies in a bowl of dark honey
bringing sweet light to someone else
your black hair slipping through my fingers
is the flash of your head going
around a corner
your smile, breaking before me,
the flippant last turn
of a revolving door,
emptying you out, changed,
away from me.

Even as I hold you
I am letting go.

ROBERT PENN
WARREN

Photo Credit: Michael V. Carlisle

Robert Penn Warren was chosen as the first Poet Laureate of the United States of America in 1986. He was born in Guthrie, Kentucky in 1905, holds degrees from Vanderbilt University and the University of California, and did graduate work at Yale University and then at Oxford as a Rhodes Scholar. Warren has received many awards for his poetry, including the Pulitzer Prize and the National Book Award. His *New and Selected Poems 1923–1985* was published in 1985.

Tell Me a Story

[A]

Long ago, in Kentucky, I, a boy, stood
By a dirt road, in first dark, and heard
The great geese hoot northward.

I could not see them, there being no moon
And the stars sparse. I heard them.

I did not know what was happening in my heart.

It was the season before the elderberry blooms,
Therefore they were going north.

The sound was passing northward.

[B]

Tell me a story.

In this century, and moment, of mania,
Tell me a story.

Make it a story of great distances, and starlight.

The name of the story will be Time,
But you must not pronounce its name.

Tell me a story of deep delight.

The Spider

The spider has more eyes than I have money.
I used to dream that God was a spider, or

Vice versa, but it is easier
To dream of a funnel, and you
The clear liquid being poured down it, forever.

You do not know what is beyond the little end of the funnel.

The liquid glimmers in darkness, you
Are happy, it pours easily, without fume.

All you have to do is not argue.

Sister Water

. . . and to begin again, the night was dark and dreary, and
The Captain said to his trusty Lieutenant, "Lieutenant,

Tell us a story." And the Lieutenant: "The night was dark and—" And I
Have heard on the creaky stairs at night an old man's

Dragging step approach my door. He pauses for breath, and I
Can hear the chain-rattle of phlegm in the painful intake,

But I never know whose father it is, or son,
Or what mission leads to my locked door. If I

Should open it, he might call me by my name. Or yours.
And if he did, then what, what might occur?

And once, not knowing where, in what room, in what city even,
You lay in the dark, and a finger,

Soft as down and with a scent
Unidentifiable but stirring your heart to tears,

Like memory, was laid to your lips. "Now—"
Comes the whisper. But is there a *now* or a *then?*

And you hear in the dark, at street level above
Your basement apartment window, tires hiss on wet asphalt.

You do not know whence they come, nor whither go,
And so lie laughing alone with a sound like a strangled loon-call,

Till, slop-gray, dawn light defines the bars of your window,
And you hear the cough and mastication of

The garbage truck in the next block. "God—"
You think, with a stab of joy, "He loves us all. He will not

Let all distinction perish." You cannot pray. But
You can wash your face in cold water.

Last Laugh

The little Sam Clemens, one night back in Hannibal,
Peeped through the dining-room keyhole, to see, outspread
And naked, the father split open, lights, liver, and all
Spilling out from that sack of mysterious pain, and the head

Sawed through, where his Word, like God's, held its deepest den,
And candlelight glimmered on blood-slick, post-mortem steel,
And the two dead fish-eyes stared steadily ceilingward—well, then,
If you yourself were, say, twelve, just how would you feel?

Oh, not that you'd loved him—that ramrod son of Virginia,
Though born for success, failing westward bitterly on.
"Armed truce"—that was all, years later, you could find to say in you.
But still, when a father's dead, an umbrella's gone

From between the son and the direful elements.
No, Sam couldn't turn from the keyhole. It's not every night
You can see God butchered in such learned dismemberments,
And when the chance comes you should make the most of the sight.

Though making the most, Sam couldn't make terms with the fact
Of the strangely prismatic glitter that grew in his eye,
Or climbing the stairs, why his will felt detached from the act,
Or why stripping for bed, he stared so nakedly

At the pore little body and thought of the slick things therein.
Then he wept on the pillow, surprised at what he thought grief,
Then fixed eyes at darkness while, slow, on his face grew a grin,
Till suddenly something inside him burst with relief,

Like a hog-bladder blown up to bust when the hog-killing frost
Makes the brats' holiday. So took then to laughing and could not
Stop, and so laughed himself crying to sleep. At last,
Far off in Nevada, by campfire or sluice or gulch-hut,

Or in roaring S.F., in an acre of mirror and gilt,
Where the boys with the dust bellied-up, he'd find words come,
His own face stiff as a shingle, and him little-built.
Then whammo!—the back-slapping riot. He'd stand, looking dumb.

God was dead, for a fact. He knew, in short, the best joke.
He had learned its thousand forms, and since the dark stair-hall

Had learned what was worth more than bullion or gold-dust-plump poke.
And married rich, too, with an extra spin to the ball;

For Livy loved God, and he'd show her the joke, how they lied.
Quite a tussle it was, but hot deck or cold, he was sly
And won every hand but the last. Then at her bedside
He watched dying eyes stare up at a comfortless sky,

And was left alone with his joke, God dead, till he died.

Evening Hour

There was a graveyard once—or cemetery
It's now more toney to say—just a field without fence
Pretty far from town, on a hill good and gravelly
So rain wouldn't stand to disturb local residents.

Though all were long past the sniffles and rheumatism:
A tract of no real estate value, where flourished not
Even thistle, and the spade at the grievous chasm
Would go *chink* on chipped flint in the dirt, for in times forgot

Here the Indian crouched to perfect his arrowhead.
And there was a boy, long after, who gathered such things
Among shiny new tombstones recording the first-planted dead,
Now and then looking up at a buzzard's high sun-glinting wings,

Not thinking of flesh and its nature, but suddenly still
For maybe two minutes; as when, up the rise, a great through-freight
Strove in the panting and clank of man's living will,
Asserting itself in the face of an ignorant date.

Not morbid, nor putting two and two together
To make any mystic, or fumblingly philosophical,
Four, he sometimes kept waiting, if decent the weather,
In a lonely way, arrowheads forgotten, till all

The lights of the town had come on. He did not know
Why the lights, so familiar, now seemed so far away,
And more than once felt the crazy impulse grow
To lay ear to earth for what voices beneath might say.

Heat Lightning

Heat lightning prowls, pranks the mountain horizon like
Memory. I follow the soundless flicker,

As ridge after ridge, as outline of peak after peak,
Is momentarily defined in the

Pale wash, the rose-flush, of distance. Somewhere—
Somewhere far beyond them—that distance. I think

Of the past and how this soundlessness, no thunder,
Is like memory purged of emotion,

Or even of meaning. I watch
The lightning wash pale beyond the night mountains, beyond

Night cumulus, like a stage set. Nothing
Is real, and I think of her, in timelessness: the clutch

In the lightless foyer, the awkward wall-propping, one ear
Cocked for footsteps, all the world

Hates a lover. It seems only a dream, the unsounding
Flicker of memory, even the episode when

Arms, encircling, had clamped arms to sides, the business
Banked on a pillow, head

Back over bed-edge, the small cry of protest—
But meanwhile, paradoxically, heels

Beating buttocks in deeper demand. Then heels stopping
In shudder and sprawl, only whites

Of eyes showing, like death. What all the tension,
The tingle, twist, tangle, the panting and pain,

What all exploitation of orifices and bruised flesh but
The striving for one death in two? I remember—

Oh, look! in that flash, how the peak
Blackens zenithward—as I said, I remember

The glutted, slack look on the face once
And the faintest blood-smear at the mouth's left corner,

And not till next day did I notice the two
symmetrical half-moons of blue marks tattooed

On my shoulder, not remembering, even then, the sensation
Of the event; and of course, not now, for heat lightning

Is thunderless. And thunderless, even,
The newspaper obit, years later, I stumbled on. Yes,

How faint that flash! And I sit in the unmooned
Dark of an August night, waiting to see

The rose-flush beyond the black peaks, and think how far,
Far away, down what deep valley, scree, scar,

The thunder redoubled, redoubling, rolls. Here silence.

Heart of the Backlog

Snug at hearthside, while heart of the backlog
Of oak simmers red in the living pulse of its own
Decay, you sit. You count
Your own heartbeat. How steady, how
Firm! What, ah, is Time! And sometimes

It is hard, after all, to decide
If the ticking you now hear is
A whisk of granules of snow,
Hard and belated on panes, or simply
The old organ, fist-size and resolute,
Now beast-like caught
In your ribcage, to pace

But go nowhere. It does,
In a ghostly sense, suggest now the sound of
Pacing, as if, in soft litter, curved claws
Were muffled. Or is it
The pace of the muffled old clock in the hall?

You watch the talus-like slide of
Consumed oak from oak yet consuming. Yes, tell me
How many the years that burn there. How delicate, dove-gray
The oak-ash that, tiny and talus-like, slides to unwink
The glowing of oak and the years unconsumed!
What is the color of years your fireplace consumes as you sit there?

But think, shut your eyes. Shut your eyes and see only
The wide stretch of world beyond your warm refuge—fields
Windless and white in full moonlight,
Snow past and now steady the stars, and, far off,
The woods-lair of darkness. Listen! is that
The great owl that you, warm at your hearthside, had heard?

How feather-frail, think, is the track of the vole
On new snow! How wide is the world! How fleeting and thin
Its mark of identity, breath
In a minuscule issue of whiteness
In air that is brighter than steel! The vole pauses, one paw
Uplifted in whiteness of moonlight.

There is no indication of what angle, or slant,
The great shadow may silkily accent the beauty of snow,
And the vole, Little One, has neither theology nor
Aesthetic—not even what you may call
Stoicism, as when the diagnostician pauses, and coughs.
Poor thing, he has only himself. And what do you have

When you go to the door, snatch it open, and, cold,
The air strikes like steel down your lungs, and you feel
The Pascalian nausea make dizzy the last stars?
Then shut the door. The backlog burns down. You sit and

Again the owl calls, and with some sadness you wonder
If at last, when the air-scything shadow descends
And needles claw-clamp through gut, heart and brain,
Will ecstasy melting with terror create the last little cry?
Is God's love but the last and most mysterious word for death?

Has the thought ever struck you to rise and go forth—yes, lost
In the whiteness—to never look upward, or back, only on,
And no sound but the snow-crunch, and breath
Gone crisp like the crumpling of paper? Listen!
Could that be the creak of a wing-joint gigantic in distance?

No, no—just a tree, far off, when ice inward bites.
No, no, don't look back—oh, I beg you!

I beg you not to look back, in God's name.

What Voice at Moth-Hour

What voice at moth-hour did I hear calling
As I stood in the orchard while the white
Petals of apple blossoms were falling,
Whiter than moth-wing in that twilight?

What voice did I hear as I stood by the stream,
Bemused in the murmurous wisdom there uttered,
While ripples at stone, in their steely gleam,
Caught last light before it was shuttered?

What voice did I hear as I wandered alone
In a premature night of cedar, beech, oak,
Each foot set soft, then still as stone
Standing to wait while the first owl spoke?

The voice that I heard once at dew-fall, I now
Can hear by a simple trick. If I close
My eyes, in that dusk I again know
The feel of damp grass between bare toes,

Can see the last zigzag, sky-skittering, high,
Of a bullbat, and even hear, far off, from
Swamp-cover, the whip-o-will, and as I
Once heard, hear the voice: *It's late! Come home.*

Heart of Autumn

Wind finds the northwest gap, fall comes.
Today, under gray cloud-scud and over gray
Wind-flicker of forest, in perfect formation, wild geese
Head for a land of warm water, the *boom*, the lead pellet.

Some crumple in air, fall. Some stagger, recover control,
Then take the last glide for a far glint of water. None
Knows what has happened. Now, today, watching
How tirelessly *V* upon *V* arrows the season's logic,

Do I know my own story? At least, they know
When the hour comes for the great wing-beat. Sky-striker,
Star-strider—they rise, and the imperial utterance,
Which cries out for distance, quivers in the wheeling sky.

That much they know, and in their nature know
The path of pathlessness, with all the joy
Of destiny fulfilling its own name.
I have known time and distance, but not why I am here.

Path of logic, path of folly, all
The same—and I stand, my face lifted now skyward,
Hearing the high beat, my arms outstretched in the tingling
Process of transformation, and soon tough legs,

With folded feet, trail in the sounding vacuum of passage,
And my heart is impacted with a fierce impulse
To unwordable utterance—
Toward sunset, at a great height.

JAMES WHITEHEAD

James Whitehead, born in St. Louis, Missouri in 1936, spent his childhood in Mississippi. He holds degrees from Vanderbilt University and the University of Iowa and is the author of two books of poetry, *Domains* and *Local Men,* and a chapbook entitled *Actual Size.* He teaches in the Program in Creative Writing at the University of Arkansas.

A Local Man Goes to the Killing Ground

They formed the ritual circle
    of Chevy trucks. Tracks were there,
    worn tires, the still prints in the mud
    and thin grass. My light could barely suggest
    the glare that fell on the men they killed.

It was an intimate thing—
    all of them drawn in so close
    they didn't bother with guns
    or the normal uses of the knife.
    It was done with boots.

I walked around that quiet place
    and tried to reclaim the energy
    that must of course remain in the earth.
    It keeps the truth to itself
    as they will, when they stride out of court.

By then it was all grey, false dawn—
    and I thought it was like stomping
    a fetus in the womb, a little
    skin between the killers, the killed,
    for the dead were curled in their passive way.

A Local Man Remembers Betty Fuller

Betty Fuller cried and said, Hit me.
I did. Which made her good and passionate
But Betty Fuller never came. Fate
Decreed that Betty Fuller would not see
The generosity a lively house
And loyal husband bring. She lost her mind
In Mendenhall. She got herself defined
As absolutely mad. A single mouse
Caused her to run exactly down the line
Of a wide road, running both north and south
With execrations pouring from her mouth.

She's out at Whitfield doing crazy time
And she can't possibly remember me
Among the rest. I'm satisfied she can't.

A Local Contractor Flees
His Winter Trouble
And Saves Some Lives
in a Knoxville Motel Room

Nobody is dead yet and won't be. Right.
Right. Right. Because I am a snake aware
Of wintertime. Out there is a hard night
To study, friends, deciding I'm still fair
Enough to keep the Remington locked up.
My dreams are bloodier than movies, buddy,
Because I'm wise enough to hide the clip.
You should be sainted when you quit on ready.

Mother is gone, dead as an animal,
And Daddy is strange—he fishes in the rain—
And my ex-wife, men, will defeat you all.
Everybody longs for where they began
Or where they've never been, you better believe.
You better believe we all end up alone.

About a Year After He Got Married
He Would Sit Alone in an Abandoned Shack
in a Cotton Field Enjoying Himself

I'd sit inside the abandoned shack all morning
Being sensitive, a fair thing to do
At twenty-three, my first son born, and burning
To get my wife again. The world was new
And I was nervous and wonderfully depressed.

The light on the cotton flowers and the child
Asleep at home was marvelous and blessed,
And the dust in the abandoned air was mild
As sentimental poverty. I'd scan
Or draw the ragged wall the morning long.

Newspaper for wallpaper sang but didn't mean.
Hard thoughts of justice were beyond my ken.
Lord, forgive young men their gentle pain,
Then bring them stones. Bring their play to ruin.

He Remembers How He Didn't Understand
What Lieutenant Dawson Meant

Lieutenant Dawson said he'd known the girl
For fifteen years
But I couldn't read his face
Or his shaved head—
He said there's something cruel
About the way these people live—Disgrace
And Violence and Crime.
He made a list
That never added up to heavy grief.
Three times he opened up then closed a fist
And said he'd known she'd never have a life.

Outside the small and mean low-ceilinged room
Where she lay dead, her pretty body torn
And ruined by the shoe and stolen ring
Her boyfriend used,
Dawson freed a groan
That wasn't clearly out of sympathy—
Then said this is your basic tragedy.

Long Tour:
The Country Music Star Explains Why
He Put off the Bus and Fired
A Good Lead Guitar in West Texas

The day I put him off the sun outside
The cafe window didn't have a mind
For anything but lighting up a road
Covered with hair and plates and guts and blood
Of animals. He always counted them.
In the jump seat he'd count the creatures dead
Three hundred miles until we'd stop at noon.
He'd add them up in a notebook he carried.
He said that eggs were almost perfect food.
He said he'd met the man that ate the toad.
His breakfast stories went from fair to bad:
A couple wanted children, tried and tried,
But they got fur and nails like little wings
And every time the little baby died:
Then once again they tried
While making love to all our pretty songs—
She gave her man a watch, he gave her rings,
And God forgave their wrongs,
And it was born alive, a nine-pound eye.
I fired him for that. And he was good.

Good Linemen Live in a Closed World

Good linemen live in a closed world—they move
Inside themselves to move themselves against
The others and their violence—they give
To interior visions whole seasons no good sense
Would approve—their insides creak and groan, crying
A thing that's trapped along the line is shrill
And curious and wants out. Bodies playing
Laugh and dream to gain the massive will
Their trade requires. These men maintain, they attack,
They suffer repetition for years and years.
Part war and similar to art, their work
Is sometimes elegant. Inside their fears
At the closed center of one fear, they move
Quickly against themselves with a massive love.

A Natural Theology

Once again a spring has come around
And many of the best I think I know
Are going crazy.
              Light on the warm ground
Is almost God requiring them to grow—
Or, at least, to change—the usual song
And arrogant demand that nature makes
Of moral, thoughtful people all gone wrong
So far as they can see.
                  Their hands hold rakes.
They comb what later are attractive lawns.
They harrow in their ways, then drive the stakes
Up which flowers and food will climb their dream
Of this one season right.
                They pick up sticks
To make the whole thing work, then plant a tree.
Spring. Spring. They take it personally.

MILLER
WILLIAMS

Miller Williams, born in 1930 in Hoxie, Arkansas, has lived and taught in Chile, Mexico and Italy and was founding editor of the *New Orleans Review*. Honors for his poetry include the Prix de Rome for literature of The American Academy of Arts and Letters and the New York Arts Fund Award for Distinguished Contribution to American Letters.

Photo Credit: Carl Hitt

The Caterpillar

Today on the lip of a bowl in the backyard
we watched a caterpillar caught in the circle
of his larval assumptions

my daughter counted
27 times he went around
before rolling back and laughing
I'm a caterpillar, look
she left him
measuring out his slow green way to some place
there must have been a picture of inside him

After supper
coming from putting the car up
we stopped to look
figured he crossed the yard

once every hour
and left him
when we went to bed
wrinkling no closer to my landlord's leaves
than when he somehow fell to his private circle

Later I followed
barefeet and doorclicks of my daughter
to the yard   the bowl
a milkwhite moonlight eye
in the black grass

it died

I said honey they don't live very long

In bed again
re-covered and re-kissed
she locked her arms and mumbling love to mine
until turning she slipped
into the deep bone-bottomed dish
of sleep

Stumbling drunk around the rim
I hold
the words she said to me across the dark

I think he thought he was
going in a straight line

Why God Permits Evil:
For Answers to This Question
of Interest to Many
Write Bible Answers Dept. E–7

—ad on a matchbook cover

Of interest to John Calvin and Thomas Aquinas
for instance and Job for instance who never got

one straight answer but only his cattle back.
With interest, which is something, but certainly not

any kind of answer unless you ask
God if God can demonstrate God's power

and God's glory, which is not a question.
You should all be living at this hour.

You had Servetus to burn, the elect to count,
bad eyes and the Institutes to write;

you had the exercises and had Latin,
the hard bunk and the solitary night;

you had the neighbors to listen to and your woman
yelling at you to curse God and die.

Some of this to be on the right side;
some of it to ask in passing, Why?

Why badness makes its way in a world He made?
How come he looked for twelve and got eleven?

You had the faith and looked for love, stood pain,
learned patience and little else. We have E–7.

Churches may be shut down everywhere,
half-written philosophy books be tossed away.

Some place on the south side of Chicago
a lady with wrinkled hose and a small gray

bun of hair sits straight with her knees together
behind a teacher's desk on the third floor

of an old shirt factory, bankrupt and abandoned
except for this just cause, and on the door:

Dept. E–7. She opens the letters
asking why God permits it and sends a brown

plain envelope to each return address.
But she is not alone. All up and down

the thin and creaking corridors are doors
and desks behind them: E–6, E–5, 4, 3.

A desk for every question, for how we rise
blown up and burned, for how the will is free,

for when is Armageddon, for whether dogs
have souls or not and on and on. On

beyond the alphabet and possible numbers
where cross-legged, naked and alone,

there sits a pale, tall and long-haired woman
upon a cushion of fleece and eiderdown

holding in one hand a hand-written answer,
holding in the other hand a brown

plain envelope. On either side, cobwebbed
and empty baskets sitting on the floor

say *in* and *out*. There is no sound in the room.
There is no knob on the door. Or there is no door.

Love and How It Becomes Important in Our Day to Day Lives

The man who tells you which is the whiter wash,
the woman who talks about her paper towels,
the woman whose coffee holds her home together,
the man who smells the air in his neighbor's house,

the man who sings a song about his socks,
the woman who tells how well her napkin fits,
the man who sells the four-way slicer-dicer,
the woman who crosses tape between her tits,

and scores beside trample my yard, a mob
demanding to be let in, like Sodomites
yelling to get at my guests but I have no guests.
I crawl across the floor and cut the lights.

"We know you're there," they say. "Open the door."
"Who are you?" I say. "What do you want with me?"
"What does it matter?" they say. "You'll let us in.
Everyone lets us in. You'll see. You'll see."

The chest against the door begins to give.
I settle against a wall. A window breaks.
I cradle a gun in the crook of my elbow.
I hear the porch collapse. The whole house shakes.

Then comes my wife as if to wake me up,
a box of ammunition in her arms.
She settles herself against the wall beside me.
"The towns are gone," she says. "They're taking the farms."

The Firebreathers at the Café Deux Magots

We sit at a sidewalk table.
Noilly Prat over ice.

A firebreather lost out of time,
his cheeks full of shadows,
takes off his shirt,
starts to spin it like a bullfighter's cape
and drops it.
He opens a blue plastic bottle,
soaks a torch, a broomstick wrapped in rags,
and waves the fire in front of him like a flag.

He seems to drink the alcohol like water.
He breathes in slowly.
He exhales a burning breath
red with yellow borders.

Flames run like liquid.
They drop in brief blazes from chin to chest.

With uncooperative hands and locked-in legs
he does this for nine silent minutes.
He bows like Pinocchio to the proper applause.
Aggressively among us he collects his coins.
His eyes when they come close
are bleary and small.
He seems to be drunk.
His hair is seared away.
His eyes don't have any lashes.
Blisters have shrunk into scars
on his chest and chin
like some exotic fruit left in the field.
One eye seems to be hunting
for something on its own.

He puts the plastic bottle
the torch and the cash
into a canvas bag and wanders away.
His feet sound like gravel poured on the pavement.

A woman plays a flute.
Her tall companion

long breasts moving like lovers
inside her blouse
comes and demands our money with great hands.

Another man,
years younger,
his green eyes lifting like fingers
the faces of women,
sheds his open shirt.

His chest is perfect and hard
and clean as marble.

Over the left nipple
one small round scar.

He opens the plastic bottle. He grins.
He tosses back the hair falling into his eyes
and then he makes a small move with his head,
a small, unconscious move,
the way one turns for a moment in mid-sentence
hearing a tumbler break in another room.

Ruby Tells All

When I was told, as Delta children were,
that crops don't grow unless you sweat at night,
I thought that it was my own sweat they meant.
I have never felt as important again
as on those early mornings, waking up,
my body slick, the moon full on the fields.
That was before air conditioning.
Farm girls sleep cool now and wake up dry,
but still the cotton overflows the fields.
We lose everything that's grand and foolish;
it all becomes something else. One by one,
butterflies turn into caterpillars
and we grow up, or more or less we do,
and, Lord, we do lie then. We lie so much
the truth has a false ring and it's hard to tell.

I wouldn't take crap off anybody
if I just knew that I was getting crap
in time not to take it. I could have won
a small one now and then if I was smarter,
but I've poured coffee here too many years
for men who rolled in in Peterbilts,
and I have gotten into bed with some
if they could talk and seemed to be in pain.
I never asked for anything myself;
giving is more blessed and leaves you free.
There was a man, married and fond of whiskey.
Given the limitations of men, he loved me.
Lord, we laid concern upon our bodies
but then he left. Everything has its time.
We used to dance. He made me feel the way
a human wants to feel and fears to.
He was a slow man and didn't expect.
I would get off work and find him waiting.
We'd have a drink or two and kiss awhile.
Then a bird-loud morning late one April
we woke up naked. We had made a child.
She's grown up now and gone though god knows where.
She ought to write, for I do love her dearly
who raised her carefully and dressed her well.

Everything has its time. For thirty years
I never had a thought about time.
Now, turning through newspapers, I pause
to see if anyone who passed away
was younger than I am. If one was
I feel hollow for a little while
but then it passes. Nothing matters enough
to stay bent down about. You have to see
that some things matter slightly and some don't.
Dying matters a little. So does pain.
So does being old. Men do not.
Men live by negatives, like don't give up,
don't be a coward, don't call me a liar,
don't ever tell me don't. If I could live
two hundred years and had to be a man
I'd take my grave. What's a man but a match,
a little stick to start a fire with?

My daughter knows this, if she's alive.
What could I tell her now, to bring her close,

something she doesn't know, if we met somewhere?
Maybe that I think about her father,
maybe that my fingers hurt at night,
maybe that against appearances
there is love, constancy, and kindness,
that I have dresses I have never worn.

On a Photograph of My Mother at Seventeen

How come to town she was, tied bright and prim,
with not a thought of me nor much of him.

Now, tied to a chair, she tries to pull free
of it and the world. Little is left of me,

I think, or him, inside her teetering head
where we lie with the half-remembered dead.

Her bones could be as hollow as a bird's
they are so light. Otherness of words.

They could be kite sticks. She could be a kite;
that's how thin her skin is. But now some light

from somewhere in the brain comes dimly through
then flickers and goes out. Or it seems to.

Maybe a door opened, where other men
and women come and go, and closed again.

How much we need the metaphors we make
to say and still not say, for pity's sake.

A Poem for Emily

Small fact and fingers and farthest one from me,
a hand's width and two generations away,
in this still present I am fifty-three.
You are not yet a full day.

When I am sixty-three, when you are ten,
and you are neither closer nor as far,
your arms will fill with what you know by then,
the arithmetic and love we do and are.

When I by blood and luck am eighty-six
and you are some place else and thirty-three
Believing in sex and god and politics
with children who look not at all like me,

some time I know you will have read them this
so they will know I love them and say so
and love their mother. Child, whatever is
is always or never was. Long ago,

a day I watched a while beside your bed,
I wrote this down, a thing that might be kept
a while, to tell you what I would have said
when you were who knows what and I was dead
which is I stood and loved you while you slept.

The Aging Actress Sees Herself
A Starlet on the Late Show

For centuries only painters, poets and sculptors
had to live with what they did as children.
Those who trod the boards—I love that—
said their first stumbling lines into air.
Some do still, but most of us who are known
and loved for being people we are not
have reels and reels of old film unrolling
behind us nearly as far as we remember.
We drag it everywhere. How would you like
your first time doing something to keep repeating
for everyone to look at all your life?

How would you like someone who used to be you
fifty years ago coming into this room?
How would you like it, never being able
to grow old all together, to have yourself
from different times of your life, running around?

How would you like never being able
to stop moving, always to be somewhere
walking, crying, kissing, slamming a door?
You can feel it, millions of images moving,
no matter how small or disguised, you get tired.
How would you like never being able
completely, really, to die? I love that.

After the Revolution for Jesus
A Secular Man Prepares His Final Remarks

What the blind lost when radio
gave way to TV,
what the deaf lost when movies
stopped spelling out words and spoke,
was a way back in. Always, this desire
to be inside again, when the doors are closed.

On the other side of the doors
our friends and parents and grandparents
work and eat and read books and make sense and love.

The thought of being disconnected
from history or place can empty the heart;
we are most afraid,
whatever else we fear,
of feeling the memory go, and of exile.
And death, which is both at once.

Still, as our lives
are the inhalations and exhalations of gods
we ought not fear those things we know will come
and ought not hope for what we know will not.
The dogs that waited for soldiers to come home
from Phillipi, New Guinea, Pennsylvania,
are all dead now whether or not the men
came back to call them.
There is no constancy but a falling away
with only love as a temporary stay
and not much assurance of that.

The desert religions are founded on sandy ways
to set ourselves free from that endless tumbling downward.
Thus we endow ourselves with gods of purpose,
the purposes of gods, and do their battles.

We are sent to war for money, but we go for god.

Prison is no place for living
but for reliving lives.
I remember a quarrel of students
proving, reproving the world;
a woman taking love

she didn't want, but needed
like a drowning swimmer
thrown a strand of barbed wire
by a kind stranger standing on the shore.

Imperfect love in that imperfect world
seemed elegant and right.
Now the old air that shaped itself to our bodies
will take the forms of others.
They will laugh with this air and pass it through their bodies
but days like ours
they will not come again to this poor planet.

I am reinventing our days together.
A man should be careful with words
at a time like this,
but lies have some attraction over the truth;
there is something in deceitful words
that sounds good to the ear.

The first layer of paint conceals the actor;
the second conceals the paint.

By which sly truth we have come to where we are.

I can hear brief choirs of rifles.
Inside my head
naked women wander toward my bed.
How gently they lie there, loving themselves to sleep.

What do we know that matters that Aeschylus did not know?

I do believe in God, the Mother and Father,
Maker of possibility, distance and dust,
who may never come to judge or quicken the dead
but does abide. We live out our lives
inside the body of God,
a heretic and breathing universe
that feeds on the falling of sparrows
and the crumbling of nations,
the rusting away of metal
and the rotting of wood.
I will be eaten by God.
There is nothing to fear.
To die, the singers believe, is to go home.
Where should I go, going home? Lord, I am here.

C.D. WRIGHT

C.D. Wright holds an M.F.A. in creative writing from the University of Arkansas. She is the author of four books of poetry, including *Further Adventures With You*. Wright is on the faculty at Brown University and runs Lost Roads Press. She is a native of northern Arkansas.

Photo Credit: Kay DuVernet

Obedience of the Corpse

The midwife puts a rag in the dead woman's hand,
Takes the hairpins out.

She smells apples,
Wonders where she keeps them in the house.
Nothing is under the sink
But a broken sack of potatoes
Growing eyes in the dark.

She hopes the mother's milk is good a while longer,
The woman up the road is still nursing—
But she remembers the neighbor
And the dead woman never got along.

A limb breaks,
She knows it's not the wind.
Somebody needs to set out some poison.

She looks to see if the woman wrote down any names,
Finds a white shirt to wrap the baby in.
It's beautiful she thinks—
Snow nobody has walked on.

Tours

A girl on the stairs listens to her father
Beat up her mother.
Doors bang.
She comes down in her nightgown.

The piano stands there in the dark
Like a boy with an orchid.

She plays what she can
Then turns the lamp on.

Her mother's music is spread out
On the floor like brochures.

She hears her father
Running through the leaves.

The last black key
She presses stays down, makes no sound,
Someone putting their tongue where their tooth had been.

Birth of the Cool

Not long ago a man was smoking on a balcony
Stripped down to his shorts
He was thinking about Amanda
Standing in his room one evening
Like a palm tree on a beach.
The smell coming from a piece of her clothing
Like a thin sheet of notepaper.
The wind rubbed his stomach
And the moon put its ice in his glass.
The waves kept going out and coming back
Like two people after a fight.
He was thinking about Amanda,
About something cold like his horns
Leaning against the wall,
And the cufflink he found in her room.

The Beautiful Urinals of Paris

Many husbands are missing tonight.
Ones who drink together to forget
And ones who drink alone and remember.
A drowned man will not reach his doorbell,
The roses waiting on the tables
Are closing their wet eyes,
Trees along the boulevard are going blind from headlights.
The finest houses have turned their back on the Seine.
All the drunk, married men of the rain
Step into the urinals like women
Entering cathedrals.
With their arms around one another
They listen to their love run out with a hiss,
Worship the steam as it rises off the drain.

Slag

The orange rivers and red dogs of Paul Gauguin
do not run through these hills.
The light that caught us here, the crazy quilts
were drawn in charcoal.
Days colder than night
avoid the foggy eyes of the clock.
This is the chilling winter of our lives.
Forty wives make forty widows.
Deep in a wound of earth
someone coughs. All of him strains
to breathe; to hear
the insomniac echo of her naked feet
as she walks the hard floor to the pump.
At the sink, she gulps from her hand.
Behind her devoted black oak
the mineralized sky weakening, glows.

CHARLES
WRIGHT

Charles Wright, born in 1935 in Pick-
wick Dam, Tennessee, holds degrees
from Davidson College and the Univer-
sity of Iowa. He is the author of seven
books of poetry, including *The Other Side
of the River,* and is a recipient of the
American Book Award for Poetry. Wright
teaches in the English department at the
University of Virginia in Charlottesville.

Photo Credit: Holly Wright

April

The plum tree breaks out in bees.
A gull is locked like a ghost in the blue attic of heaven.
The wind goes nattering on,
Gossipy, ill at ease, in the damp rooms it will air.
I count off the grace and stays
My life has come to, and know I want less—

Divested of everything,
A downfall of light in the pine woods, motes in the rush,
Gold leaf through the undergrowth, and come back
As another name, water
Pooled in the black leaves and holding me there, to be
Released as a glint, as a flash, as a spark . . .

Cloud River

The unborn children are rowing out to the far edge of the sky,
Looking for warm beds to appear in. How lucky they are, dressed
In their lake-colored gowns, the oars in their oily locks
Taking them stroke by stroke to circumference and artery . . .

I'd like to be with them still, pulling my weight,
Blisters like small white hearts in the waxed palms of my hands.
I'd like to remember my old name, and keep the watch,
Waiting for something immense and unspeakable to uncover its face.

Clear Night

Clear night, thumb-top of a moon, a back-lit sky.
Moon-fingers lay down their same routine
On the side deck and the threshold, the white keys and the black keys.
Bird hush and bird song. A cassia flower falls.

I want to be bruised by God.
I want to be strung up in a strong light and singled out.
I want to be stretched, like music wrung from a dropped seed.
I want to be entered and picked clean.

And the wind says "What?" to me.
And the castor beans, with their little earrings of death, say "What?" to me.
And the stars start out on their cold slide through the dark.
And the gears notch and the engines wheel.

October

The leaves fall from my fingers.
Cornflowers scatter across the field like stars,
                          like smoke stars,
By the train tracks, the leaves in a drift

Under the slow clouds
                   and the nine steps to heaven,
The light falling in great sheets through the trees,
Sheets almost tangible.

The transfiguration will start like this, I think,
                         breathless,
Quick blade through the trees,
Something with red colors falling away from my hands,

The air beginning to go cold . . .
                       And when it does
I'll rise from this tired body, a blood-knot of light,
Ready to take the darkness in.

—Or for the wind to come
And carry me, bone by bone, through the sky,
Its wafer a burn on my tongue,
                     its wine deep forgetfulness.

Arkansas Traveller

On the far side of the water, high on a sand bar,
Grandfathers are lolling above the Arkansas River,
Guitars in their laps, cloth caps like Cagney down over their eyes.
A woman is strumming a banjo.
                        Another adjusts her bow tie
And boiled shirtwaist.
And in the half-light the frogs begin from their sleep
To ascend into darkness,
Vespers recalibrate through the underbrush,
                     the insect choir

Offering its clear soprano
Out of the vaulted gum trees into the stained glass of the sky.

———————

Almost 95 years to the day I saw
Elison Smythe passed out
                              on the back seat of an Oldsmobile 88
In the spring of 1952 in Biltmore Forest, N.C.,
Who then rose up from the dark of his 16th year
And said to the nothingness:
                              Where are we,
Who's driving this goddamn thing?
My great-grandfather stepped off the boat
                              from the archduchy of Upper Austria
And headed north to the territory.
And into another war
                              here, just past the Mississippi,
On the Arkansas.
                              I don't know that it was such a great blessing
Sending us to Arkansas,
But it was so regarded at the time, and we're grateful to Gen. Jackson.
Still, don't let me die as grandmother did,
                              suddenly on a steamboat
Stuck fast on a sand bar unable to get to Little Rock.
And was four years later a volunteer captain
In the Confederacy,
                              and took a Minie ball in his palate
At Chickamauga he carried there till his death
Almost half a century afterwards.
                              And wrote a poem back
To the widow of one of his men about a sure return
"Where life is not a breath,
Nor life's affections, transient fire . . . in heaven's light."
And was captured again,
                              and wounded again, confined for two years
At Rock Island prison.
And came back to Little Rock and *began his career.*
And died at 66,
                              a ticket to Cuba stored flat in his jacket pocket.

———————

When Jesus walked on the night grass
                              they say not even the dew trembled.
Such intricate catechisms of desire.
Such golden cars down the wrong side of the sky.

Each summer in Little Rock,
                              like a monk in his cell
Saying the lesson over and over
Until it is shining, all day I'd prove up my childhood till lights out
Snapped on the fireflies who floated
Like miniature jellyfish
                              off the reefs of the sleeping porch
Whose jasmine and rose-scented air broke over me back and forth
Before I could count the half of them,
                              and settled me under.
This was before I was 10.
That year my grandfather, my look-alike on the sand bar, died,
The war ended, and nothing was ever the same way
Again.
        His mantelpiece clock sits on my dresser now,
Still gilded and 19th century.
Devotion, remember, is what counts.
Without it you're exiled, twisted and small.

The next morning we'd play golf,
                              four holes on the back side,
Trailing our footprints like paired bodies emptied and left out to dry
In the web of sunlight and wet grass
                              behind us over the clipped fairways,
My grandmother and I up before anyone else
Each day I was there,
                              the sun already a huge, hot thumb
At 7 o'clock on our bare heads.
Later, its print still warm on my forehead,
Sunset like carrot juice down the left pane of the sky
Into the indeterminacy of somewhere else,
I'd roll the tarpaulin down and up
On the sleeping porch,
                              the frog-shrill and the insect-shrill
Threading out of the bushes
                              as palpable as a heartstring,
Whatever that was back then, always in memory . . .

To speak of the dead is to make them live again:
                              we invent what we need.

Knot by knot I untie myself from the past
And let it rise away from me like a balloon.
What a small thing it becomes.
What a bright tweak at the vanishing point, blue on blue.

The Other Side of the River

Easter again, and a small rain falls
On the mockingbird and the housefly,
                                on the Chevrolet
In its purple joy
And the TV antennas huddled across the hillside—

Easter again, and the palm trees hunch
Deeper beneath their burden,
                          the dark puddles take in
Whatever is given them,
And nothing rises more than halfway out of itself—

Easter with all its little mouths open into the rain.

                _____

There is no metaphor for the spring's disgrace,
No matter how much the rose leaves look like bronze dove hearts,
No matter how much the plum trees preen in the wind.

For weeks I've thought about the Savannah River,
For no reason,
        and the winter fields around Garnett, South Carolina
My brother and I used to hunt
At Christmas,
                Princess and Buddy working the millet stands
And the vine-lipped face of the pine woods
In their langourous zig-zags,
The quail, when they flushed, bursting like shrapnel points
Between the trees and the leggy shrubs
                                into the undergrowth,
Everything else in motion as though under water,
My brother and I, the guns, their reports tolling from far away

Through the aqueous, limb-filtered light,
December sun like a single tropical fish
Uninterested anyway,
                    suspended and holding still
In the coral stems of the pearl-dusked and distant trees . . .

There is no metaphor for any of this,
Or the meta-weather of April,
The vinca blossoms like deep bruises among the green.

———————

It's linkage I'm talking about,
                    and harmonies and structures
And all the various things that lock our wrists to the past.

Something infinite behind everything appears,
                    and then disappears.

It's a matter of how
                    you narrow the surfaces.
It's all a matter of how you fit in the sky.

———————

Often, at night, when the stars seem as close as they do now, and as full,
And the trees balloon and subside in the way they do
                    when the wind is right,
As they do now after the rain,
                    the sea way off with its false sheen,
And the sky that slick black of wet rubber,
I'm 15 again, and back on Mt. Anne in North Carolina
Repairing the fire tower,
Nobody else around but the horse I packed in with,
                    and five days to finish the job.
Those nights were the longest nights I ever remember,
The lake and pavilion 3,000 feet below
                    as though modeled in tinfoil,
And even more distant than that,
The last fire out, the after-reflection of Lake Llewellyn
Aluminum glare in the sponged dark,
Lightning bugs everywhere,
                    the plump stars
Dangling and falling near on their black strings.

These nights are like that,
The silvery alphabet of the sea
                              increasingly difficult to transcribe,
And larger each year, everything farther away, and less clear,
Than I want it to be,
                              not enough time to do the job,
And faint thunks in the earth,
As though somewhere nearby a horse was nervously pawing the ground.

I want to sit by the bank of the river,
                              in the shade of the evergreen tree,
And look in the face of whatever,
                              the whatever that's waiting for me.

There comes a point when everything starts to dust away
More quickly than it appears,
                              when what we have to comfort the dark
Is just that dust, and just its going away.

25 years ago I used to sit on this jut of rocks
As the sun went down like an offering through the glaze
And backfires of Monterey Bay,
And anything I could think of was mine because it was there
                              in front of me, numinously everywhere,
Appearing and piling up . . .

So to have come to this,
                              remembering what I did do, and what I
                  didn't do,
The gulls whimpering over the boathouse,
                                        the monarch butterflies
Cruising the flower beds,
And all the soft hairs of spring thrusting up through the wind,
And the sun, as it always does,
                  dropping into its slot without a click,
Is a short life of trouble.

INDEX OF TITLES